I0465172

Naughty Young Girls

1845 - 1890

Historische Aktfotografie

1

Jürgen Prommersberger: Naughty Young Girls 1845 - 1890
Regenstauf , Februar 2016

Alle Rechte am Werk liegen beim Autor:
Jürgen Prommersberger
Händelstr 17
93128 Regenstauf

Erstauflage
Herstellung: CreateSpace Independent Publishing Platform

HINWEIS:
Diese Bilder stammen aus der Anfangszeit der Fotografie. Die Fotografie machte damals ihre ersten Schritte und daher sind die folgenden Bilder etwas Außergewöhnliches. Die ältesten Bilder sind somit schon 150 – 160 Jahre alt. Ich möchte darauf hinweisen, dass aus diesem Grund die Qualität (Tiefenschärfe, Kontrast) dieser Bilder nicht mit Aufnahmen neueren Datums vergleichbar ist. Zum technischen Hintergrund der fotografischen Möglichkeiten schließe ich nach den Aktbildern ein kurzes Kapitel an.

NOTICE:
These pictures are from the early days of photography. The photograph made then its first steps and therefore, the following images are something extraordinary. The oldest images are already 150-160 years old. I want to point out that for this reason the quality (Focus, High Contrast) of these images can not be compared with recent images. I will add a short chapter about the technical background of the photographic opportunities after the pictures.

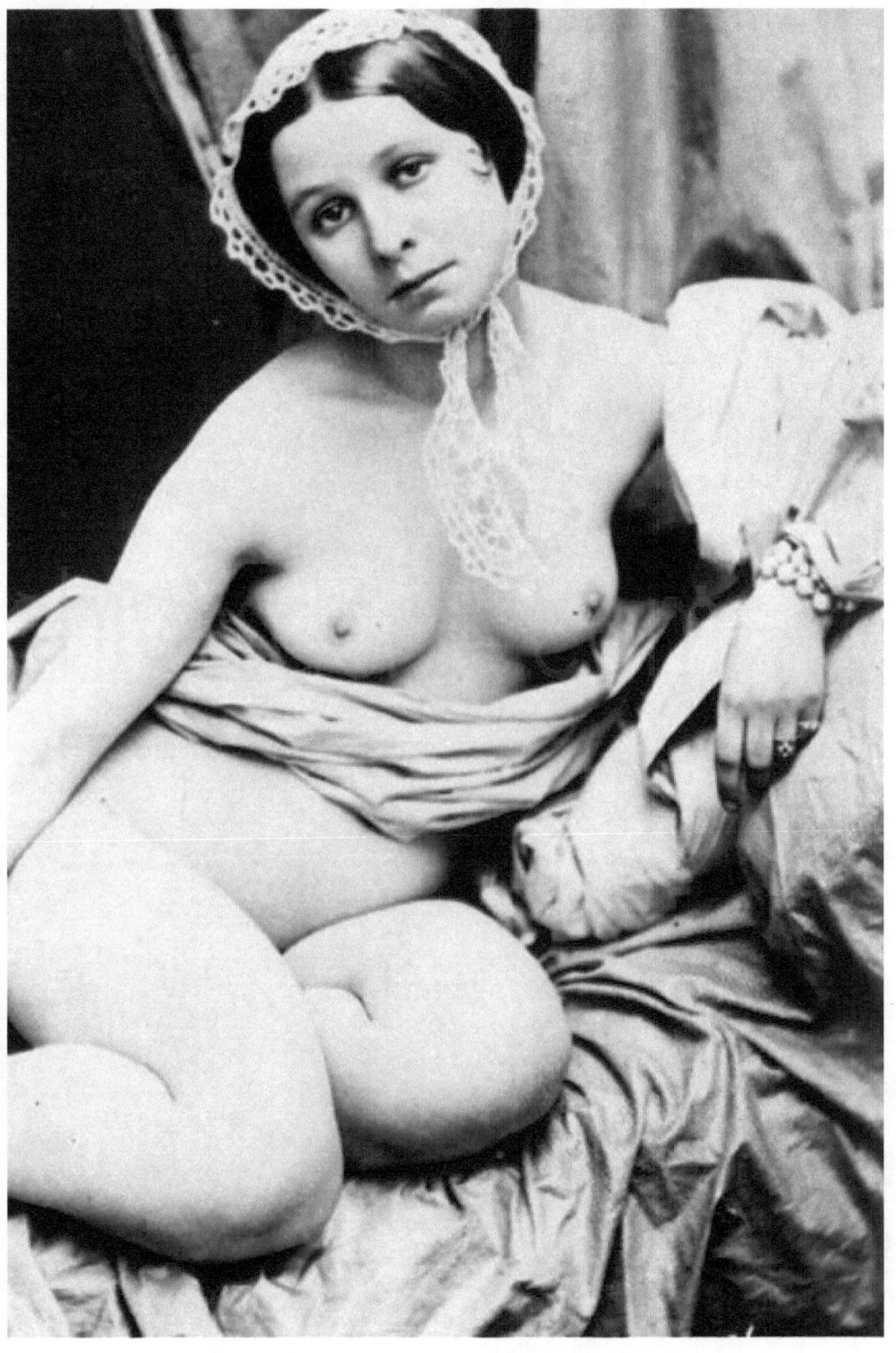

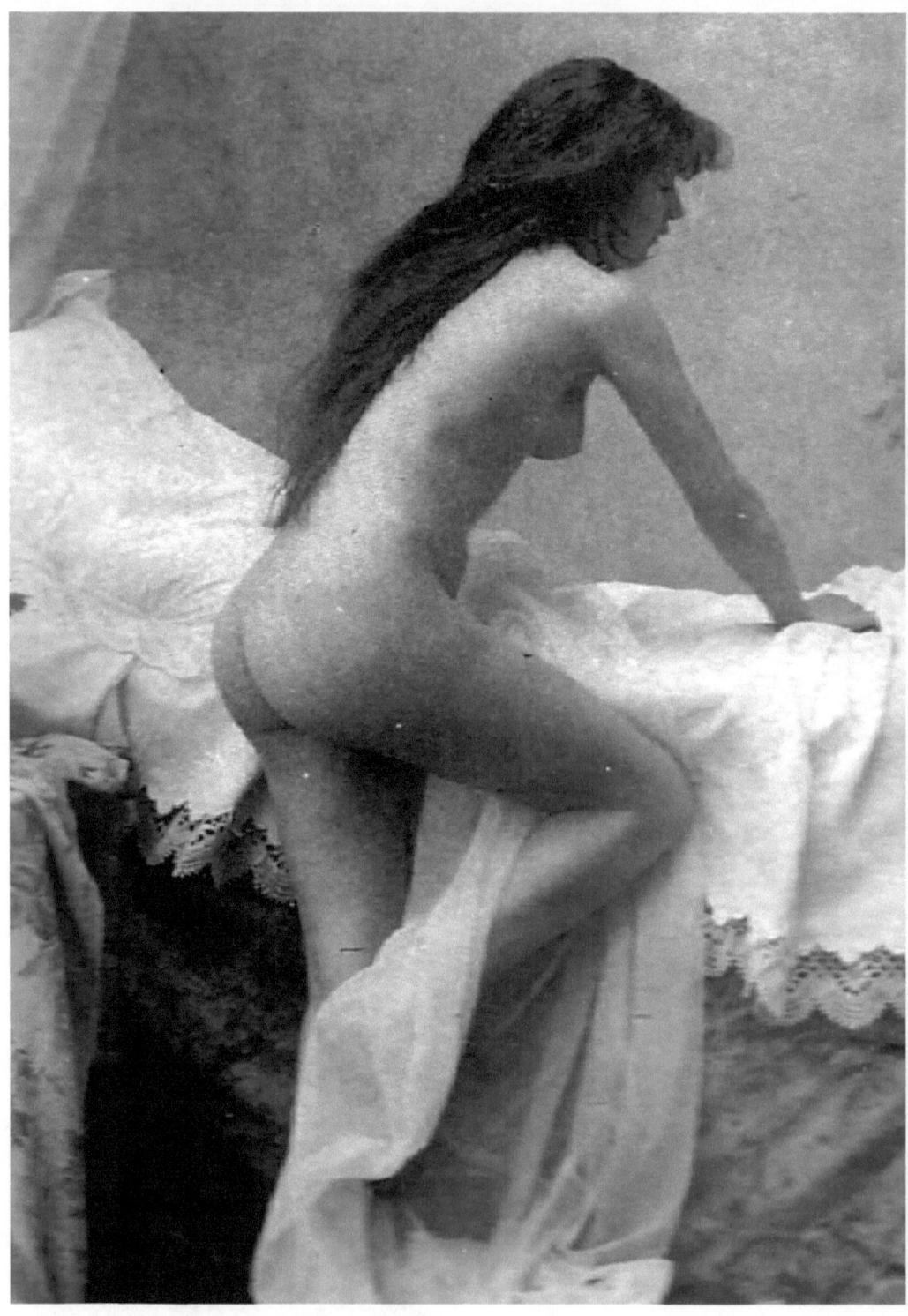

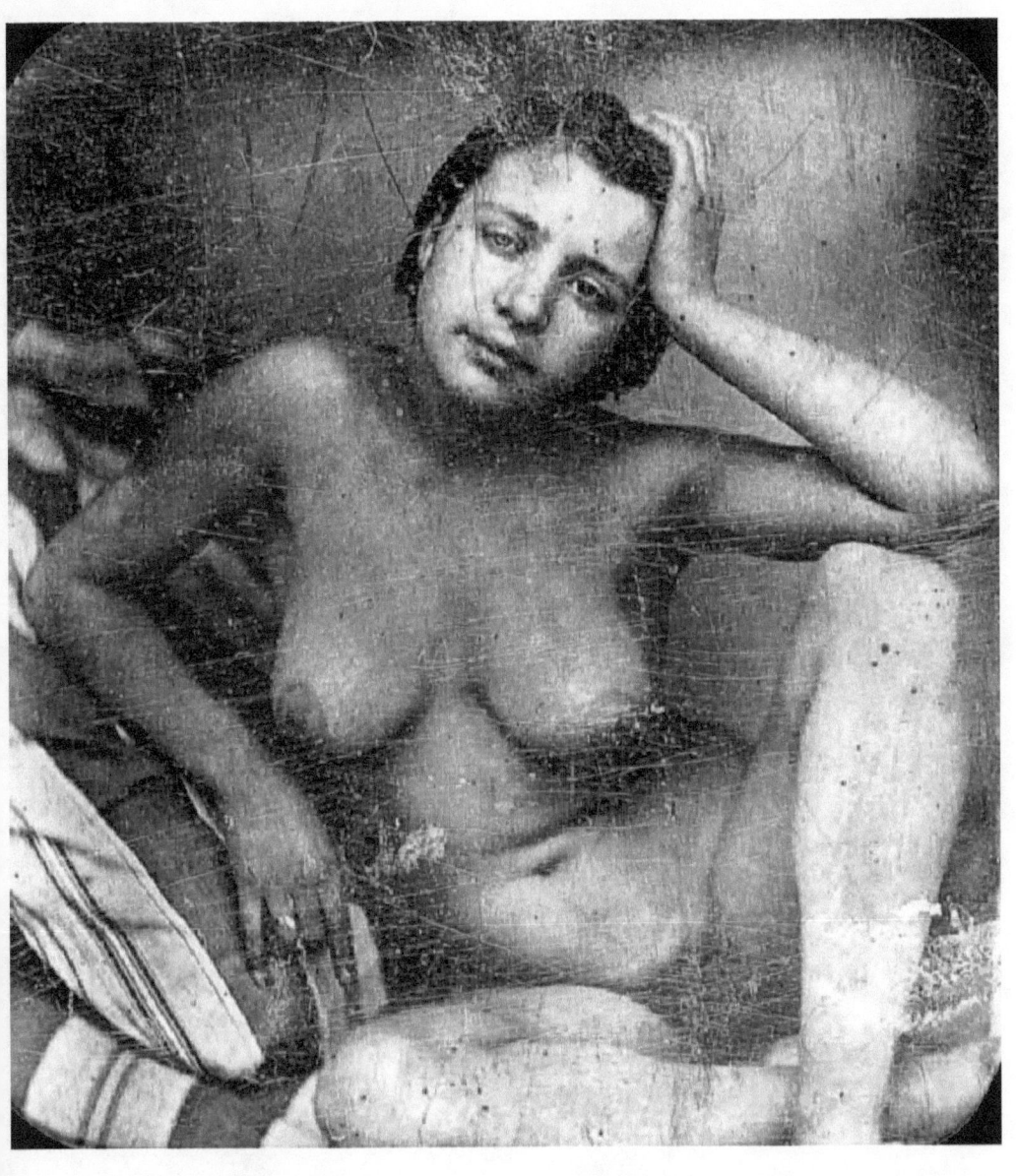

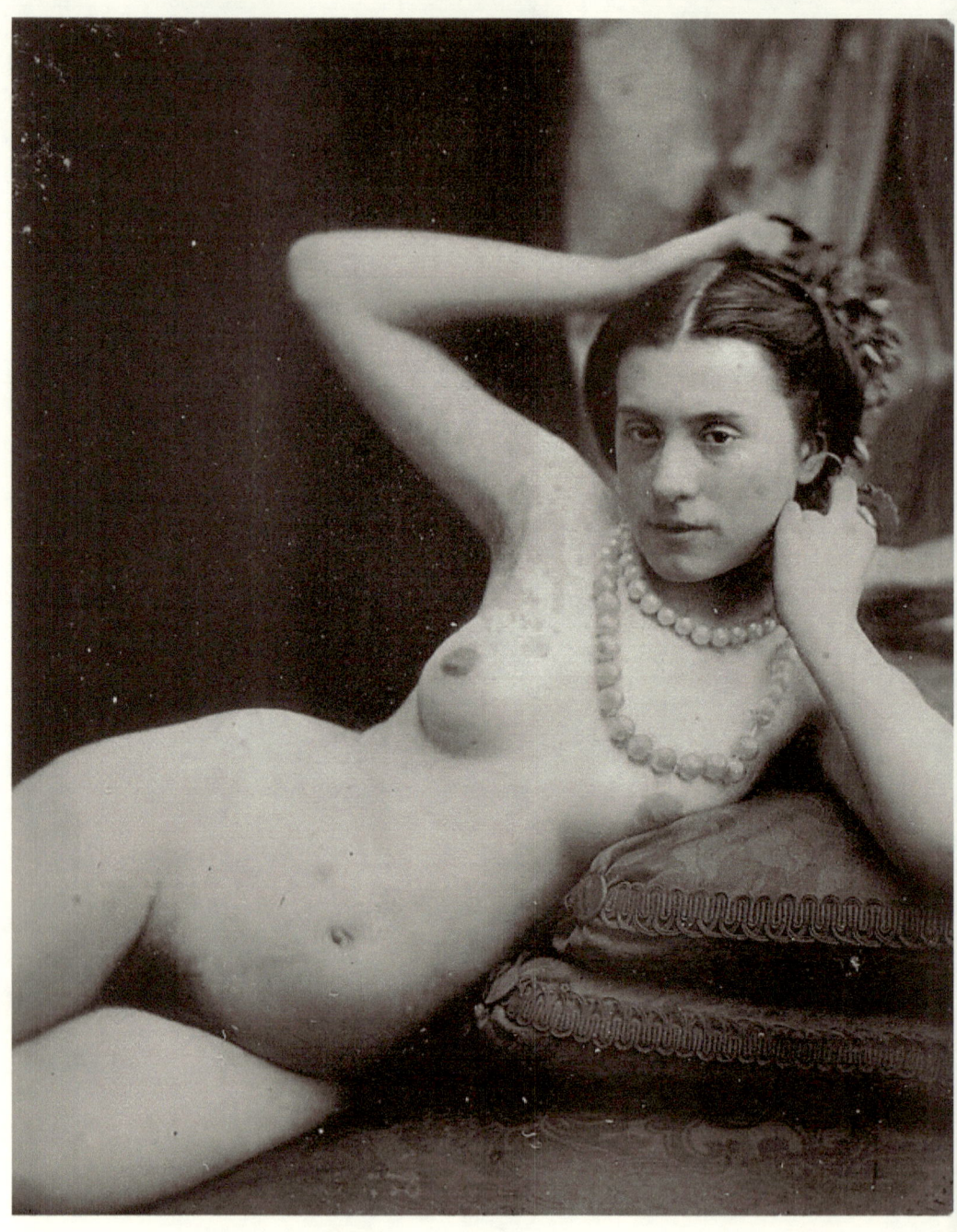

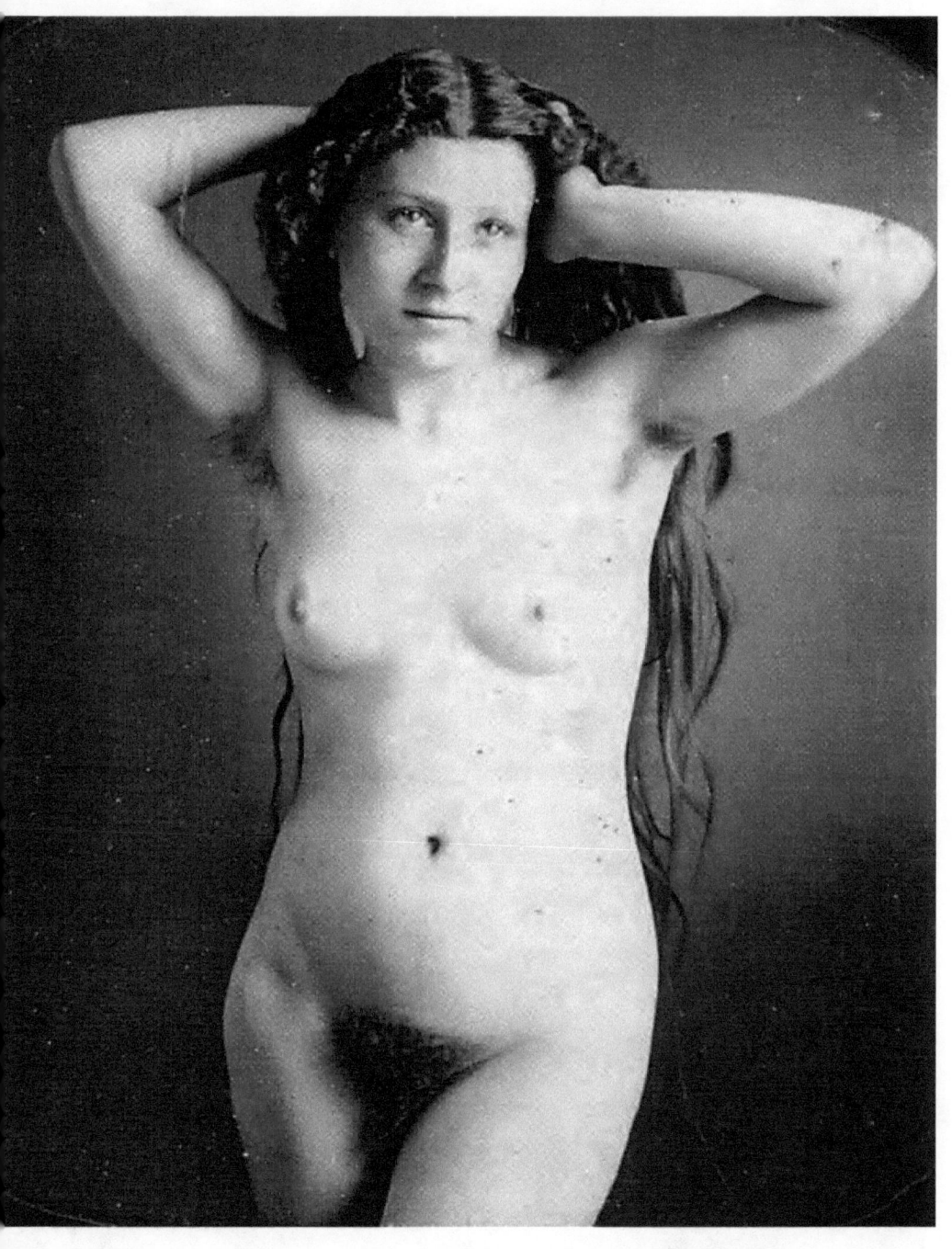

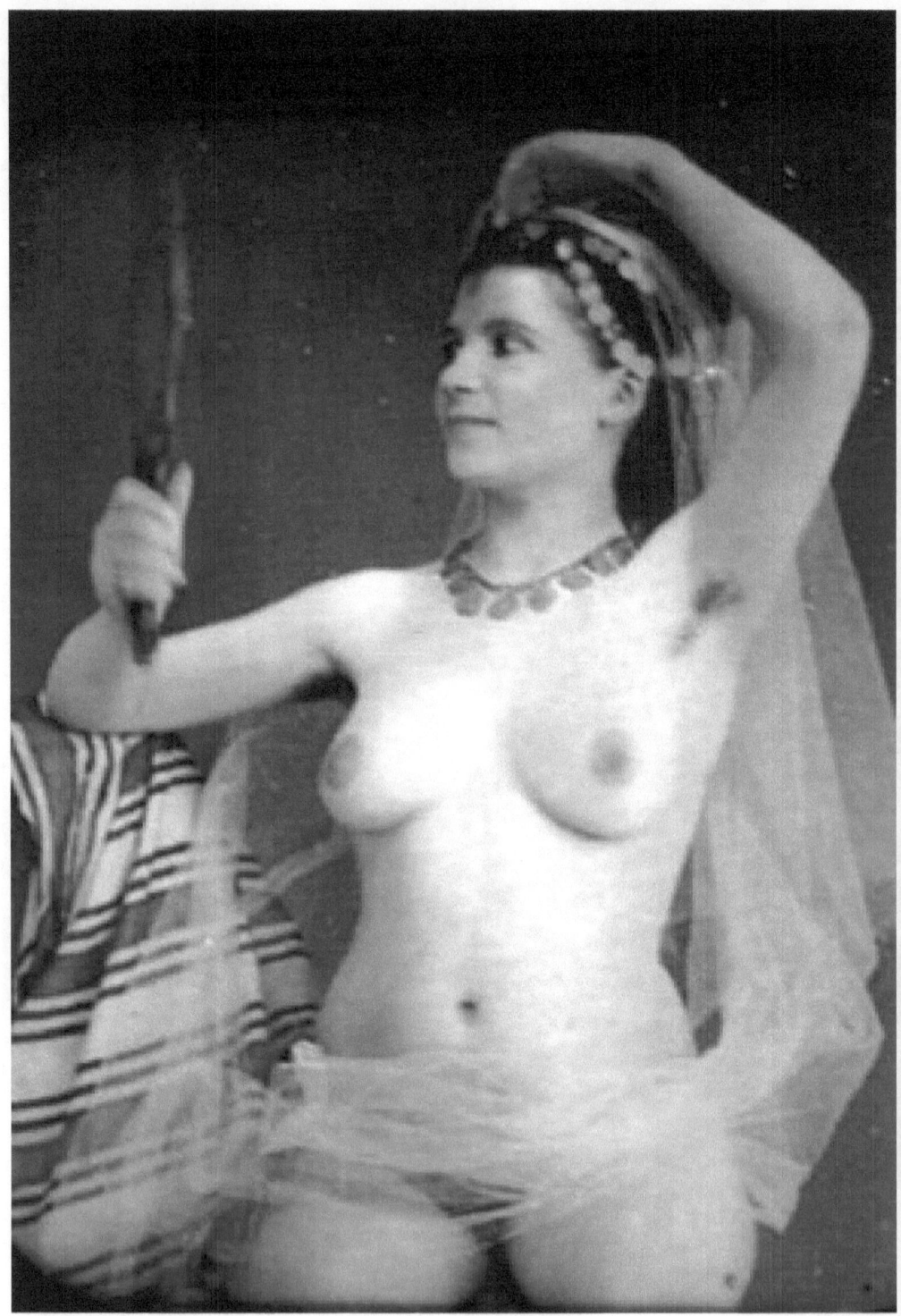

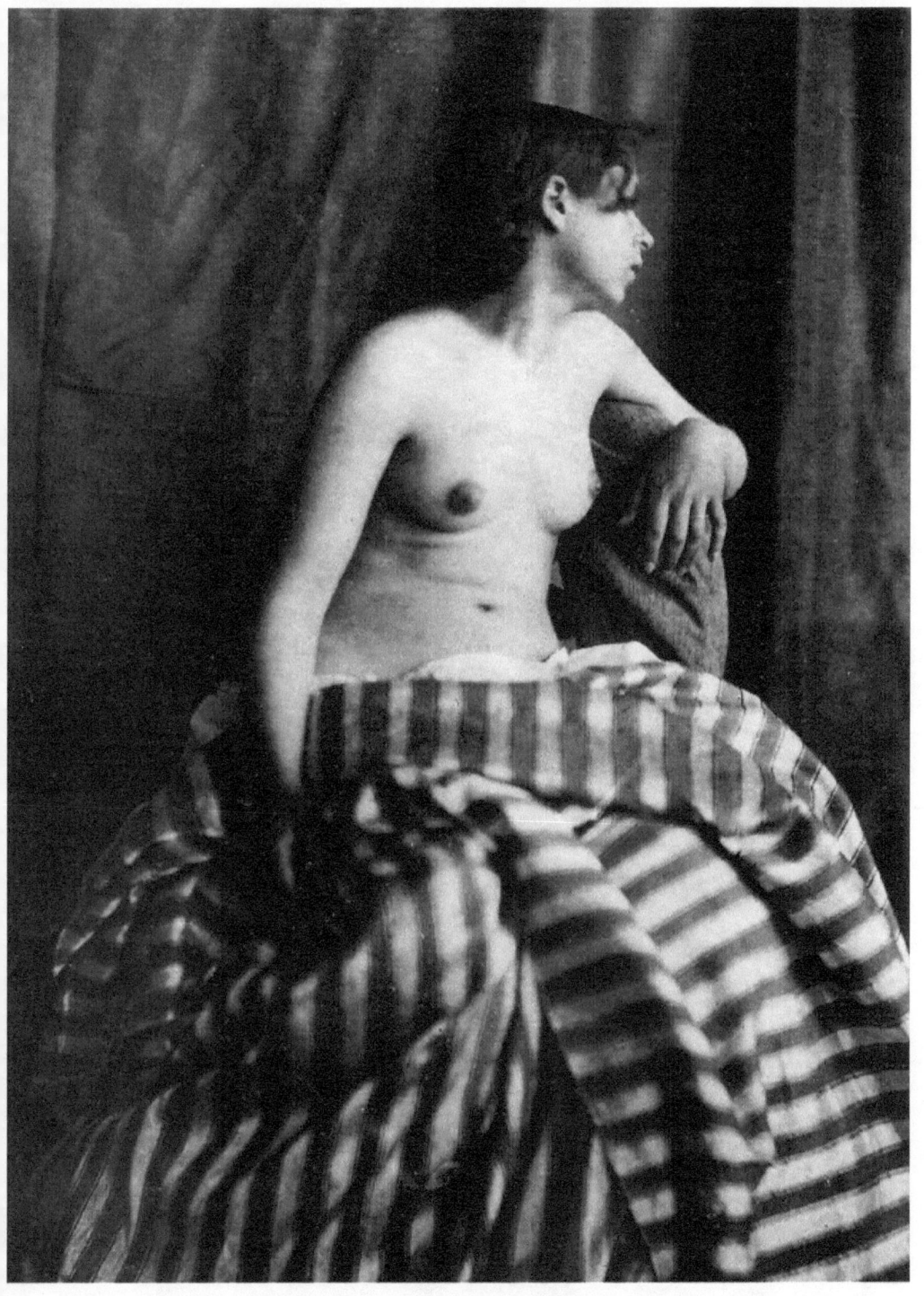

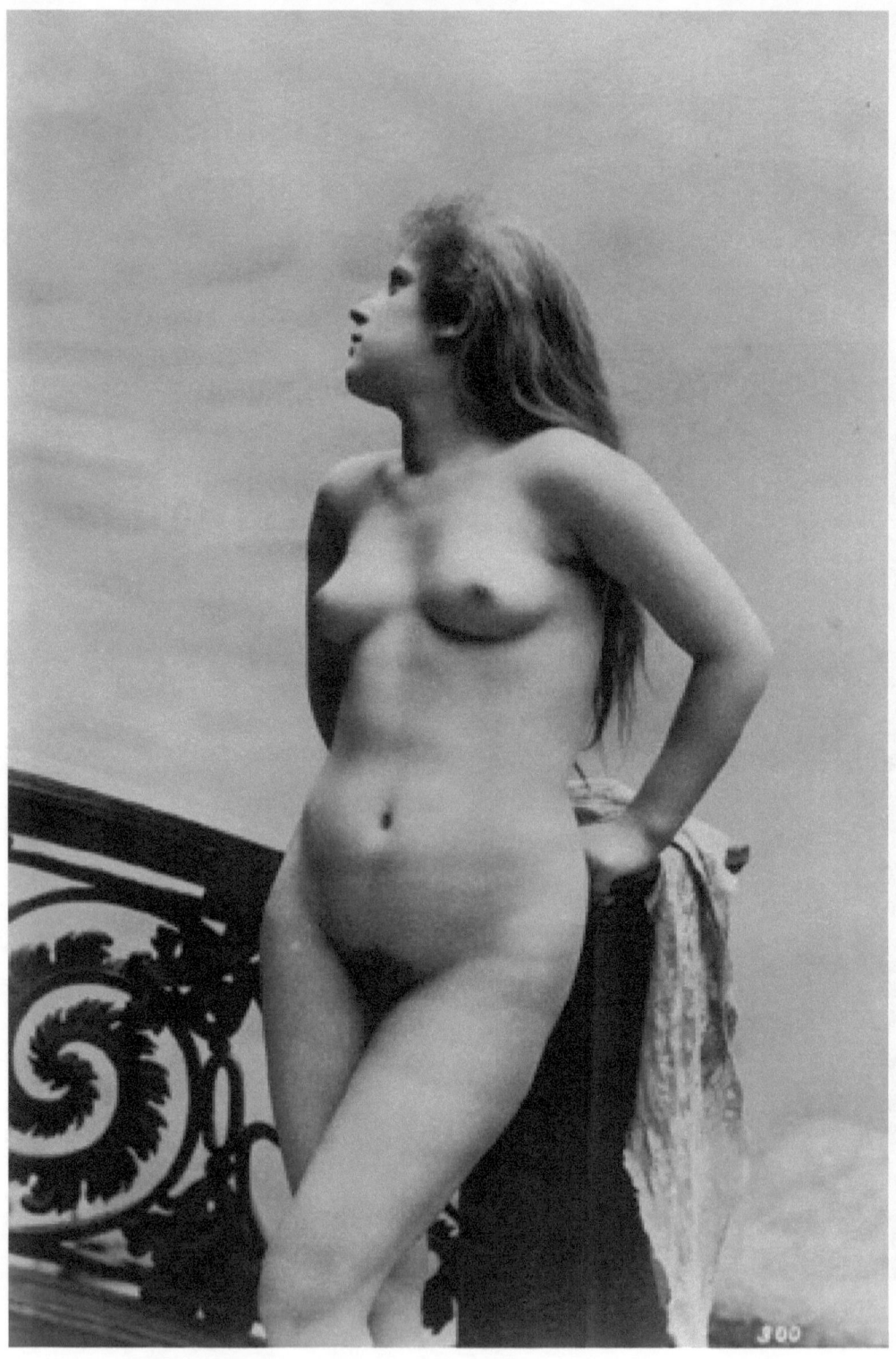

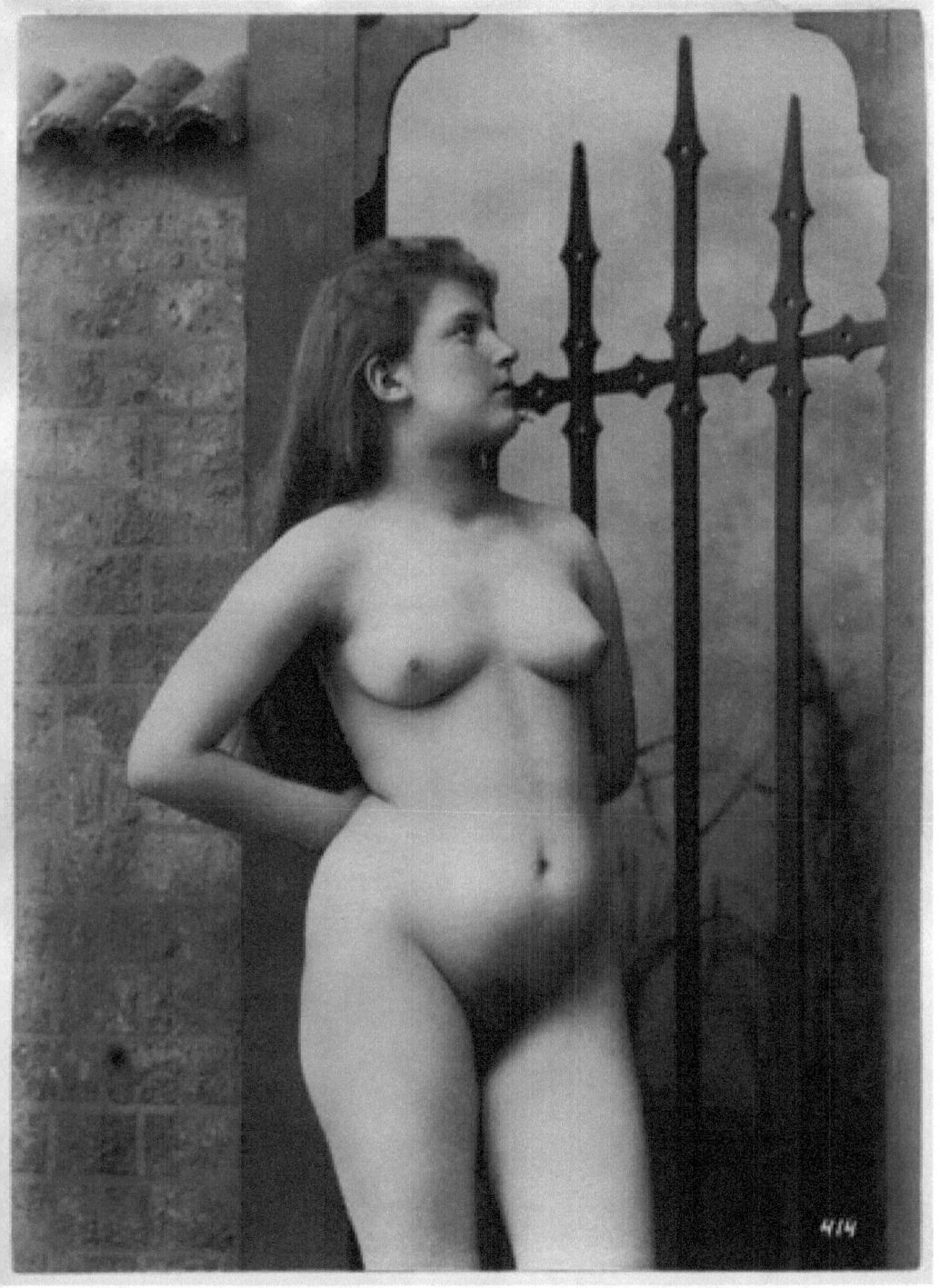

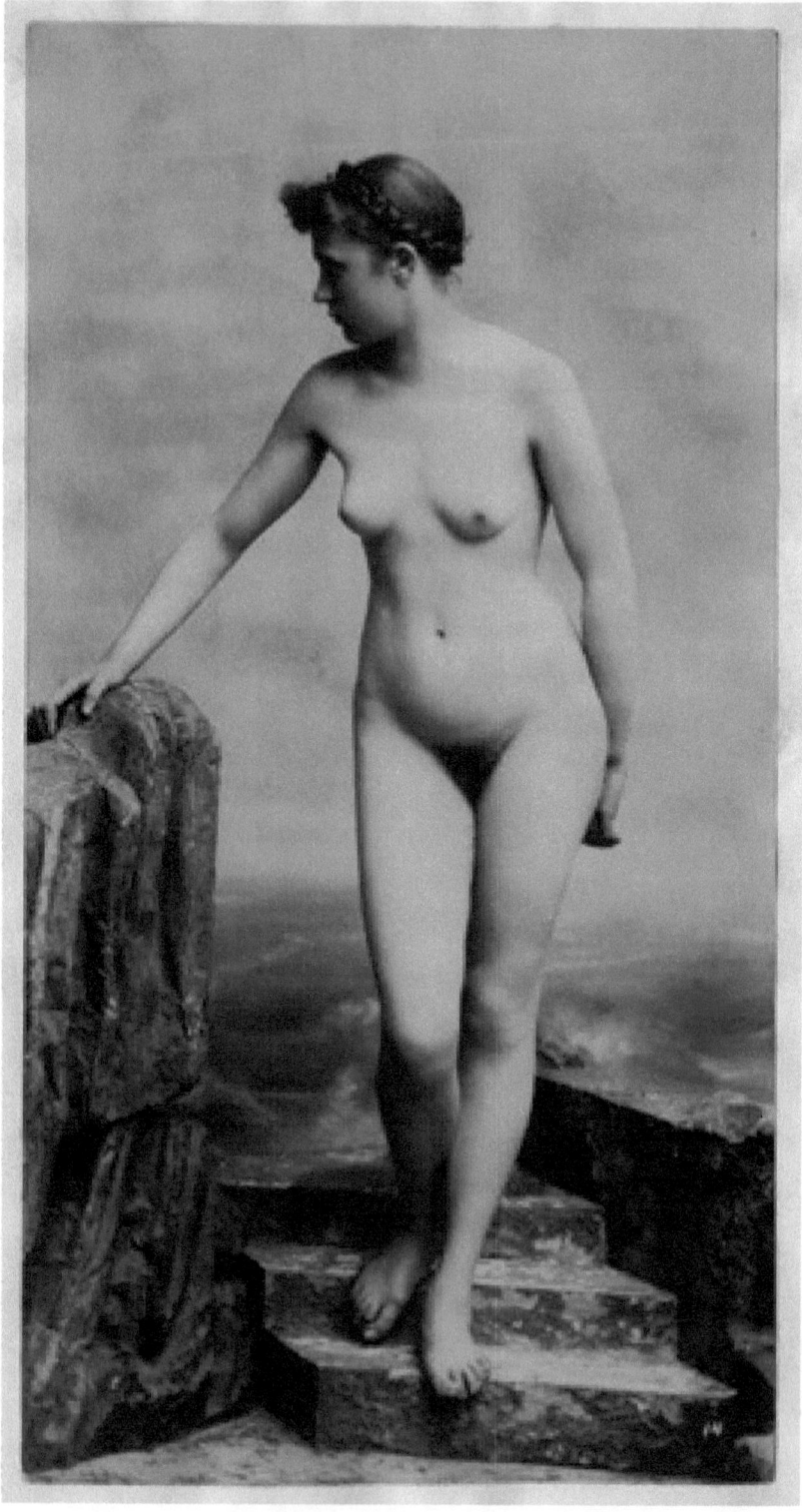

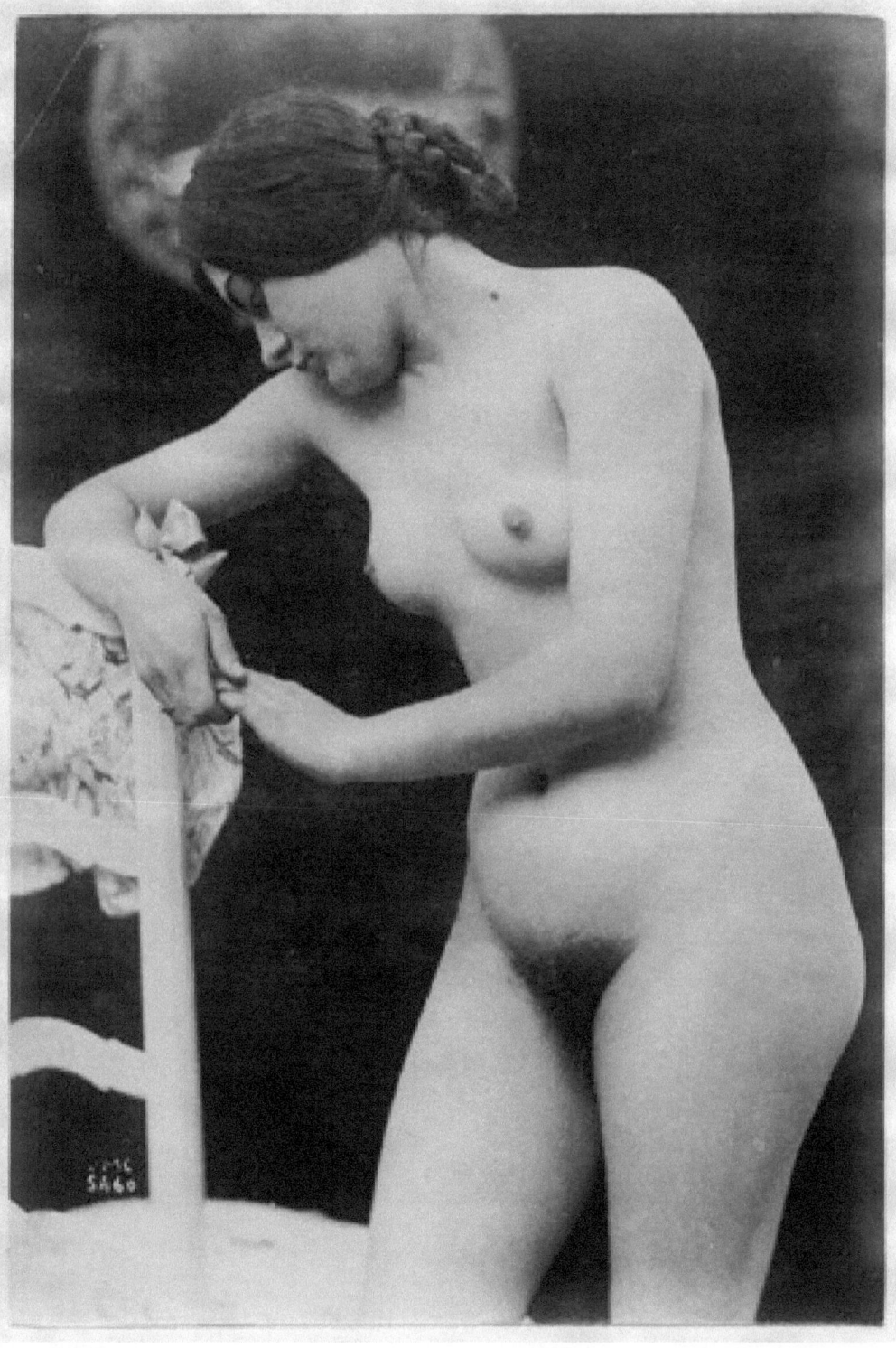

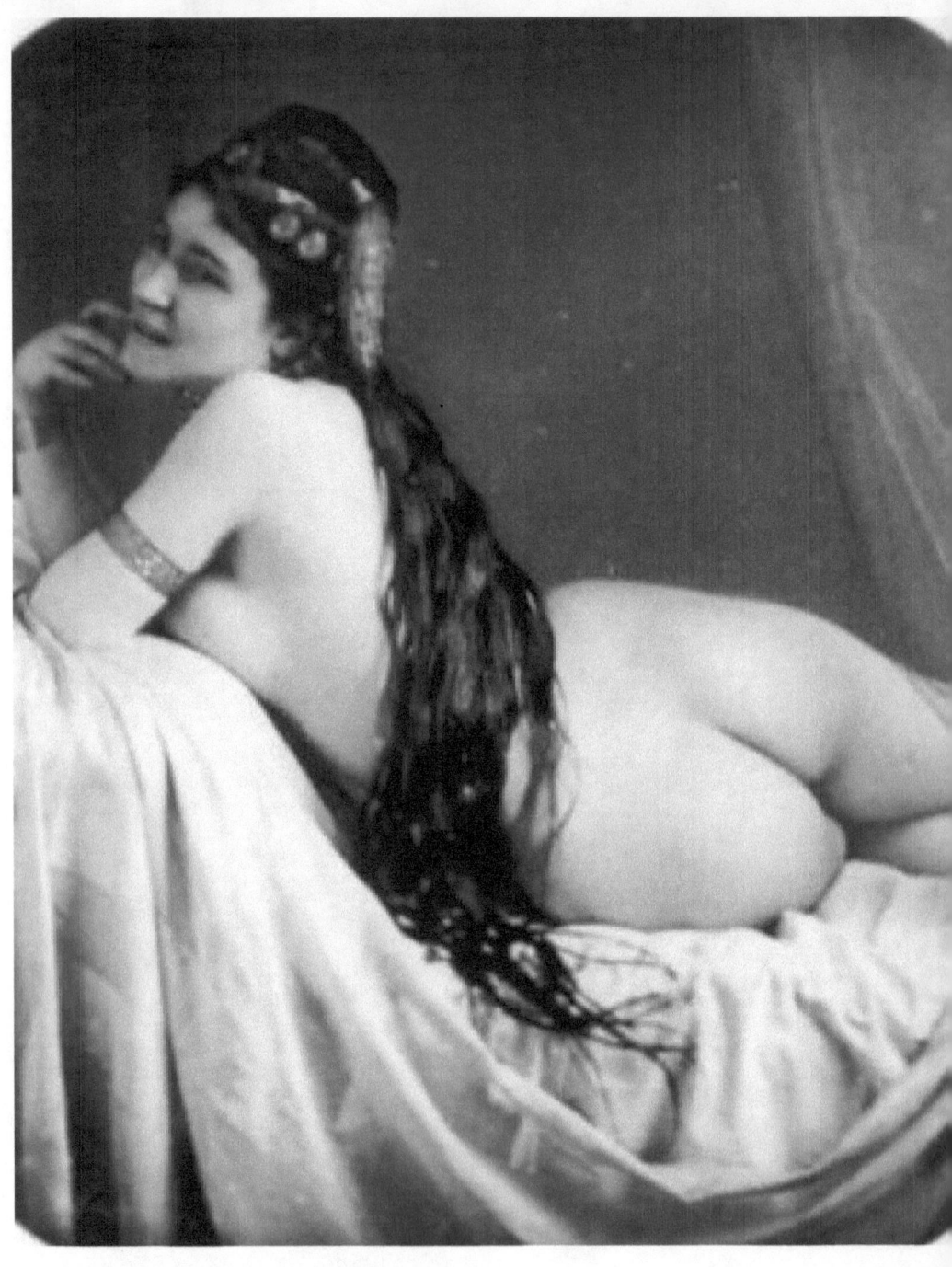

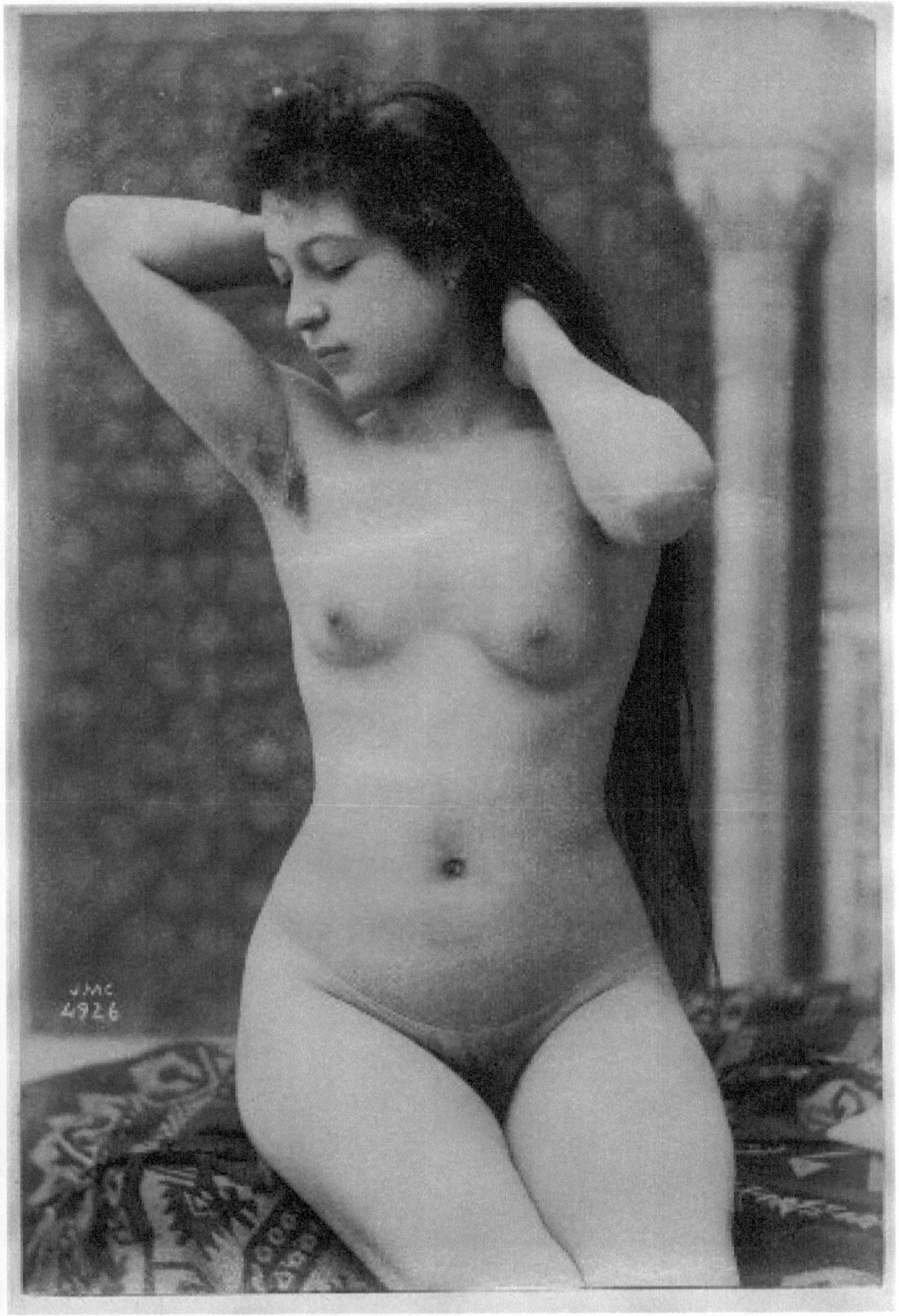

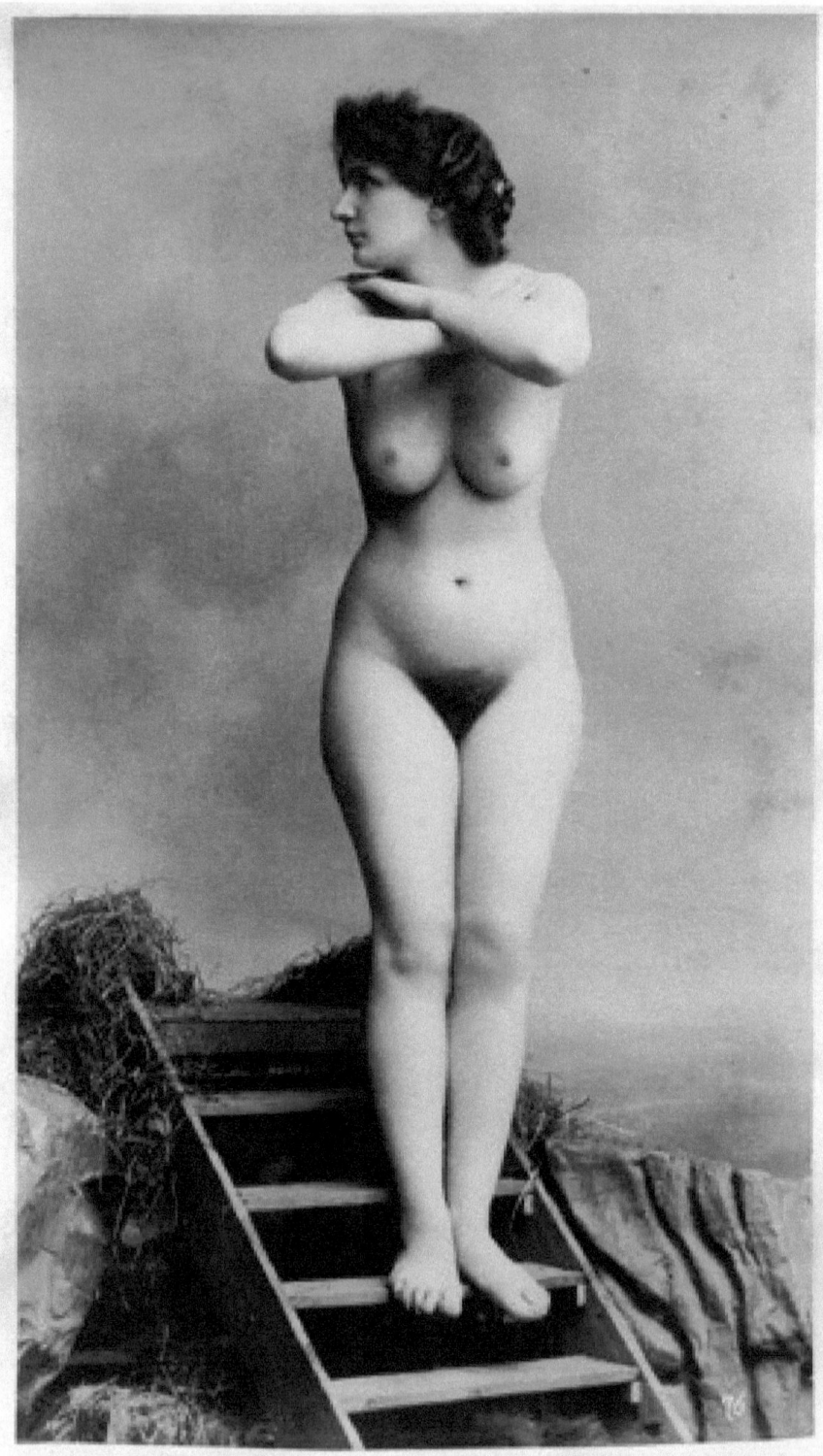

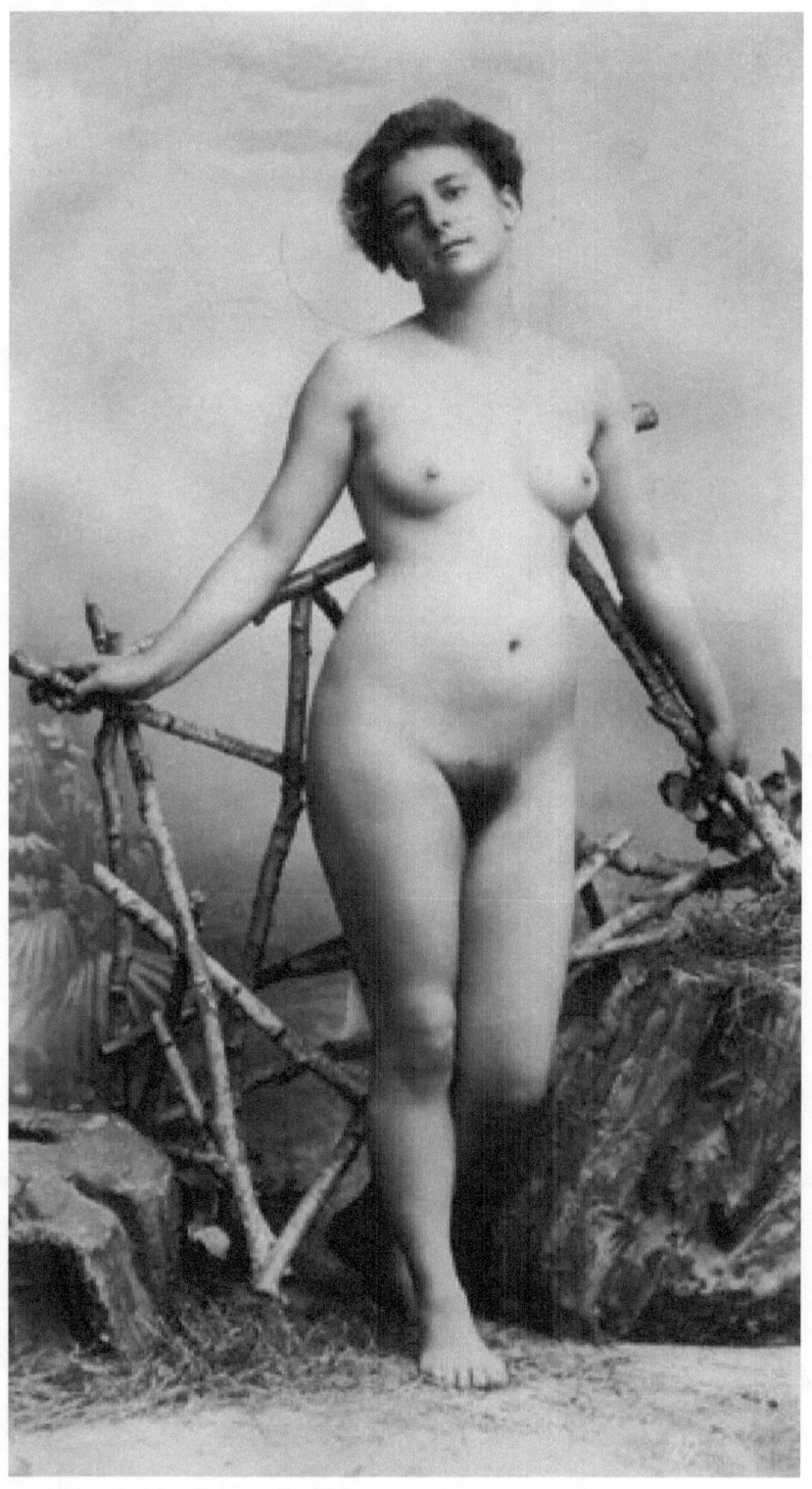

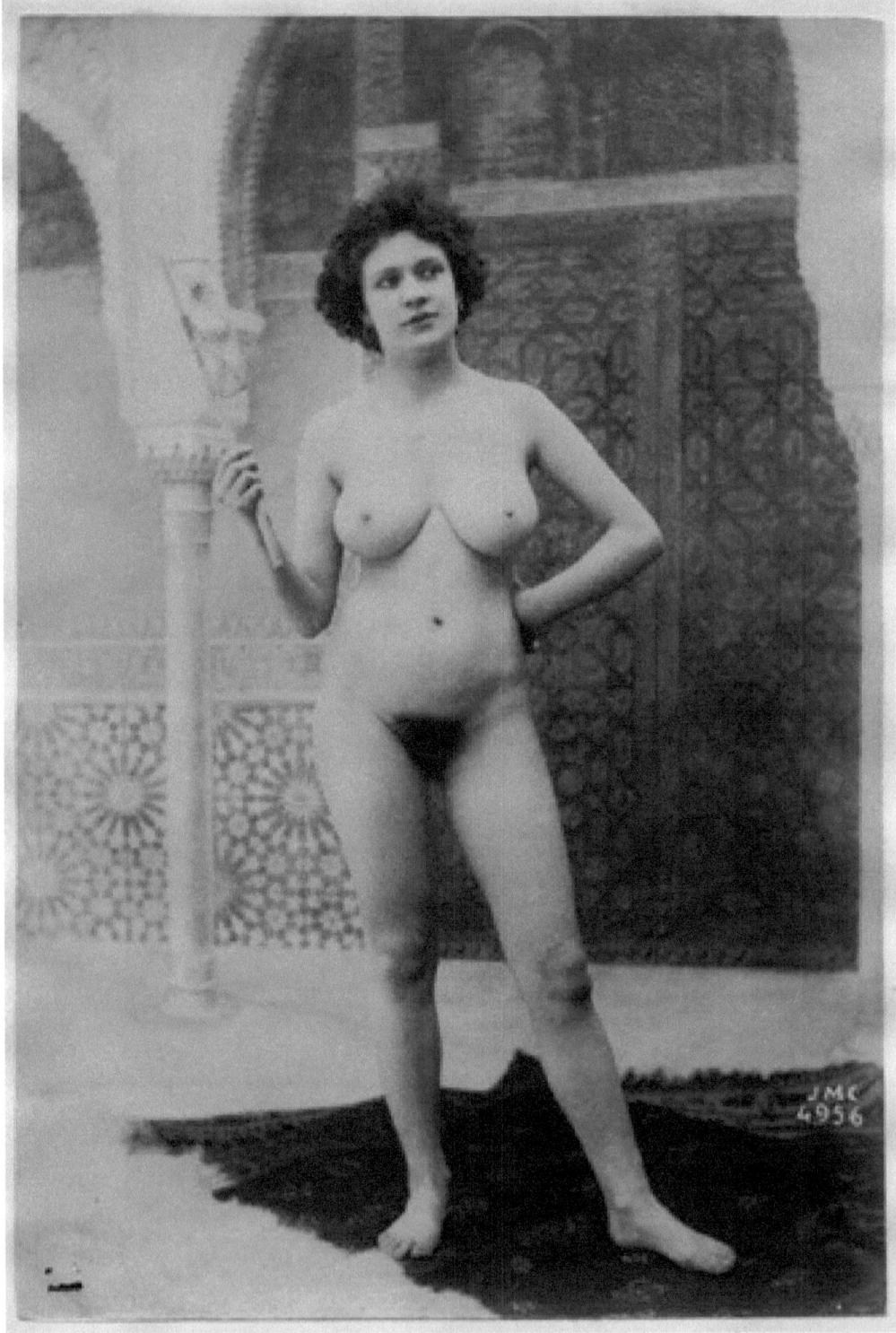

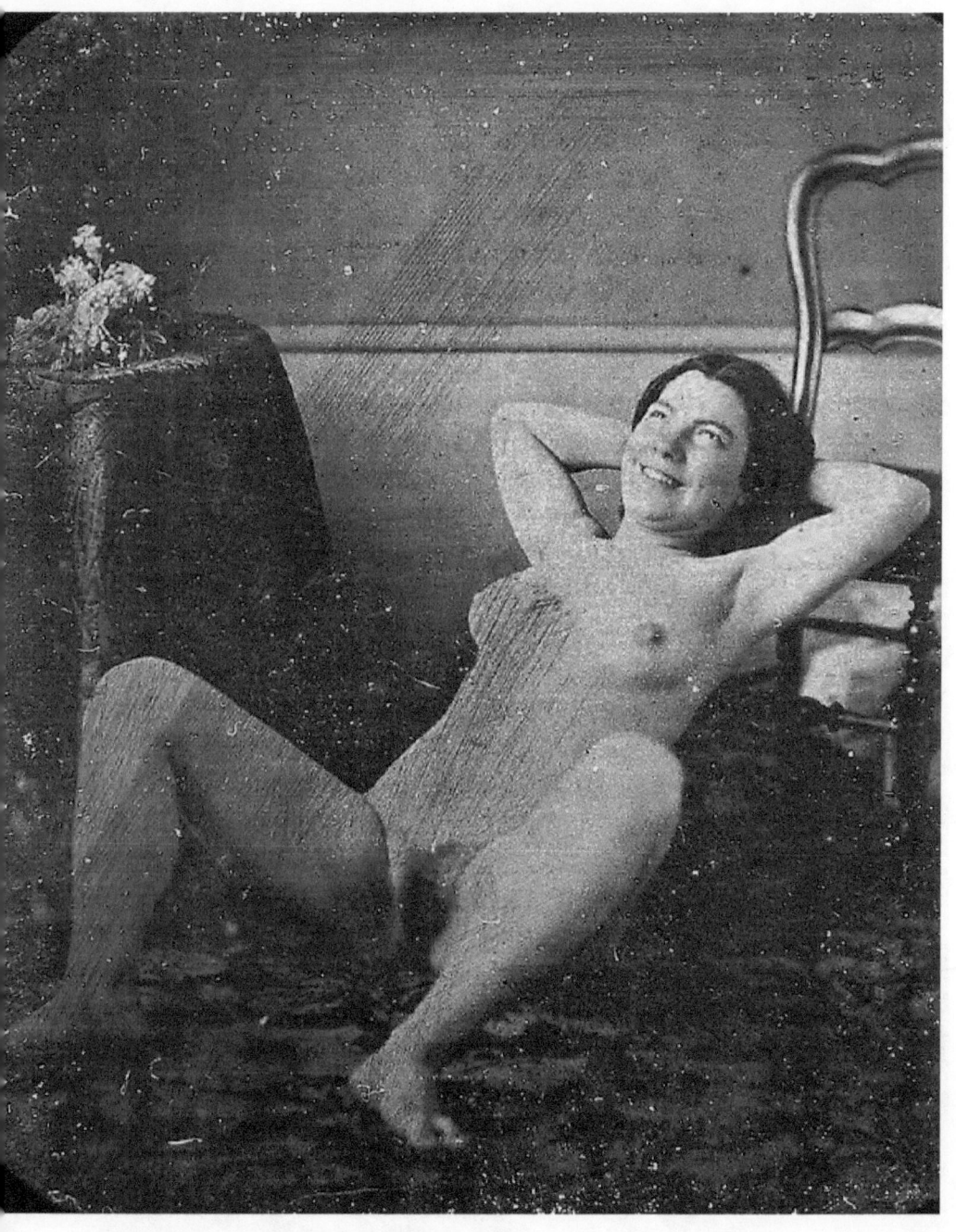

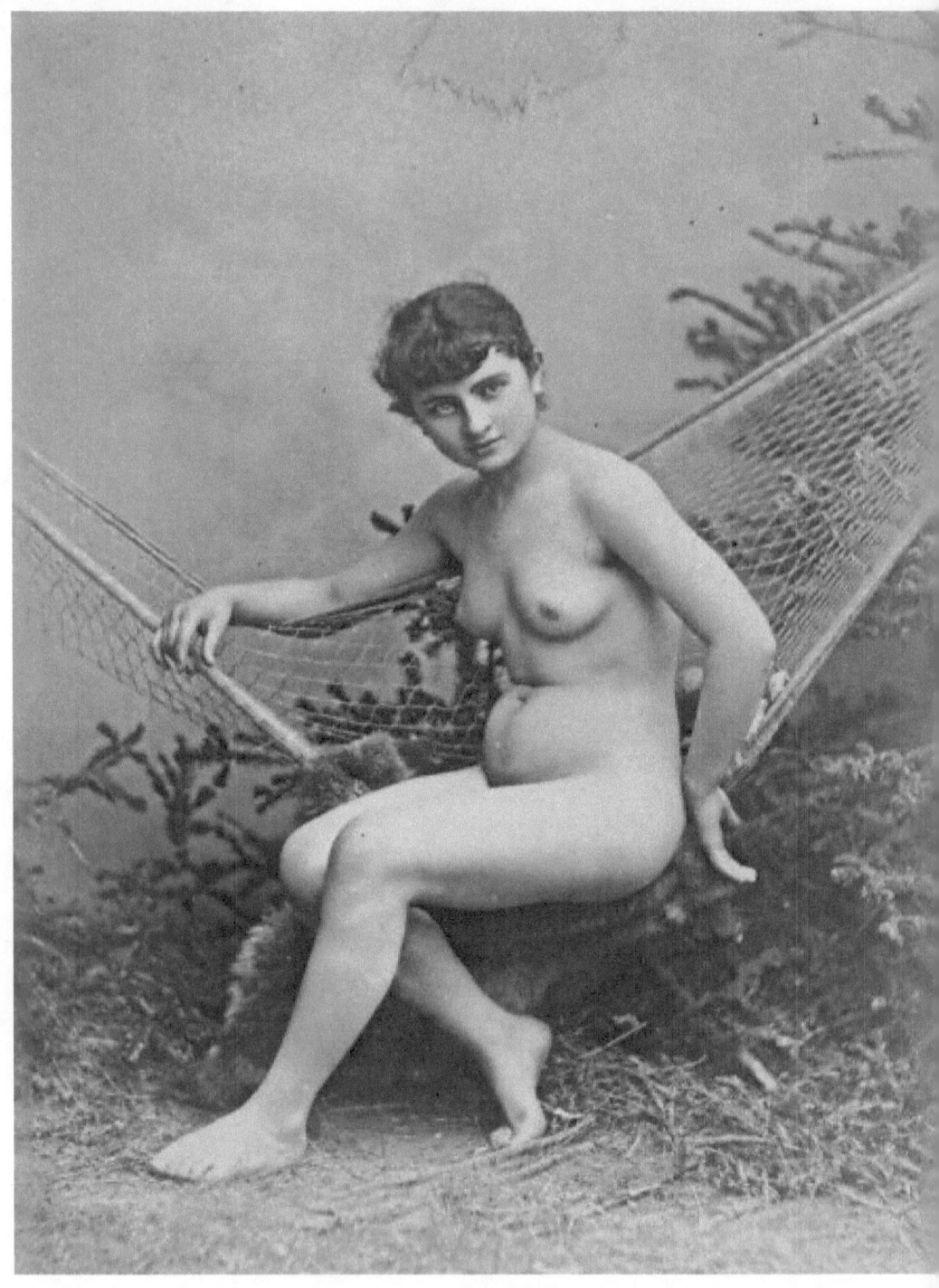

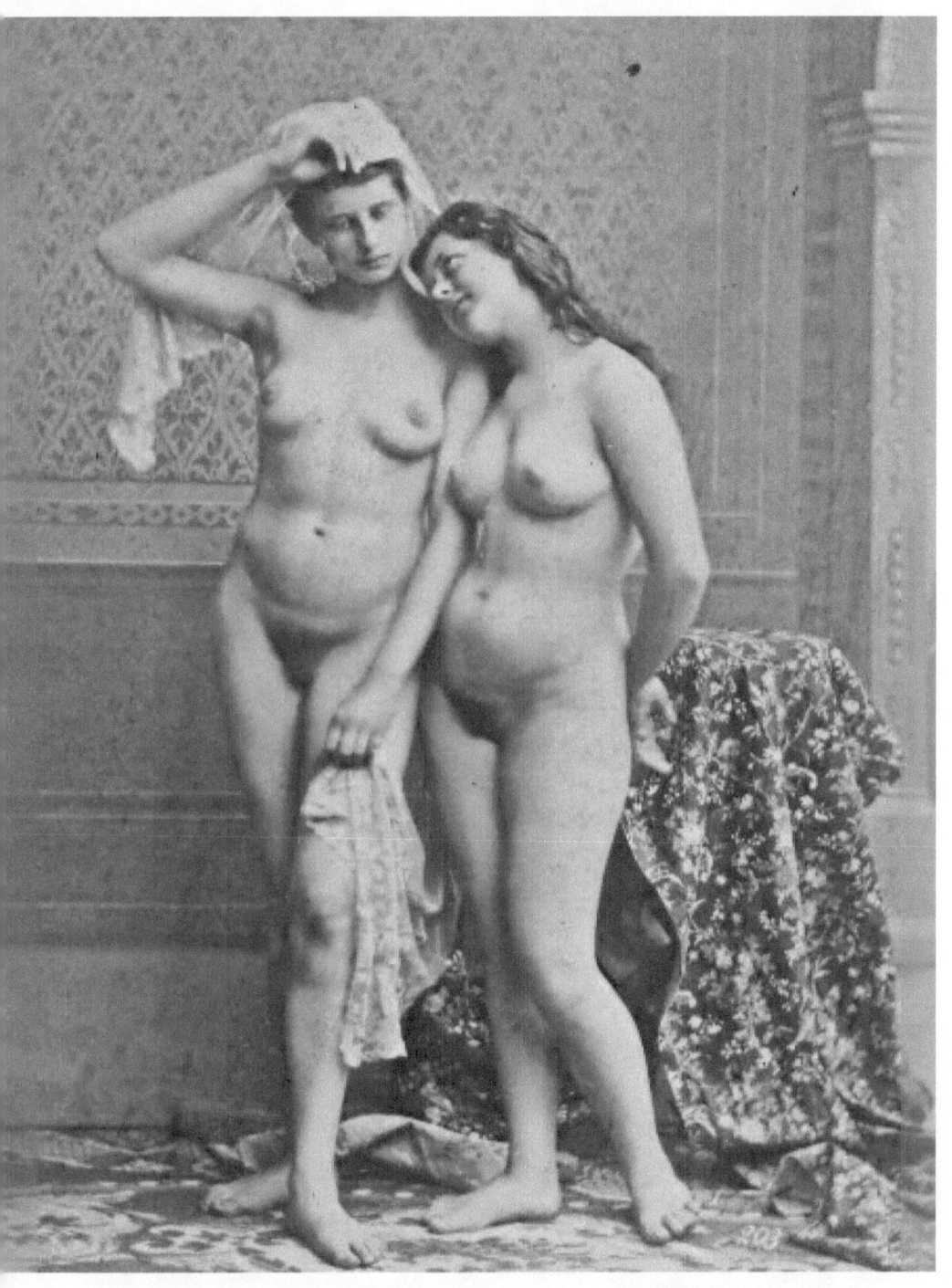

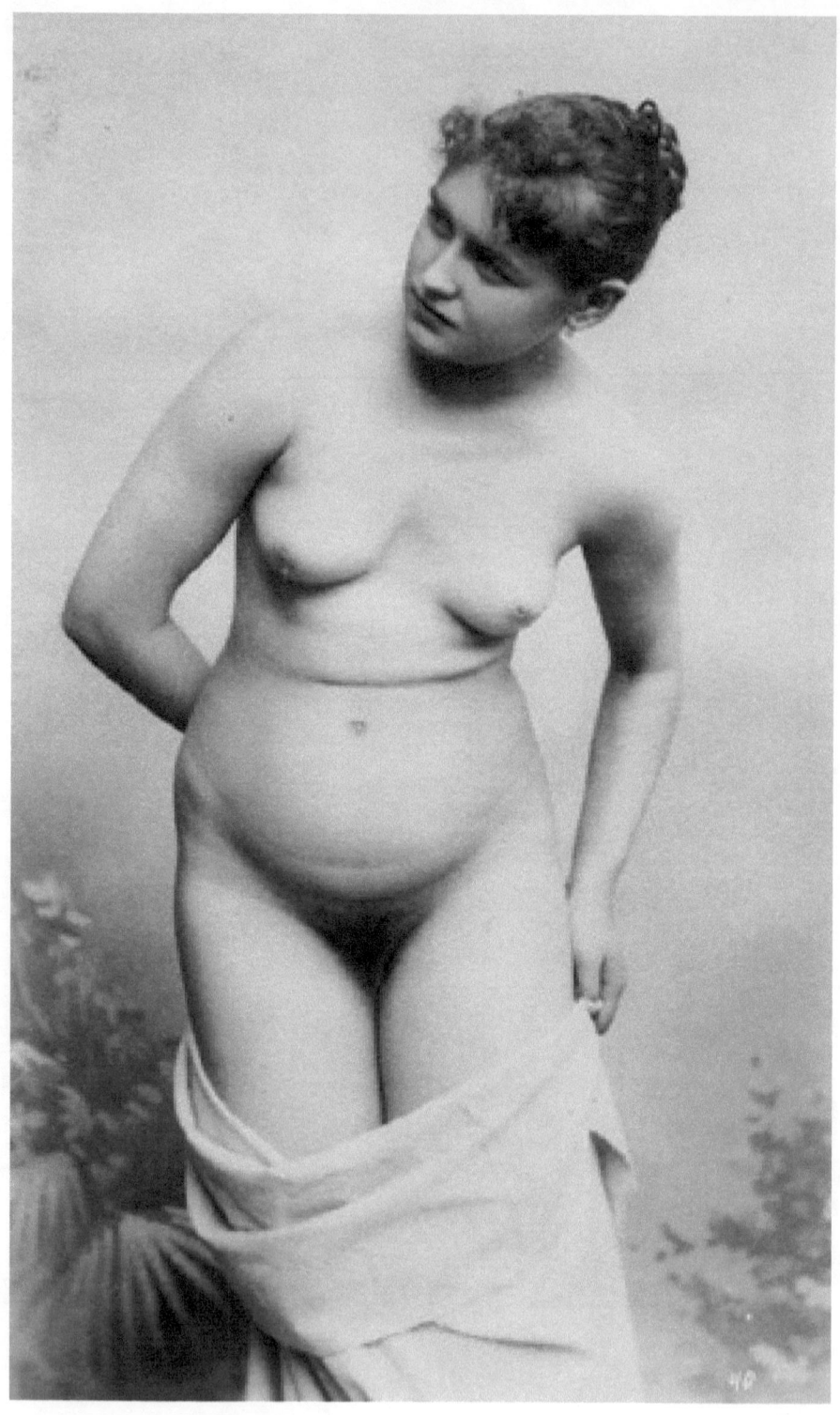

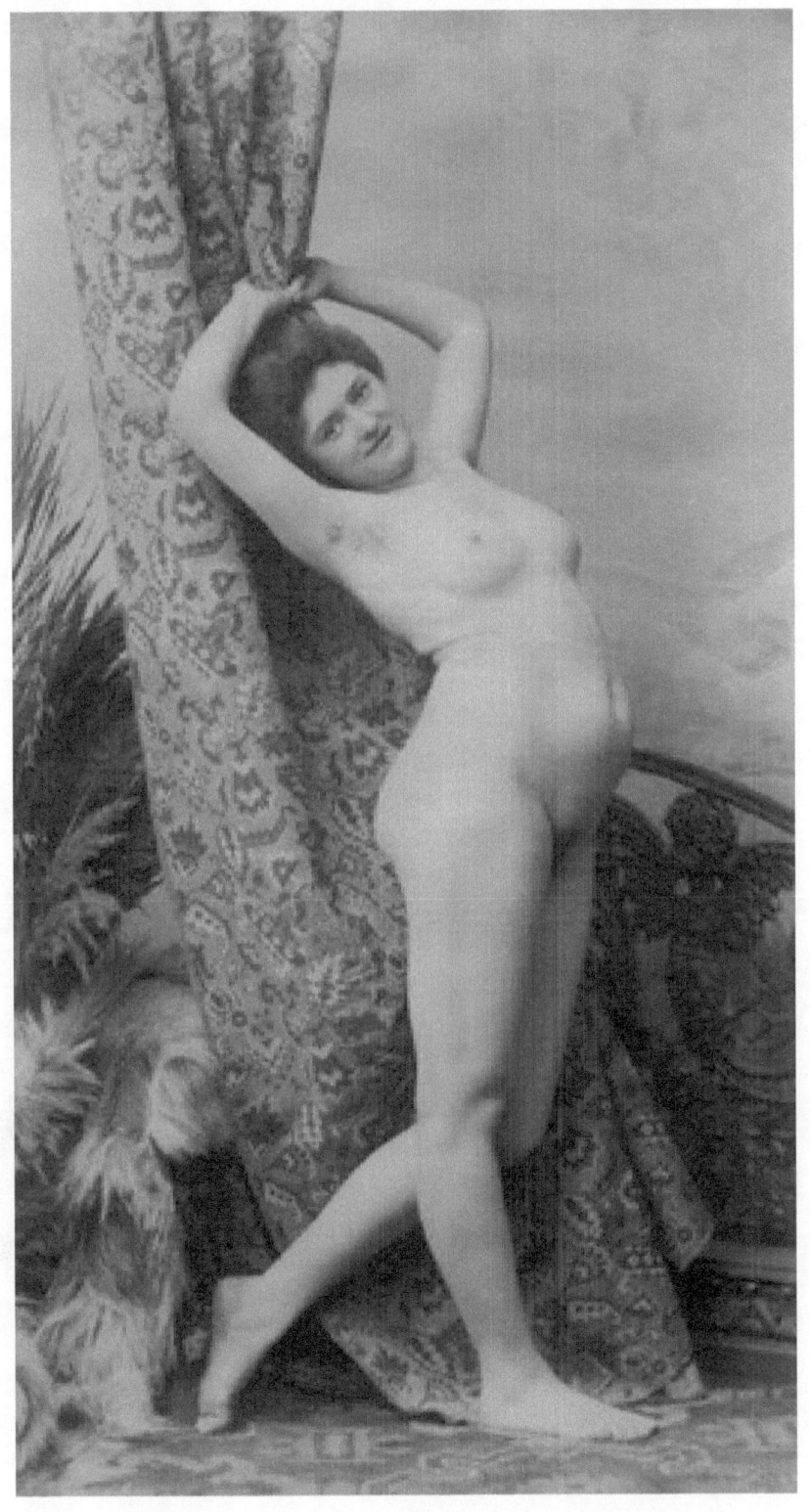

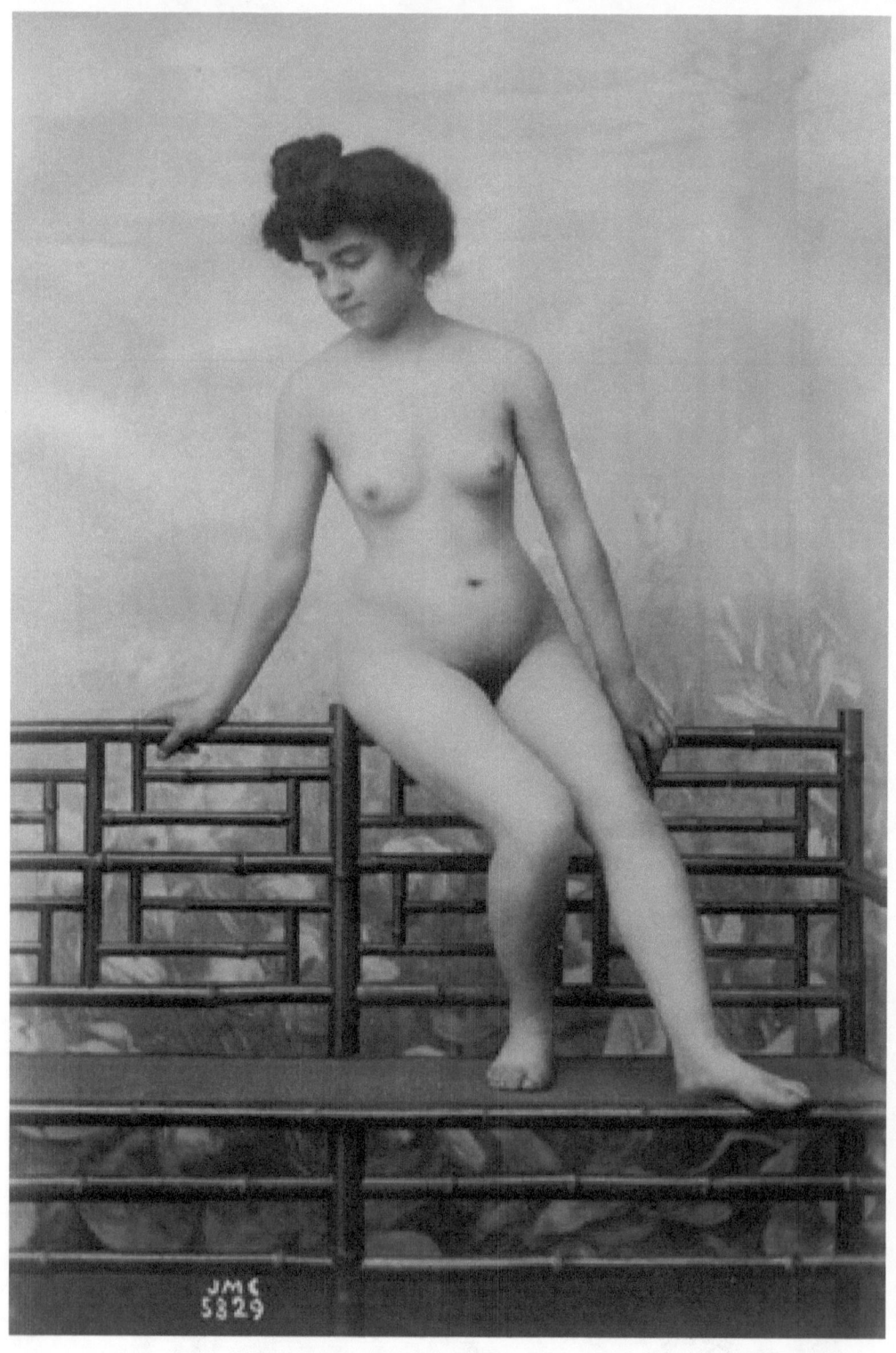

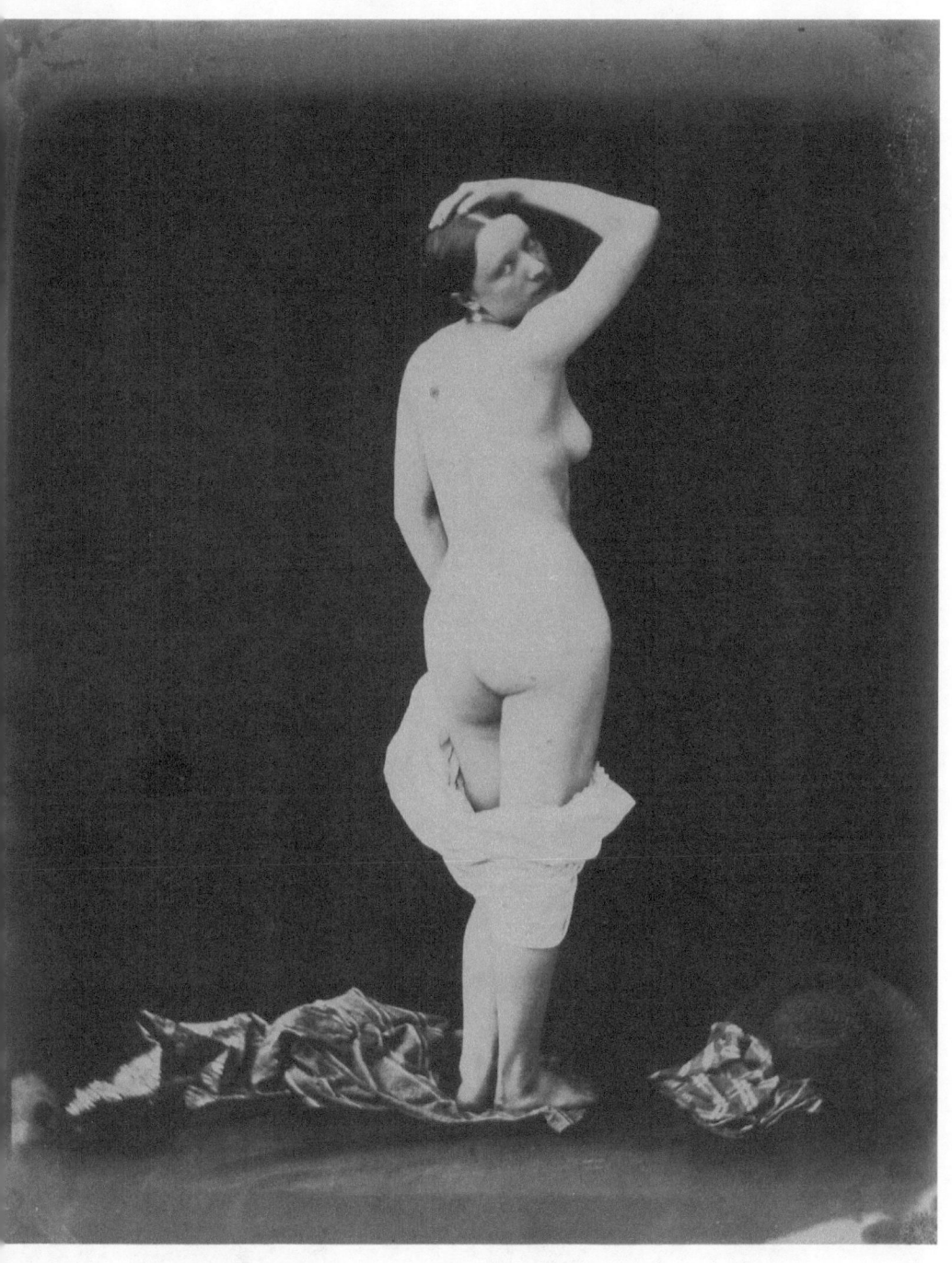

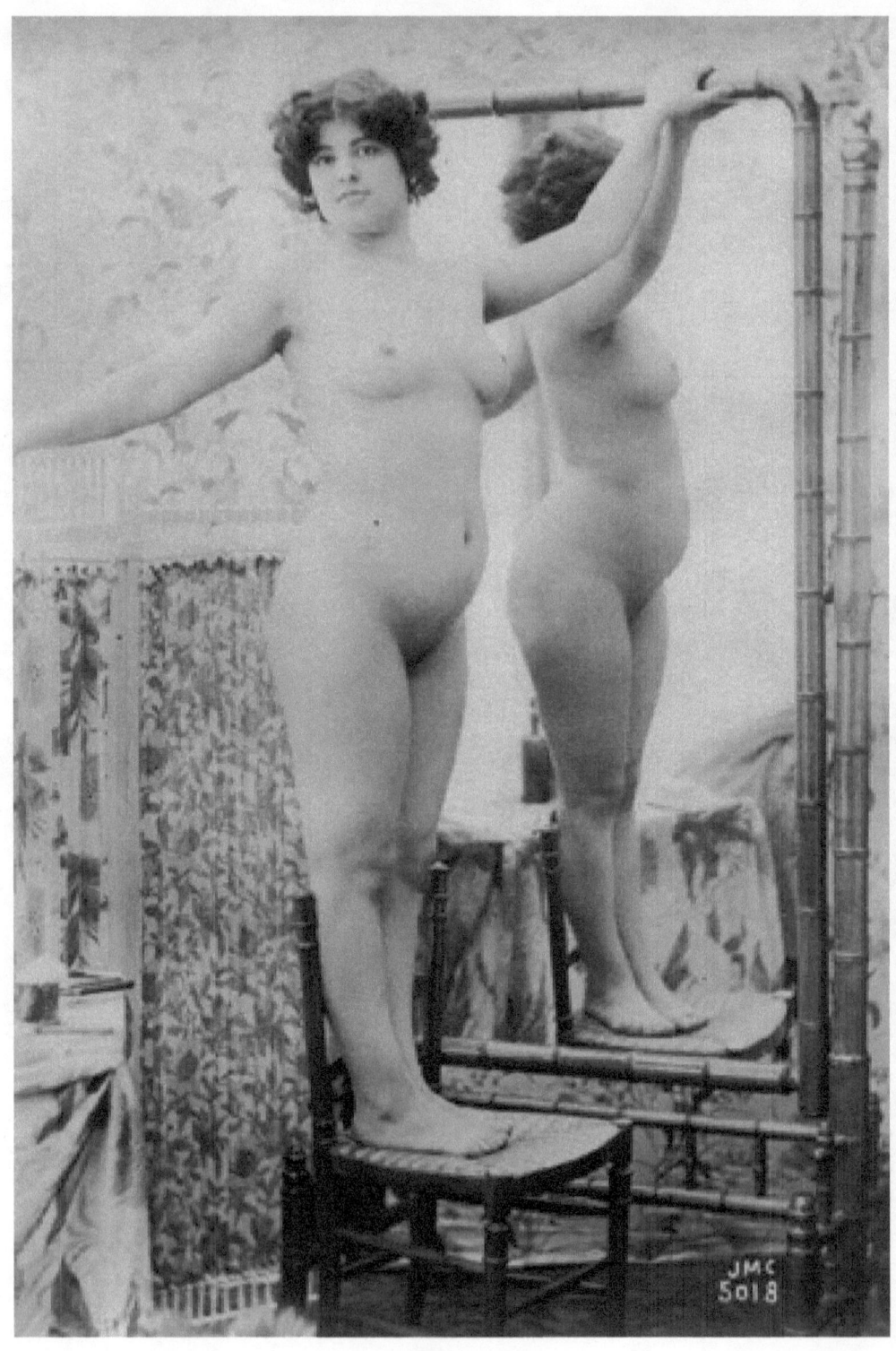

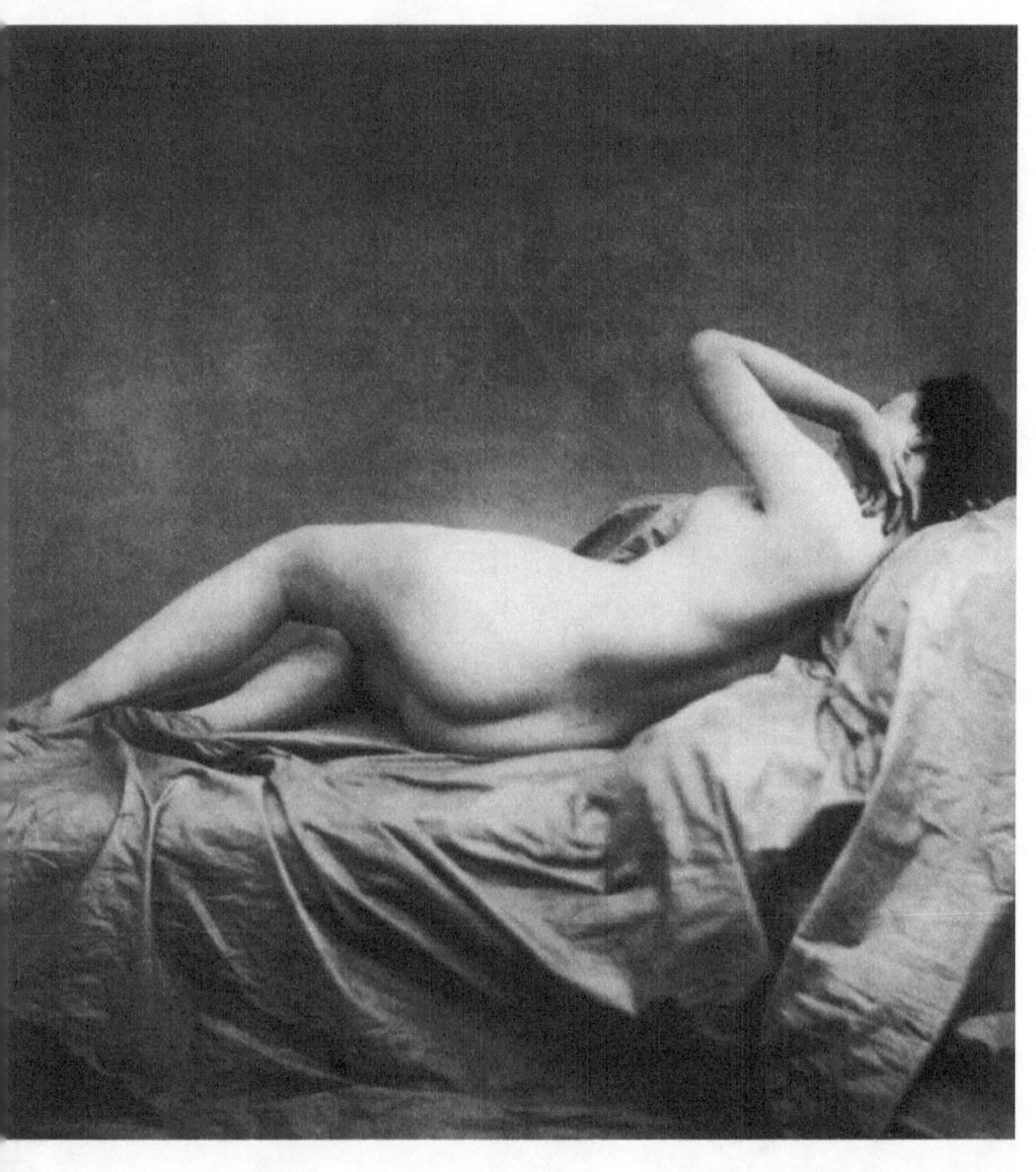

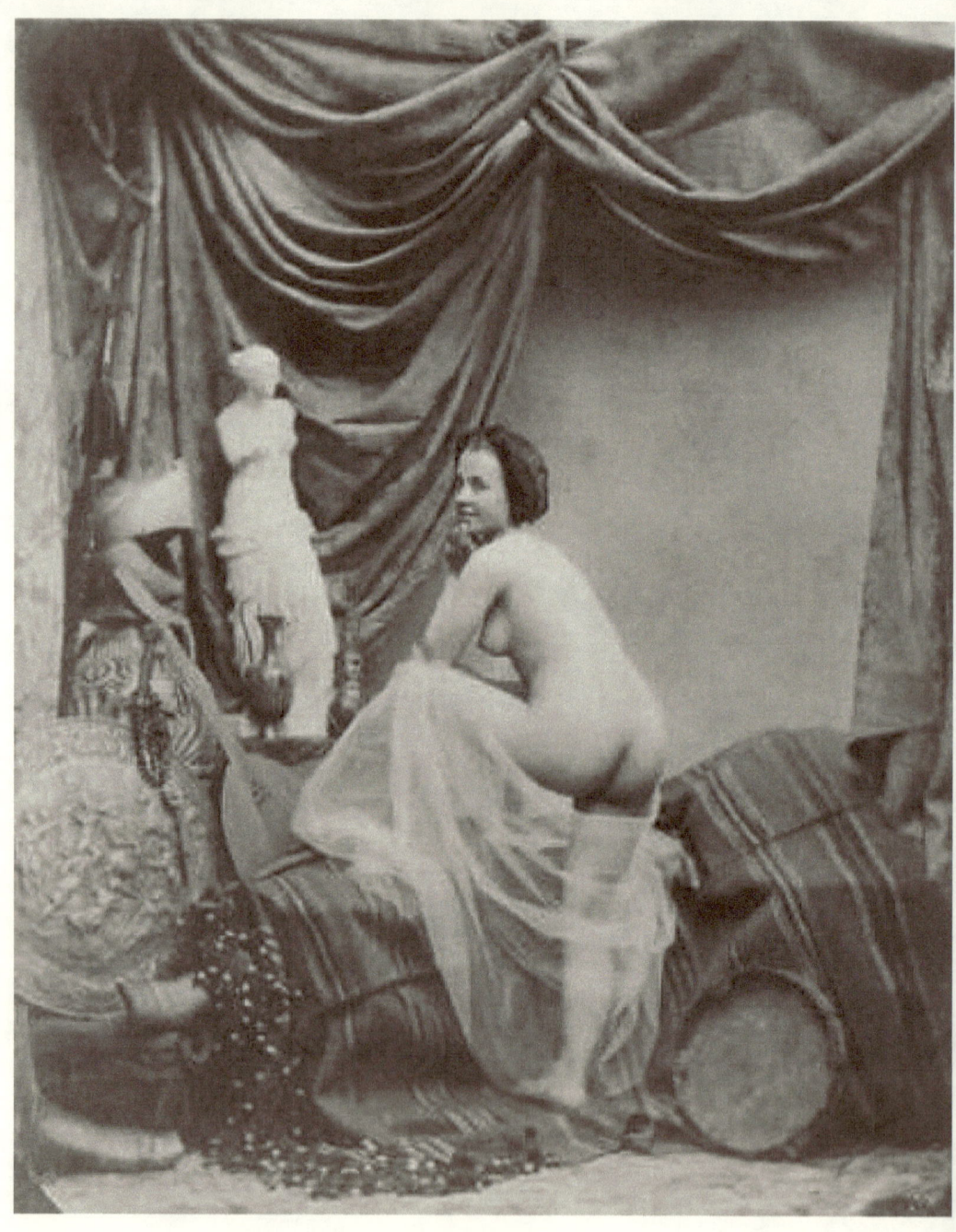

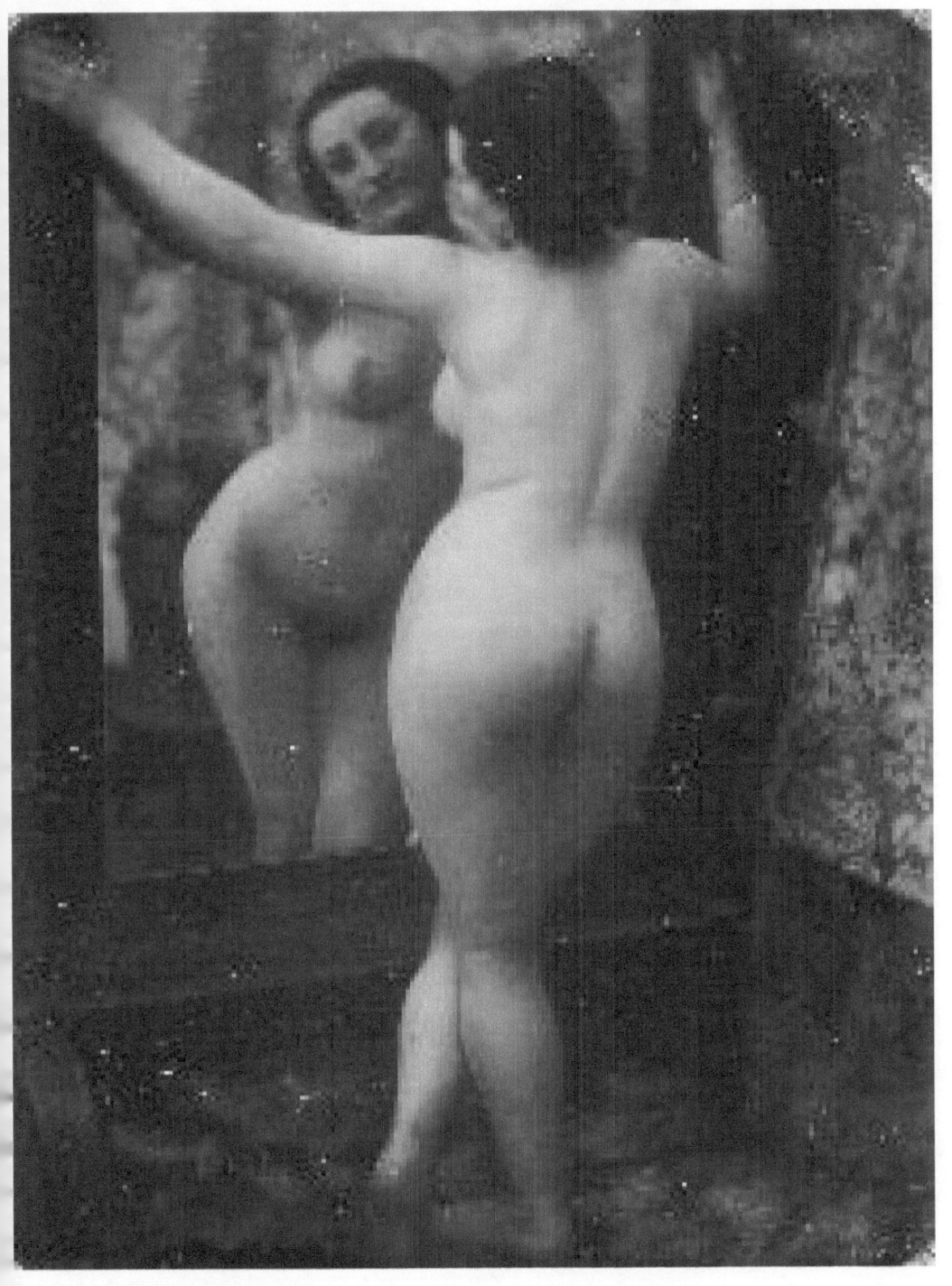

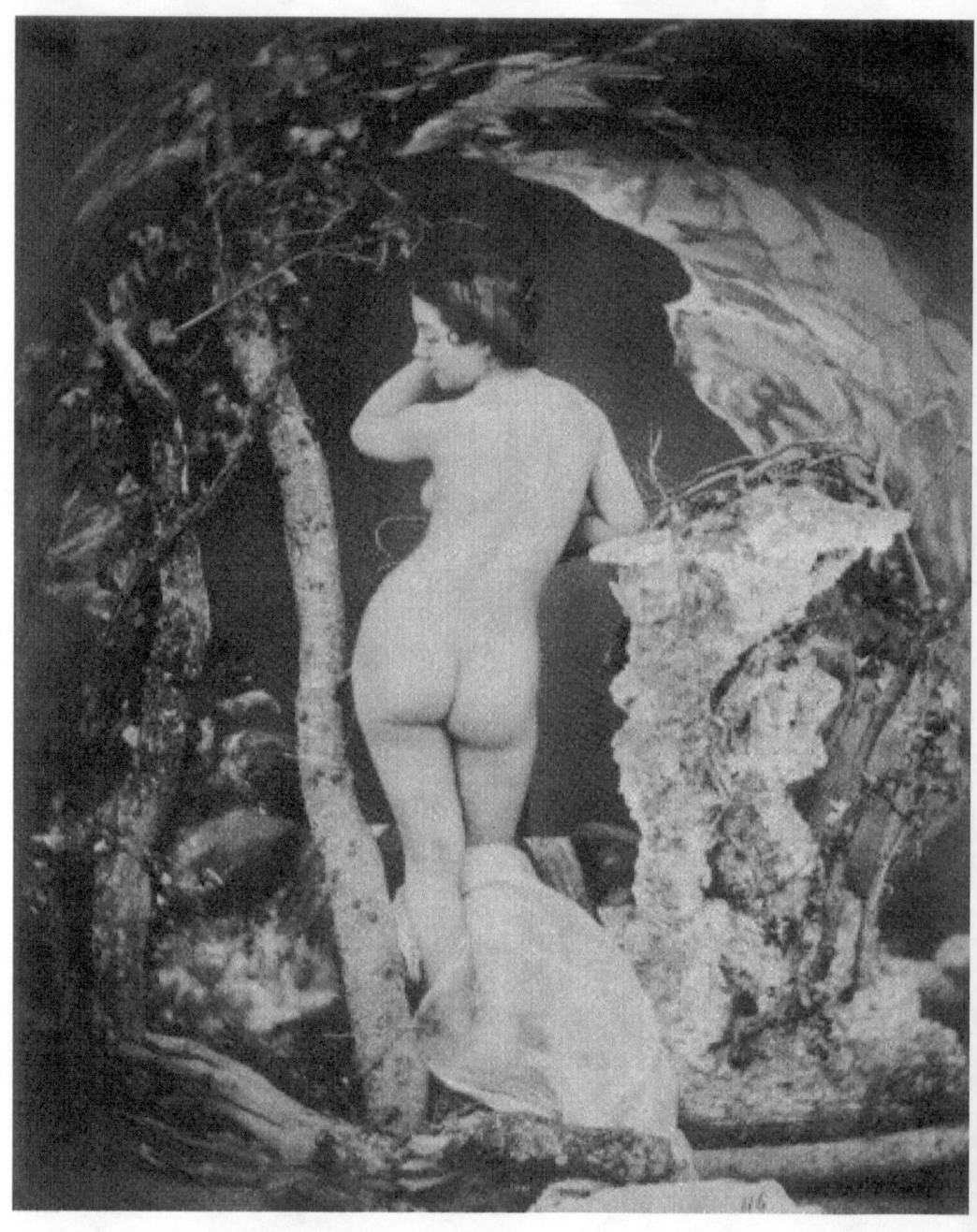

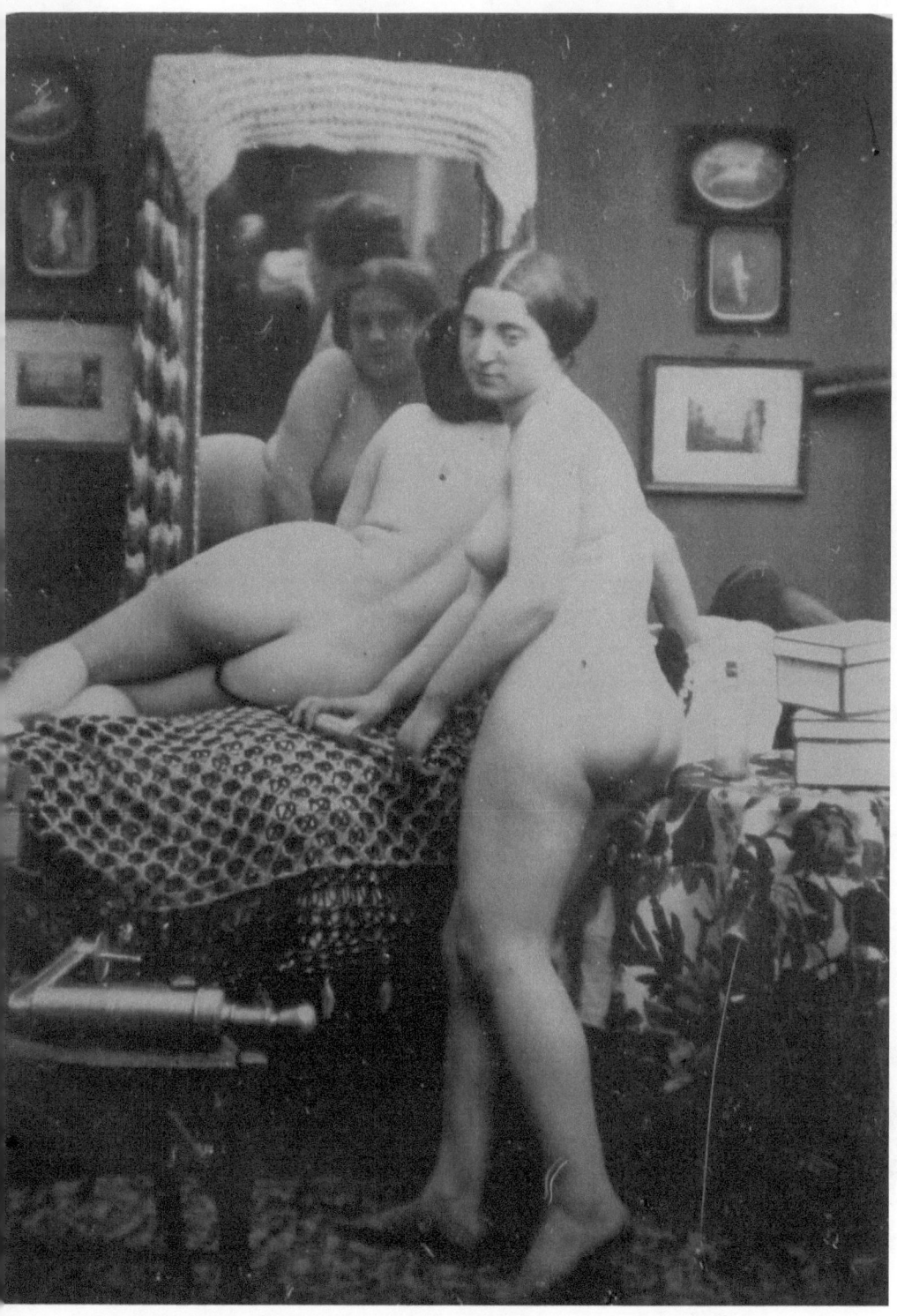

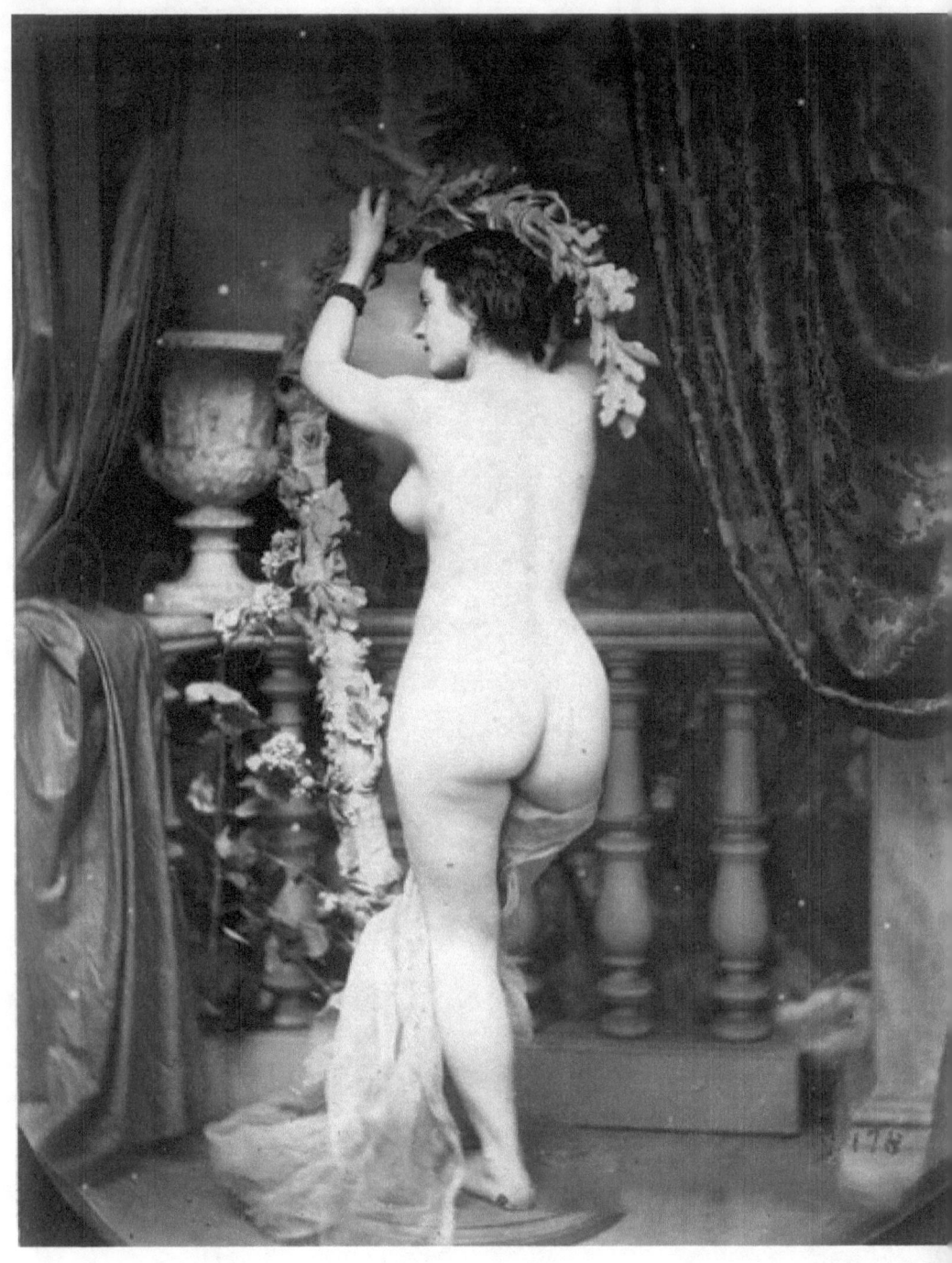

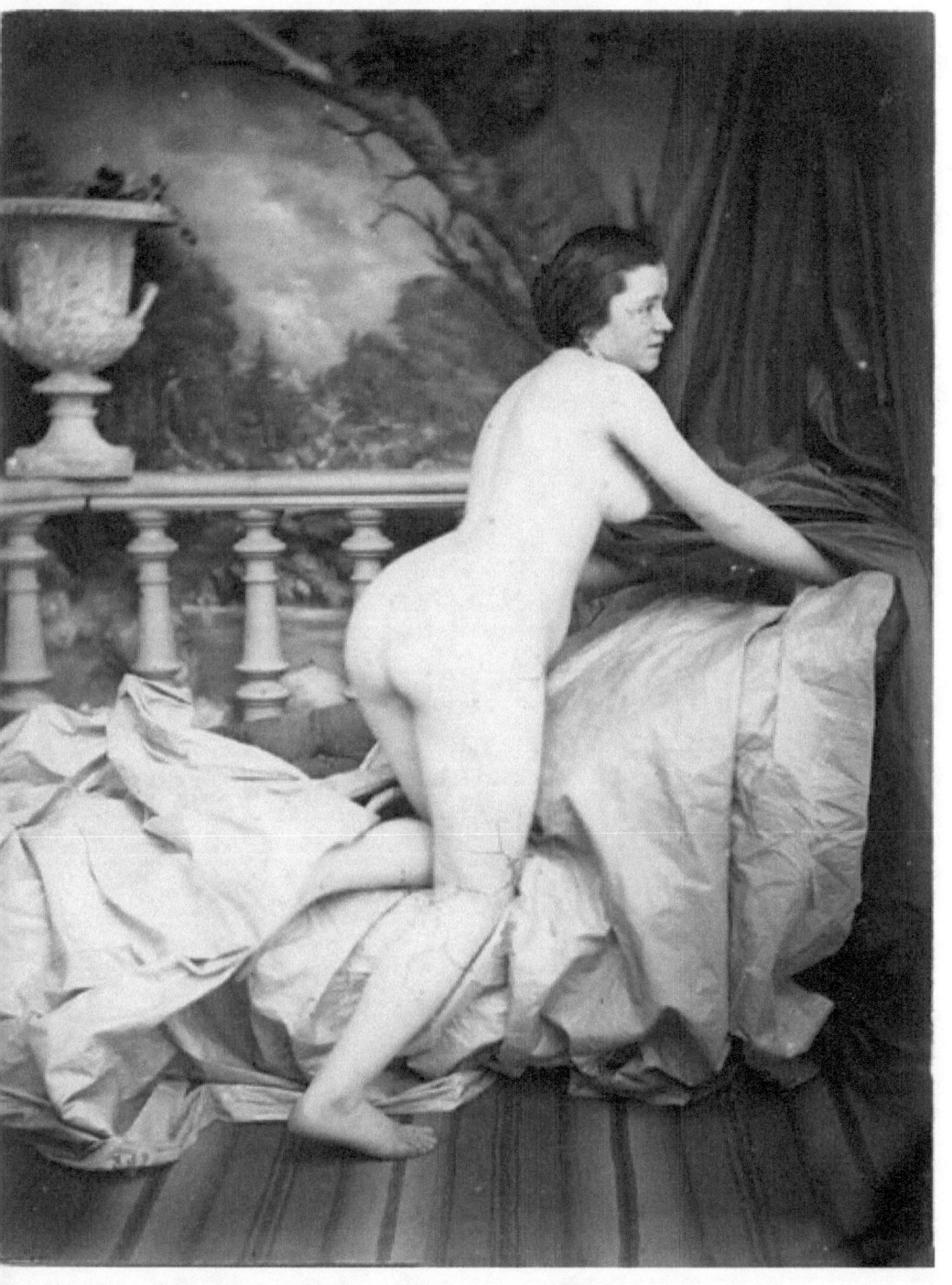

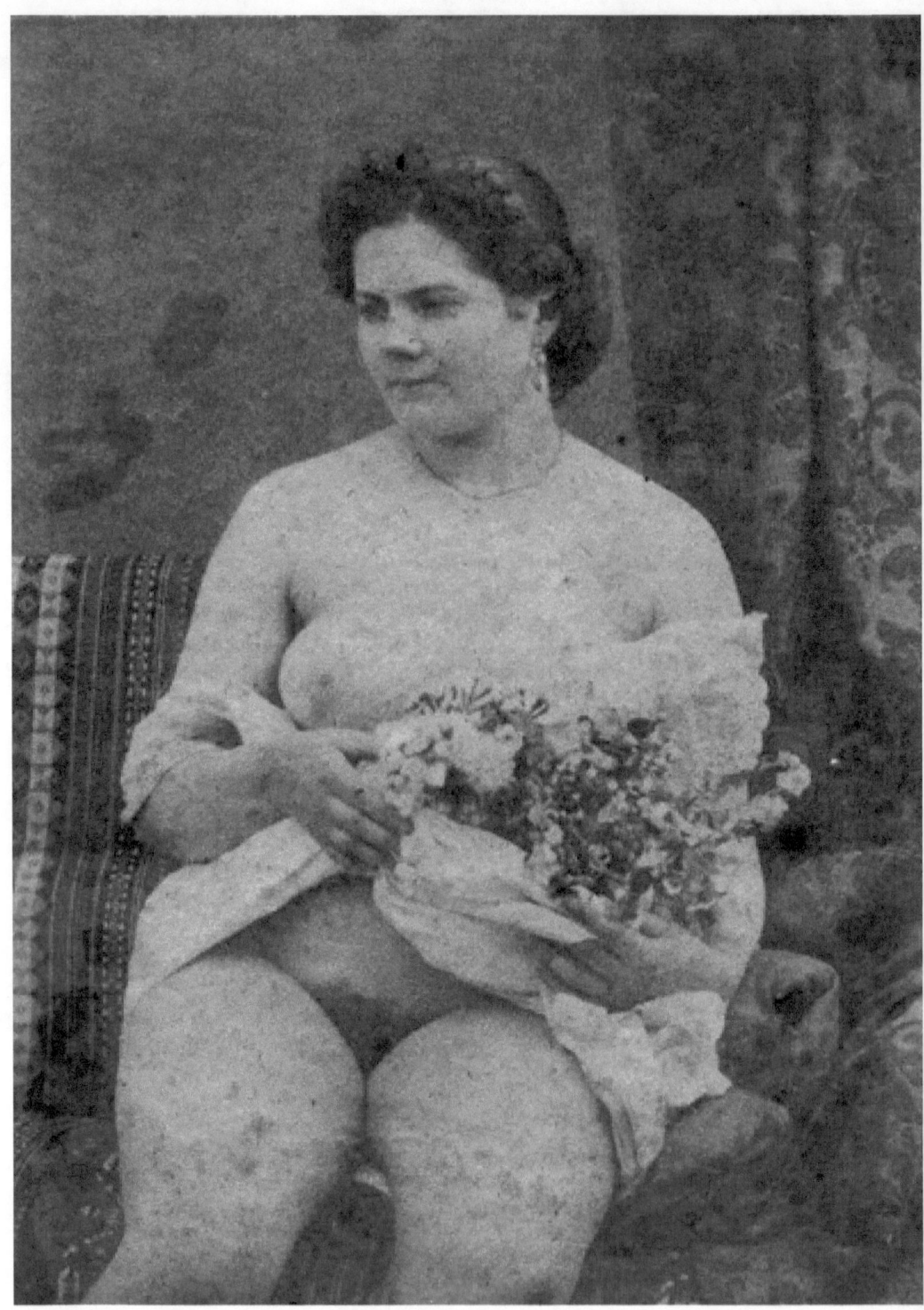

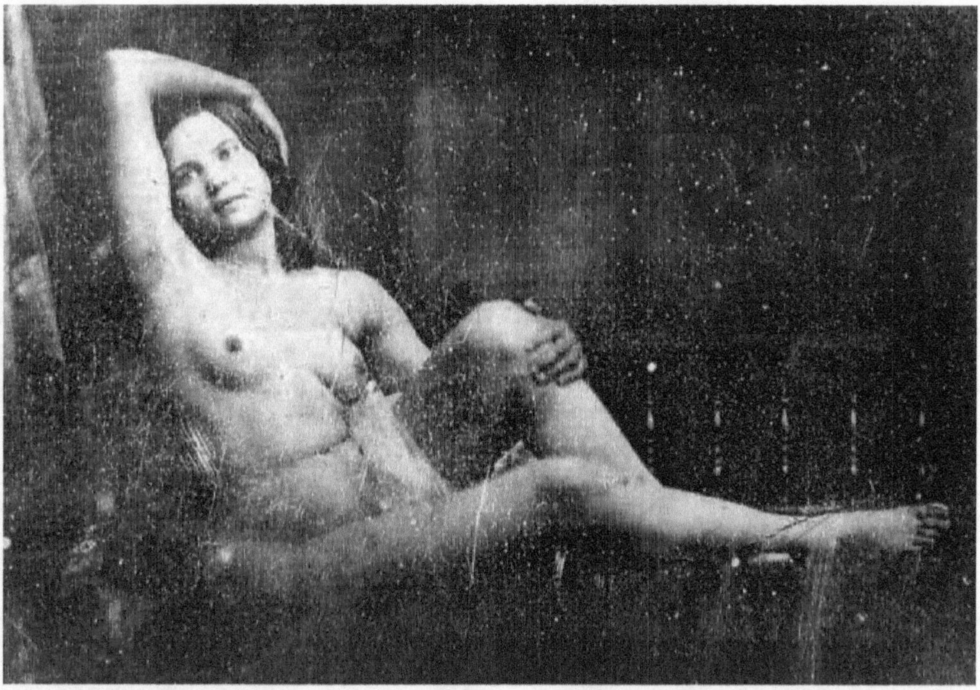

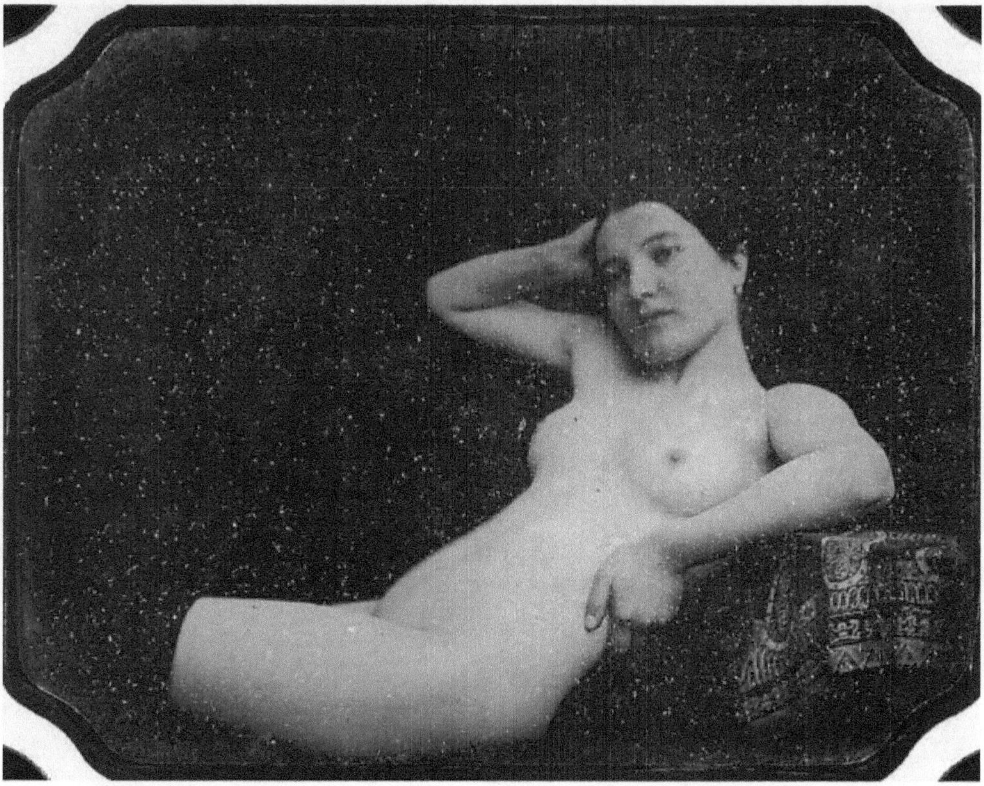

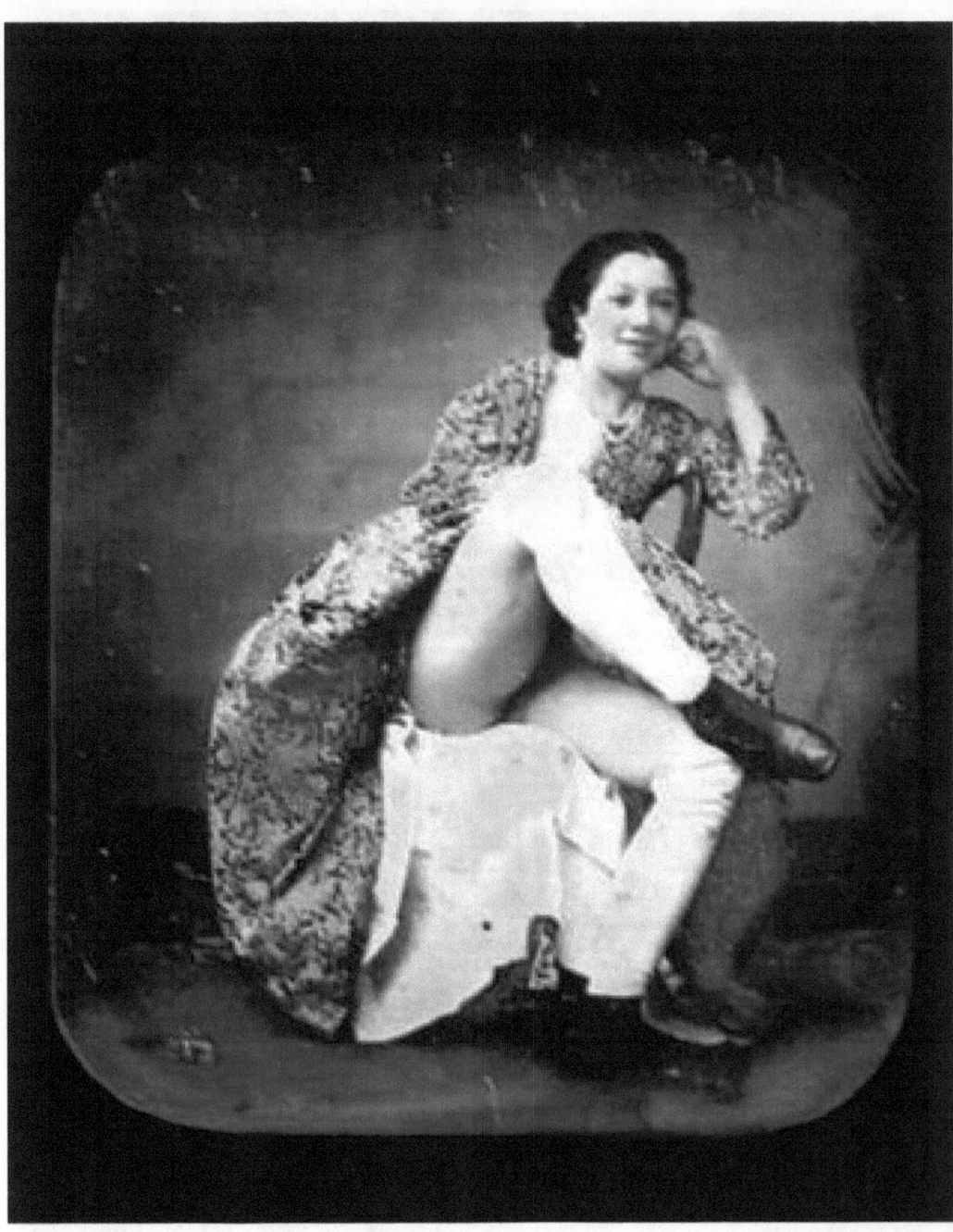

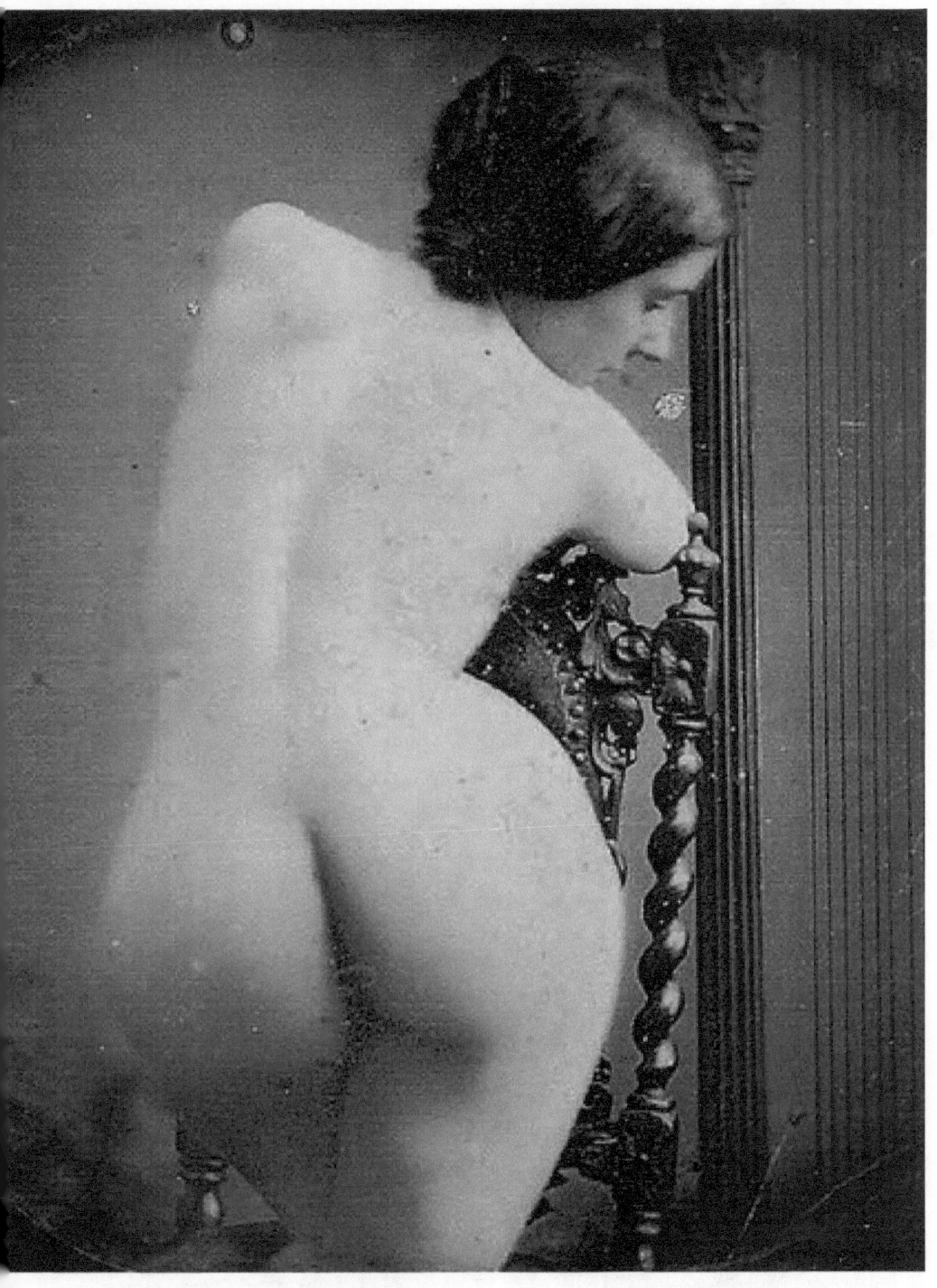

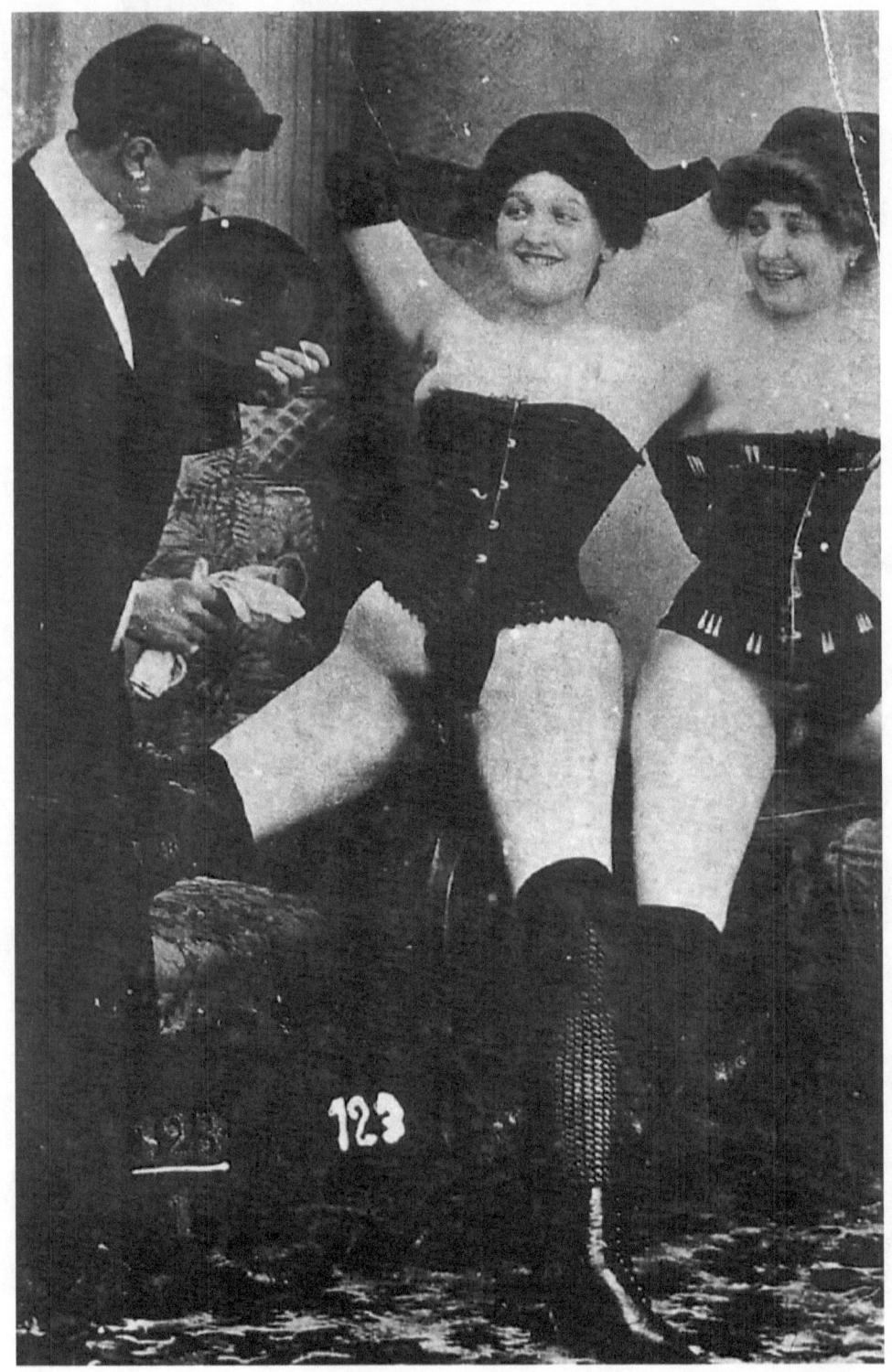

123

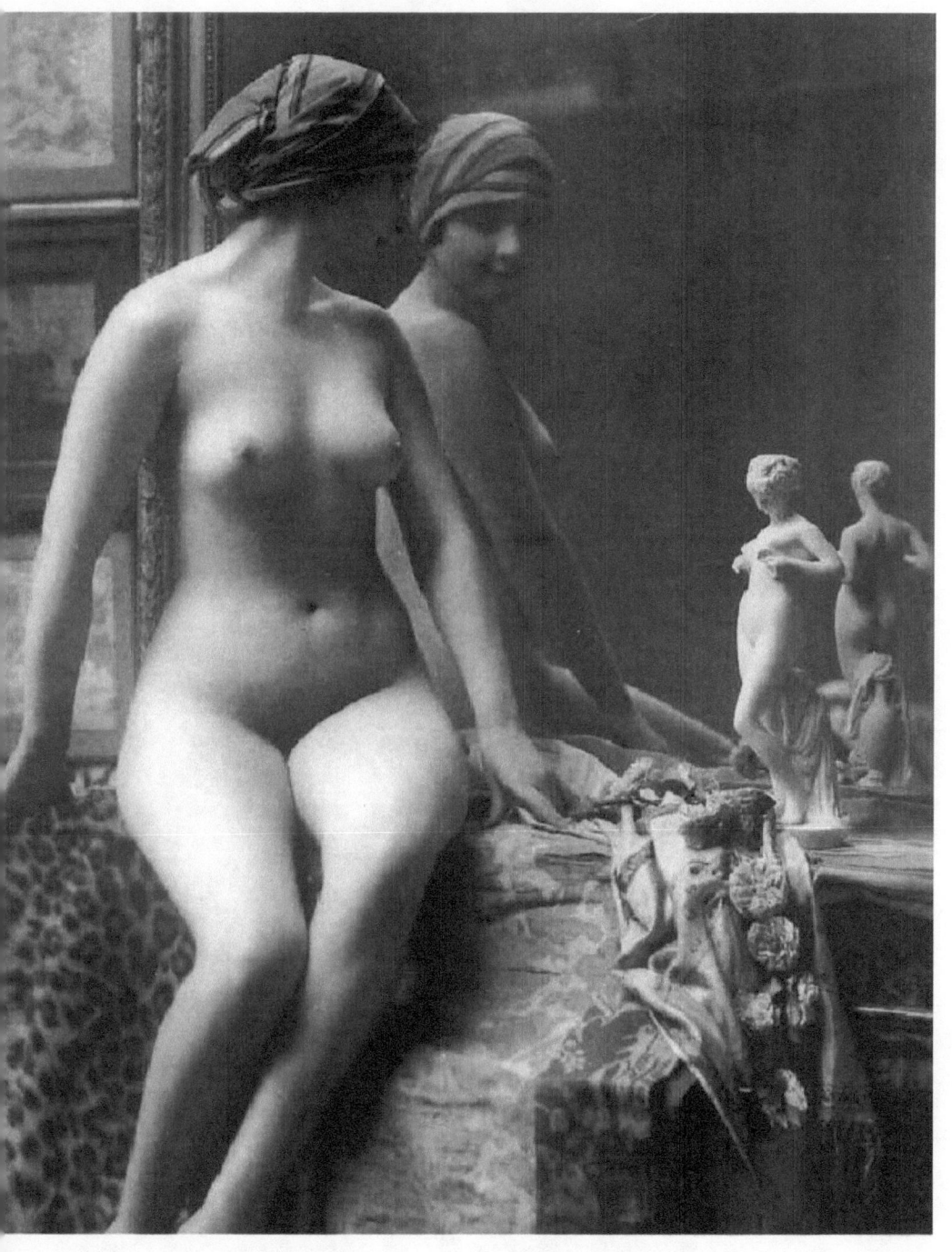

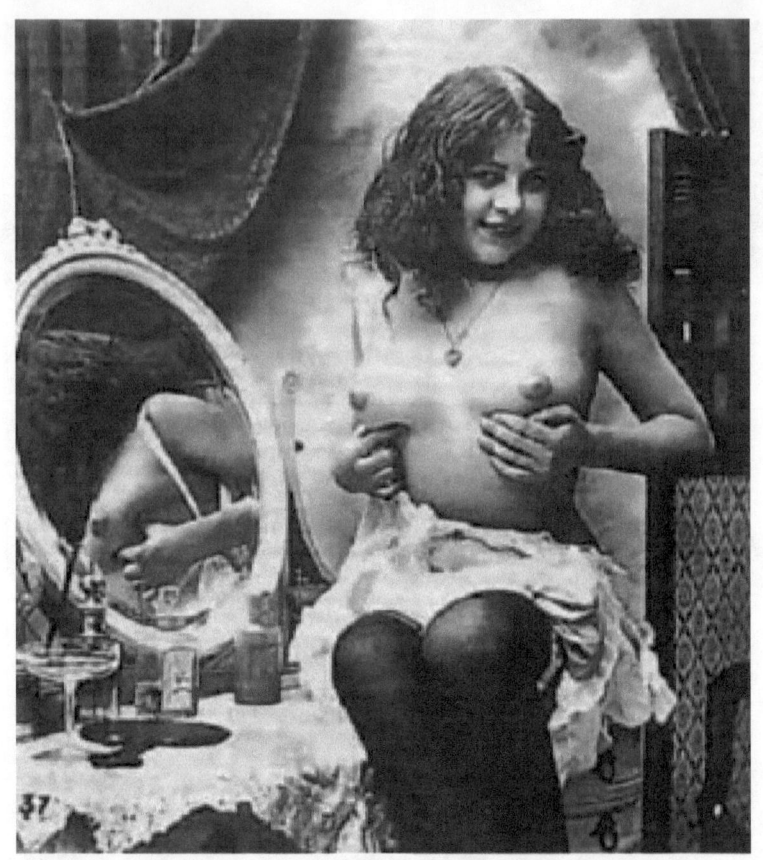

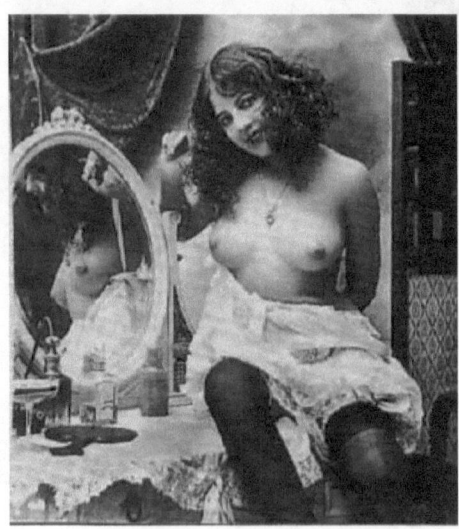

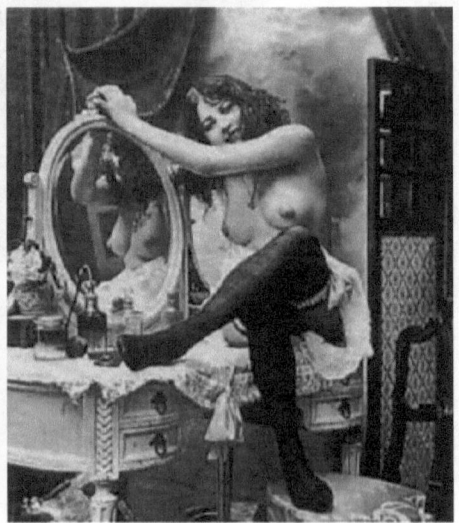

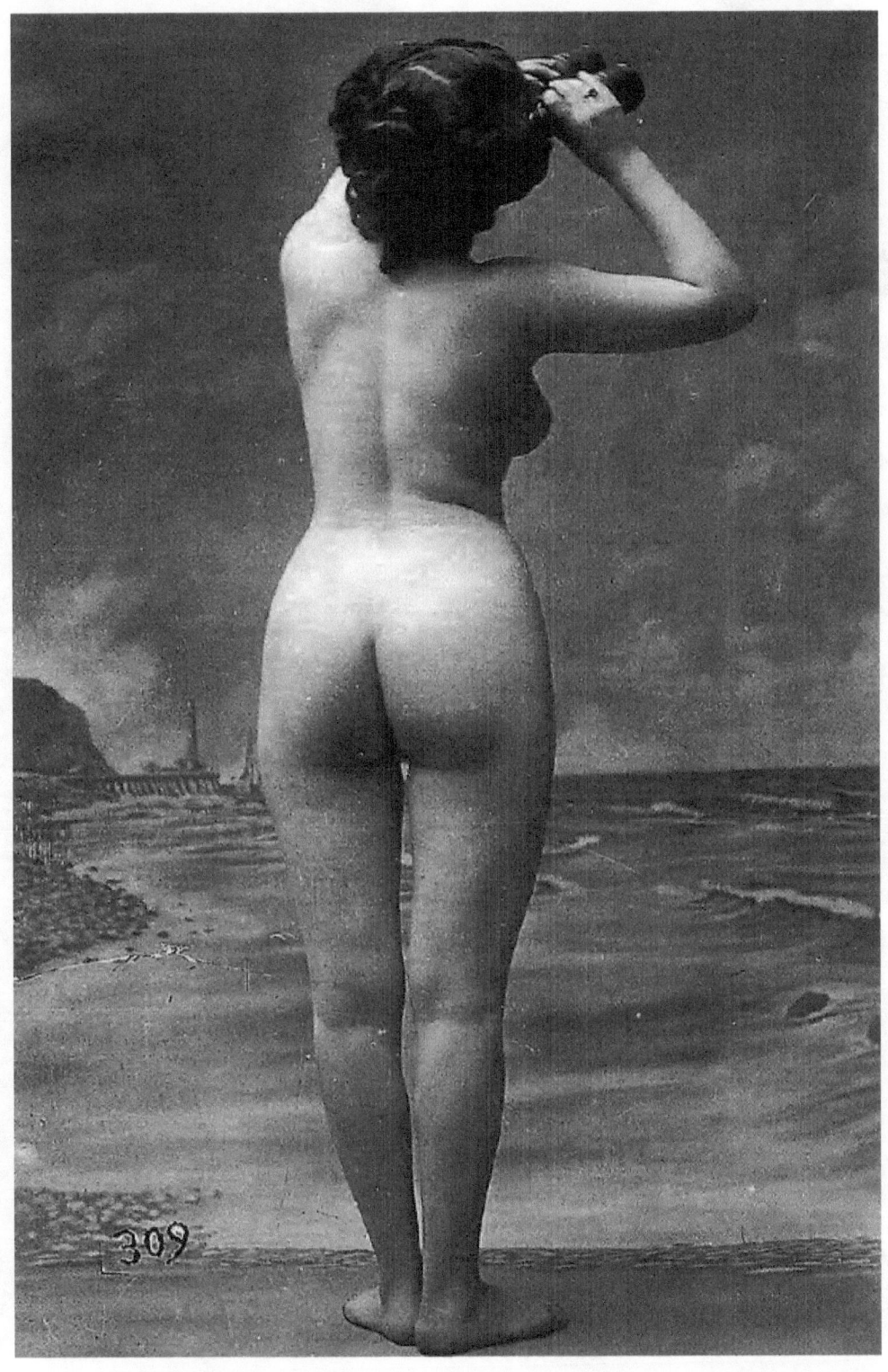

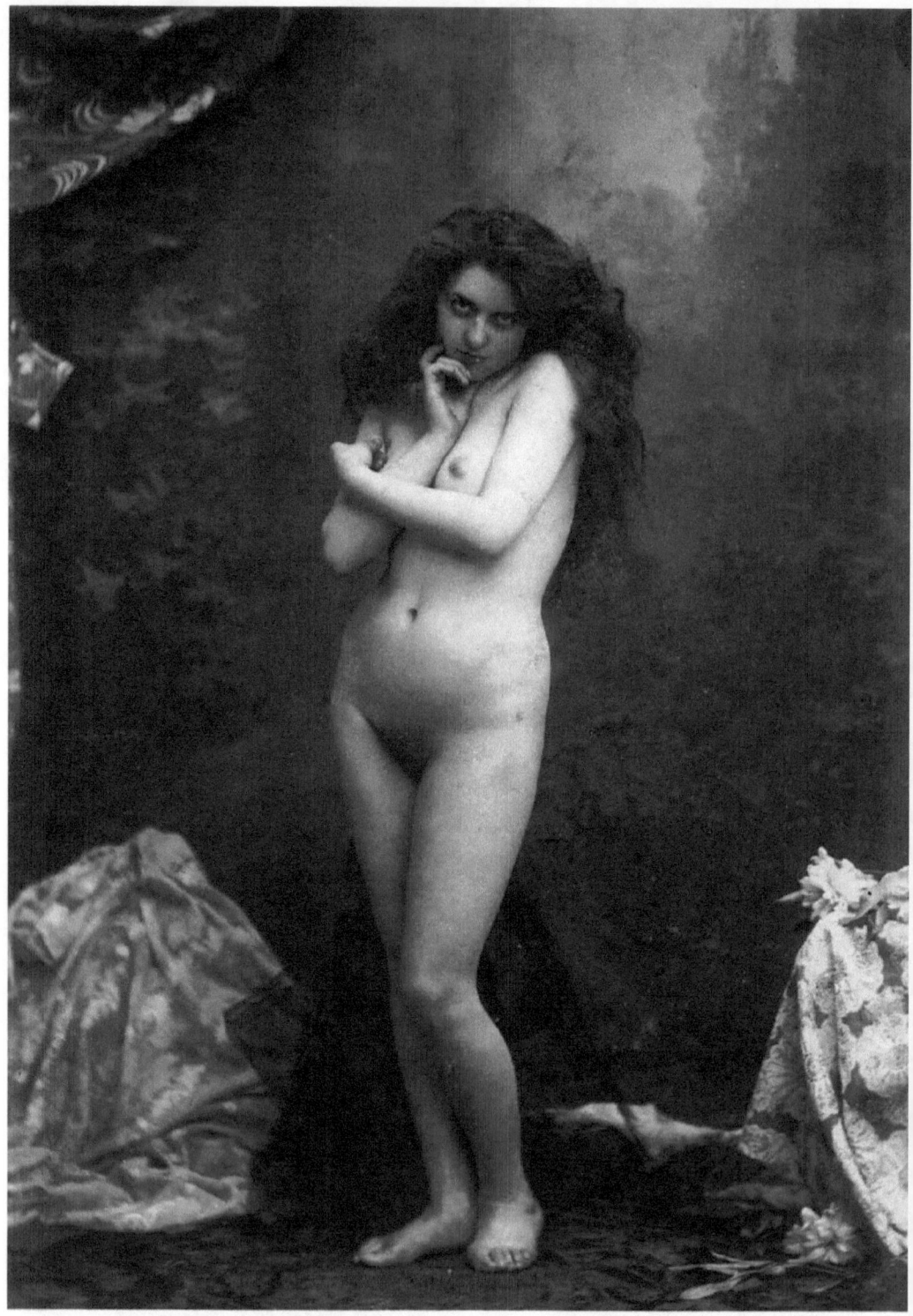

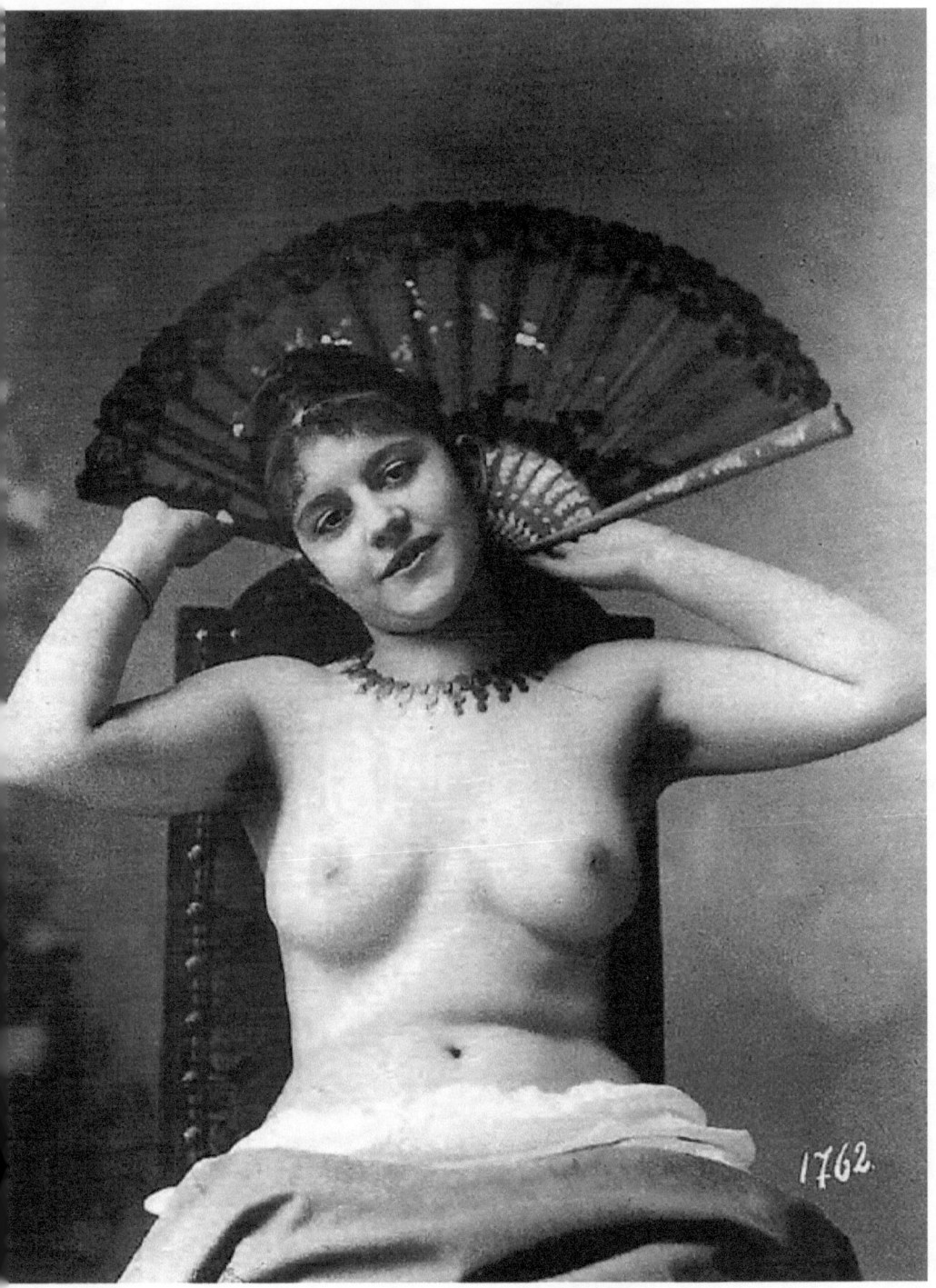

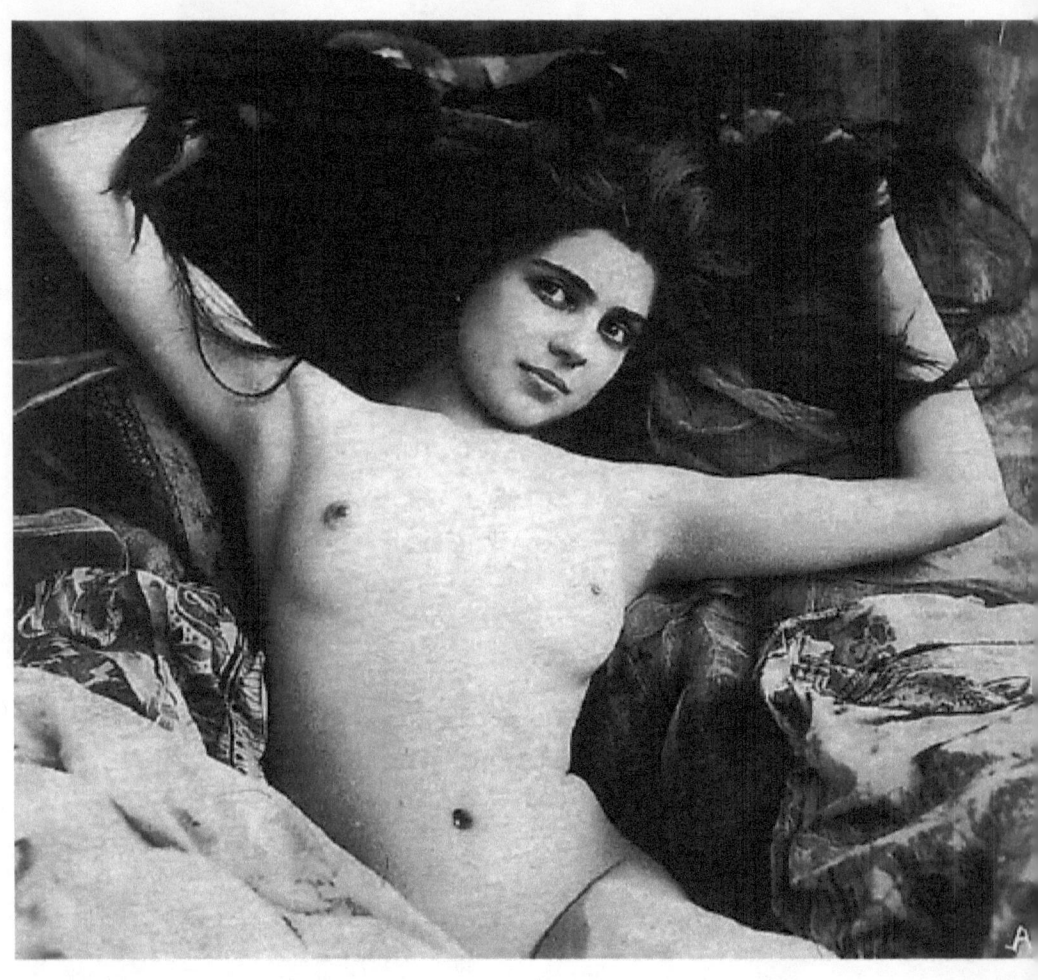

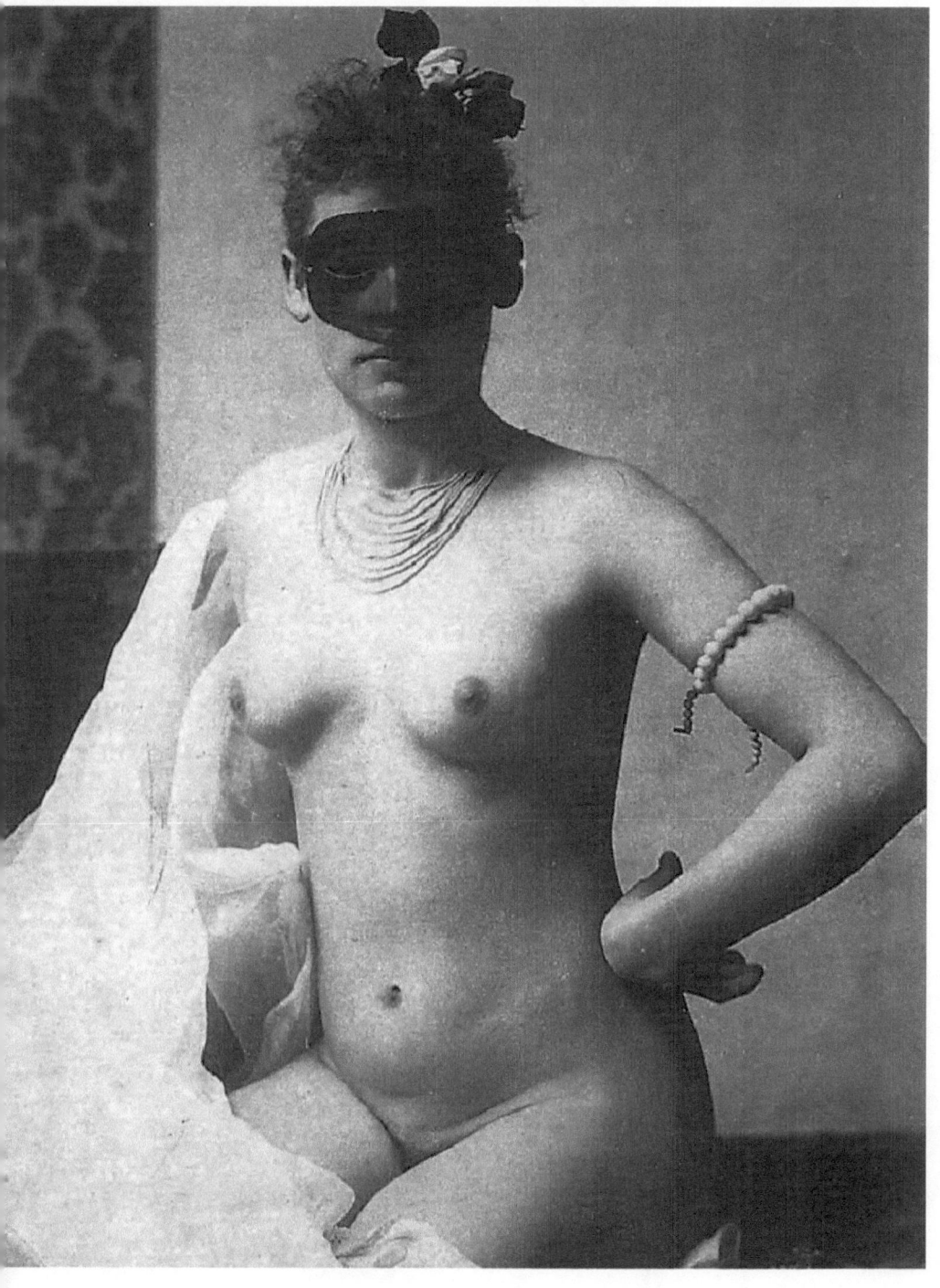

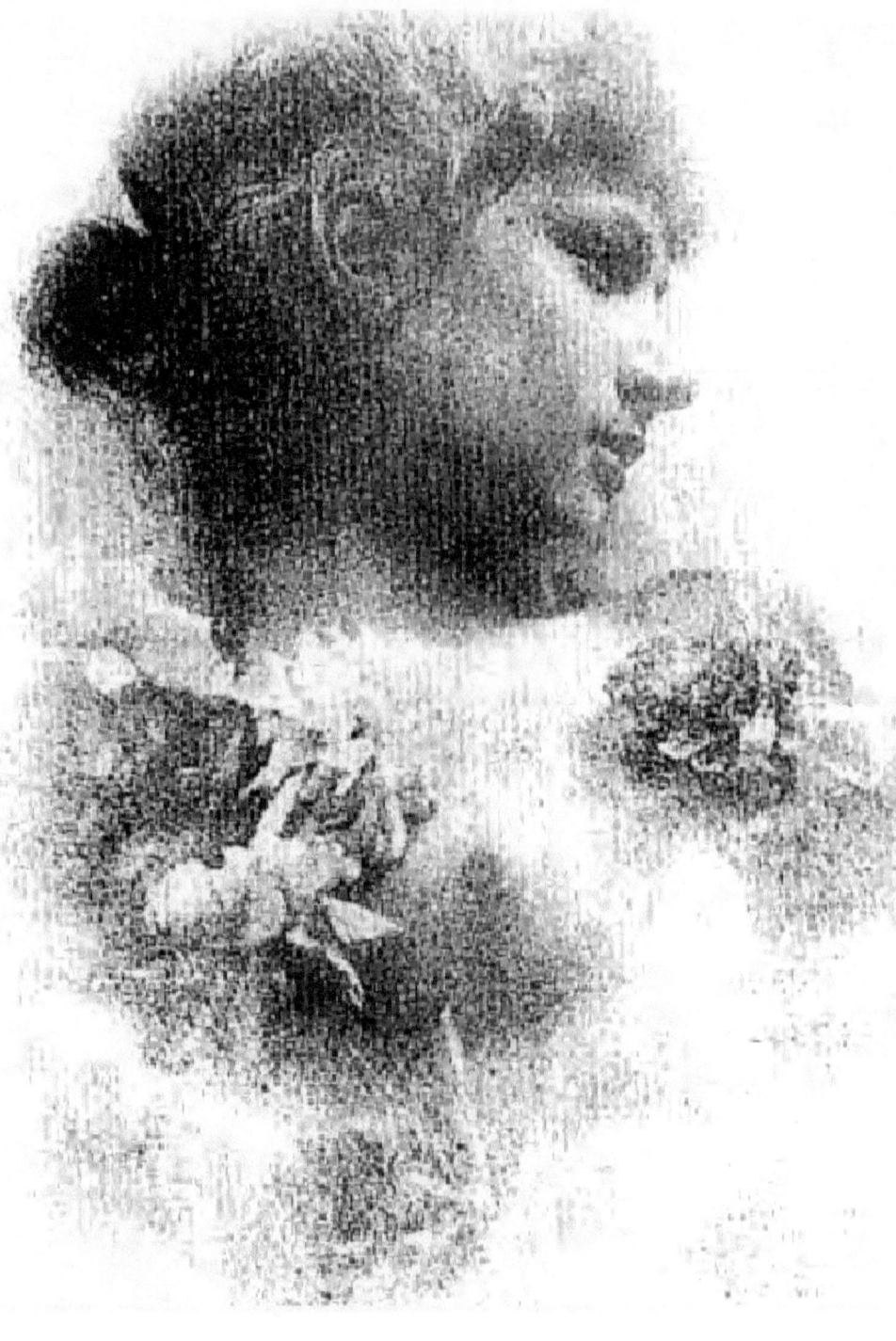

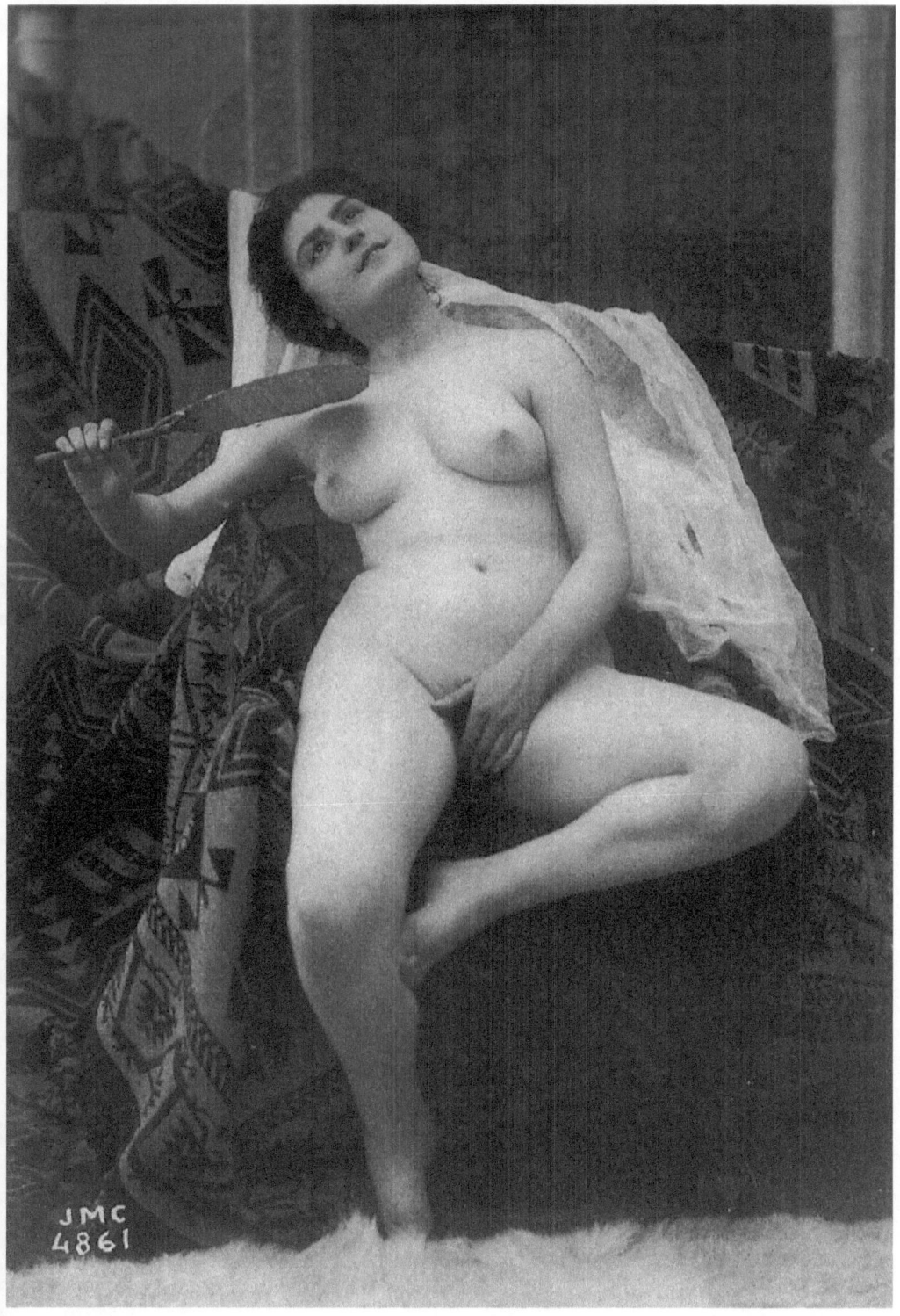

JMC
4861

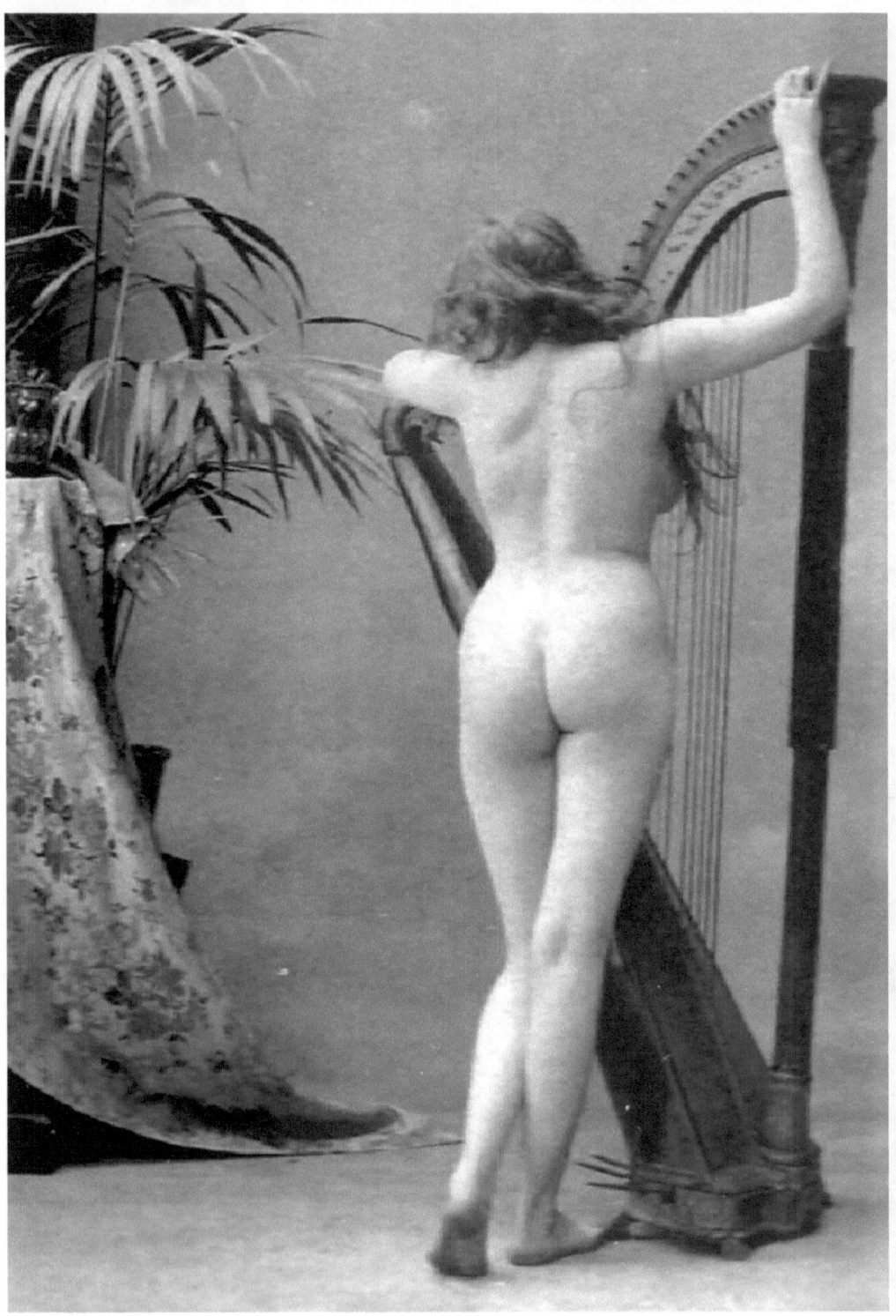

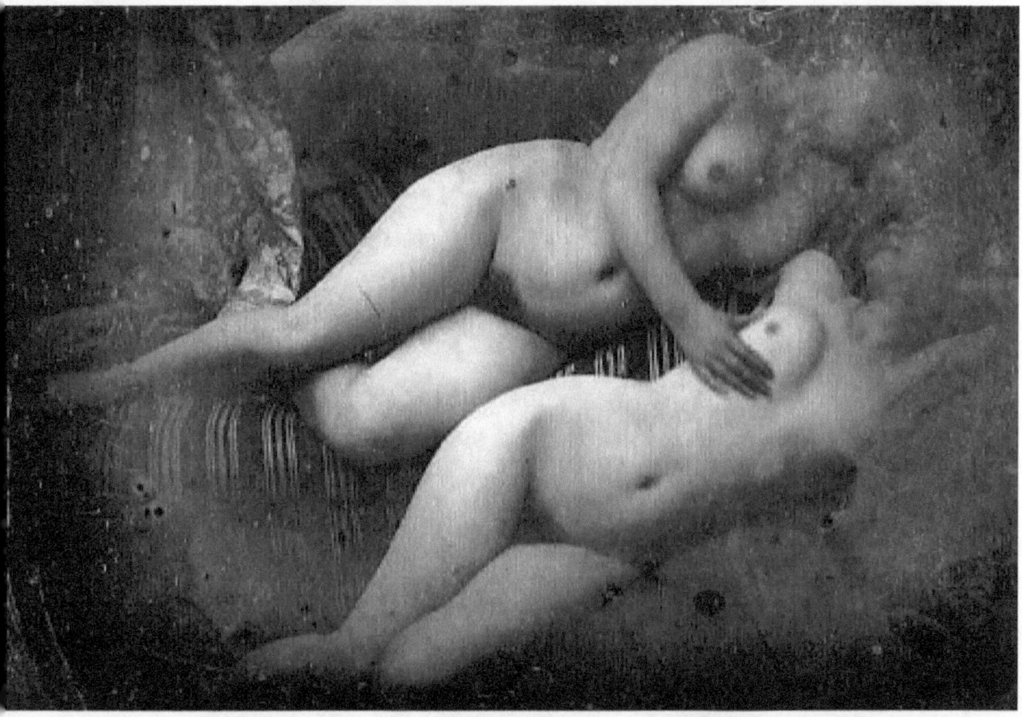

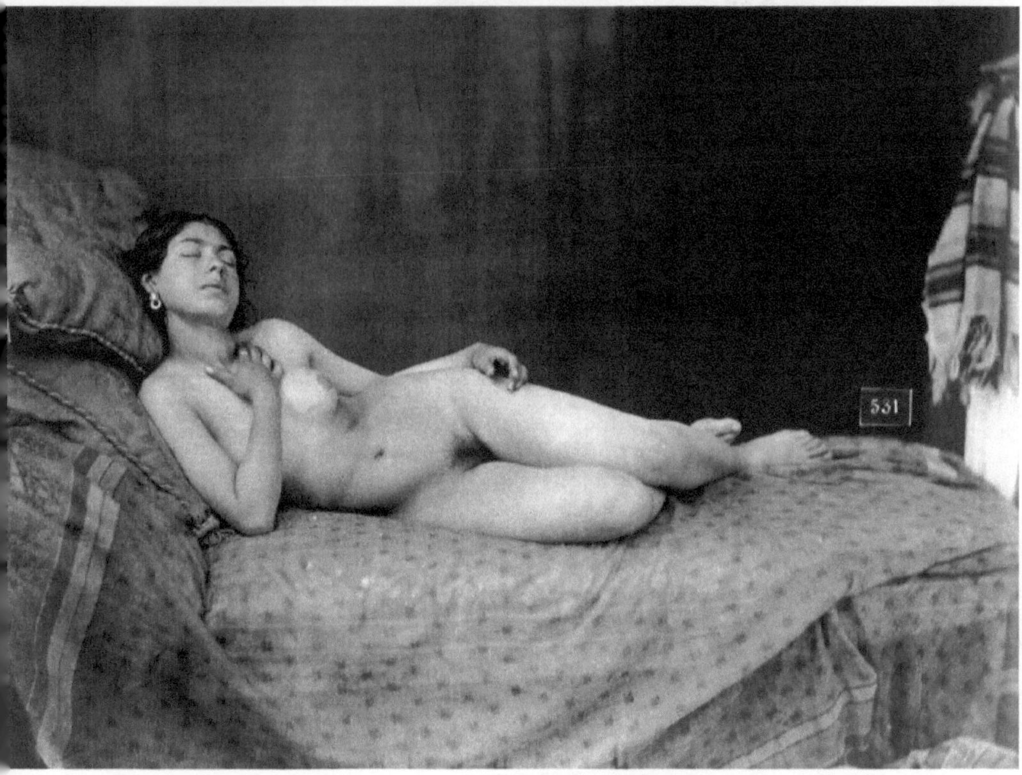
531

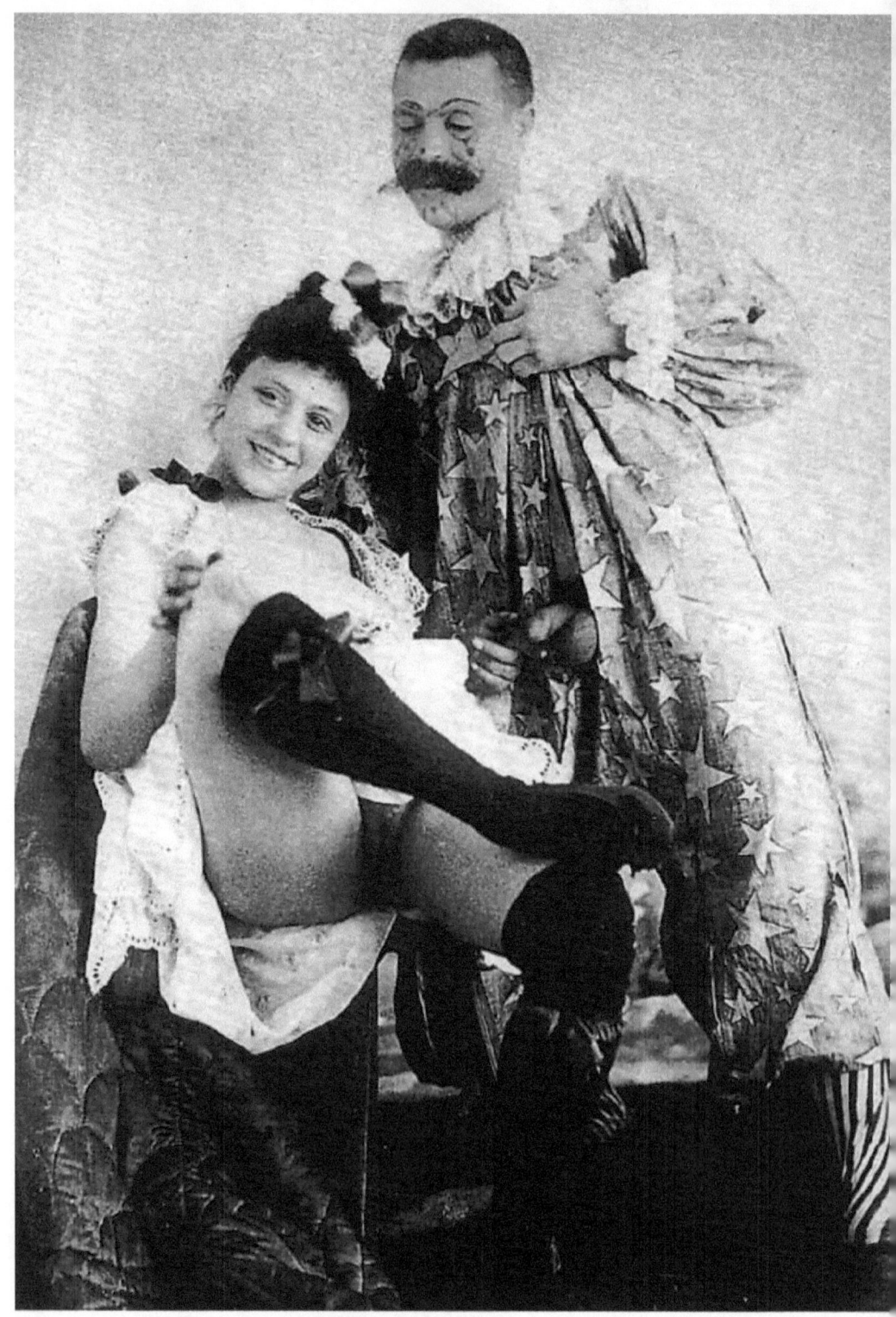

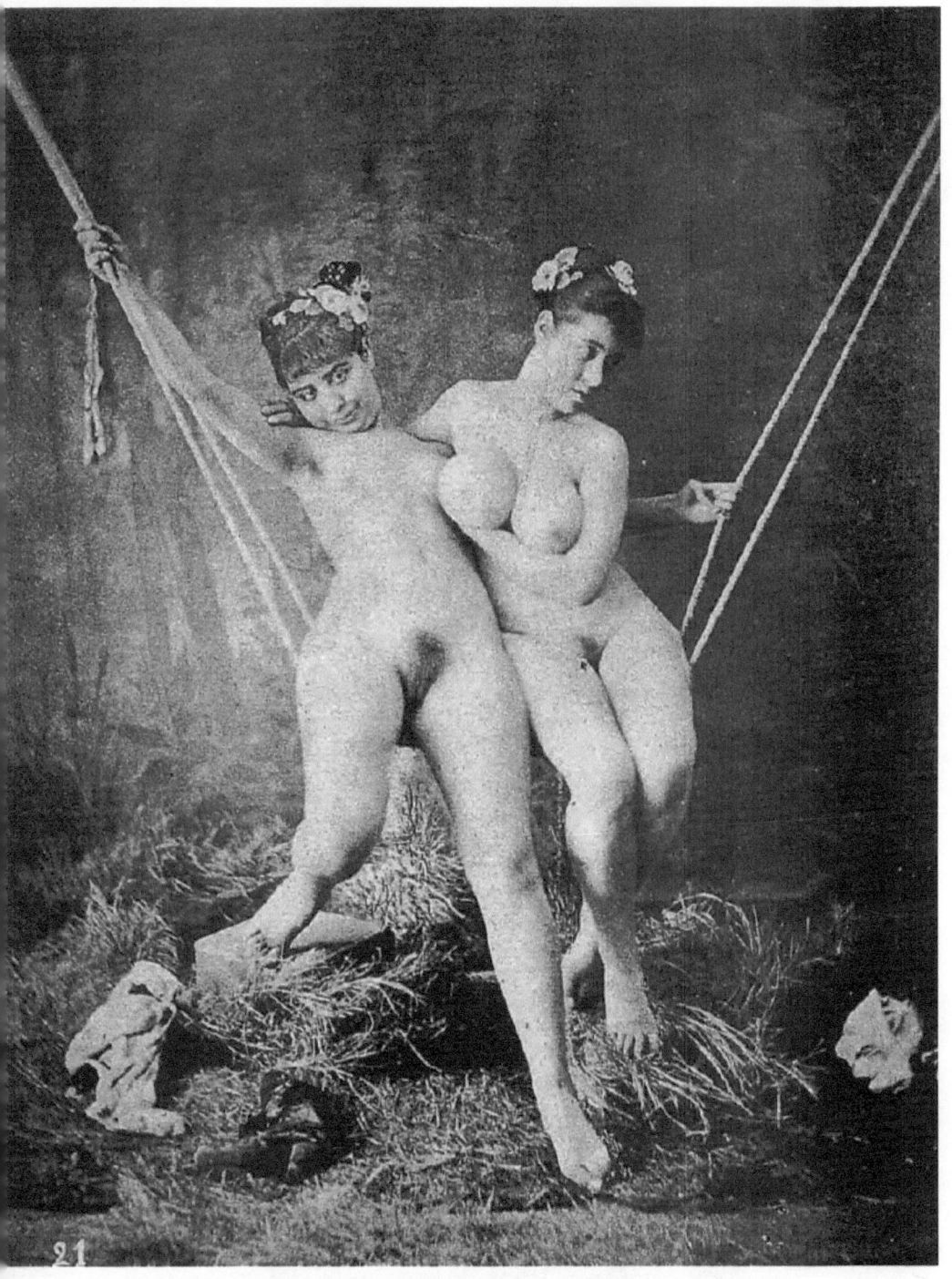

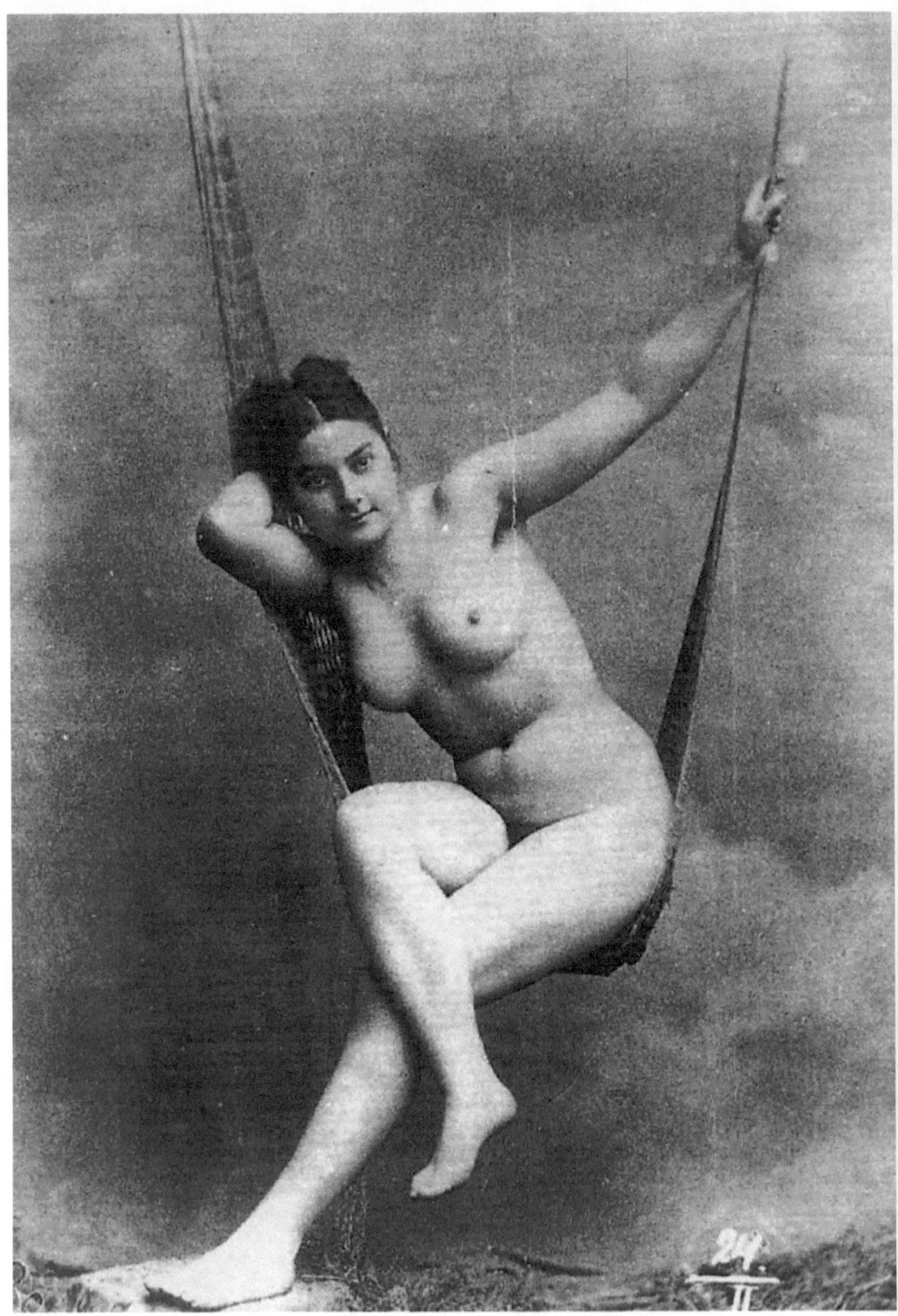

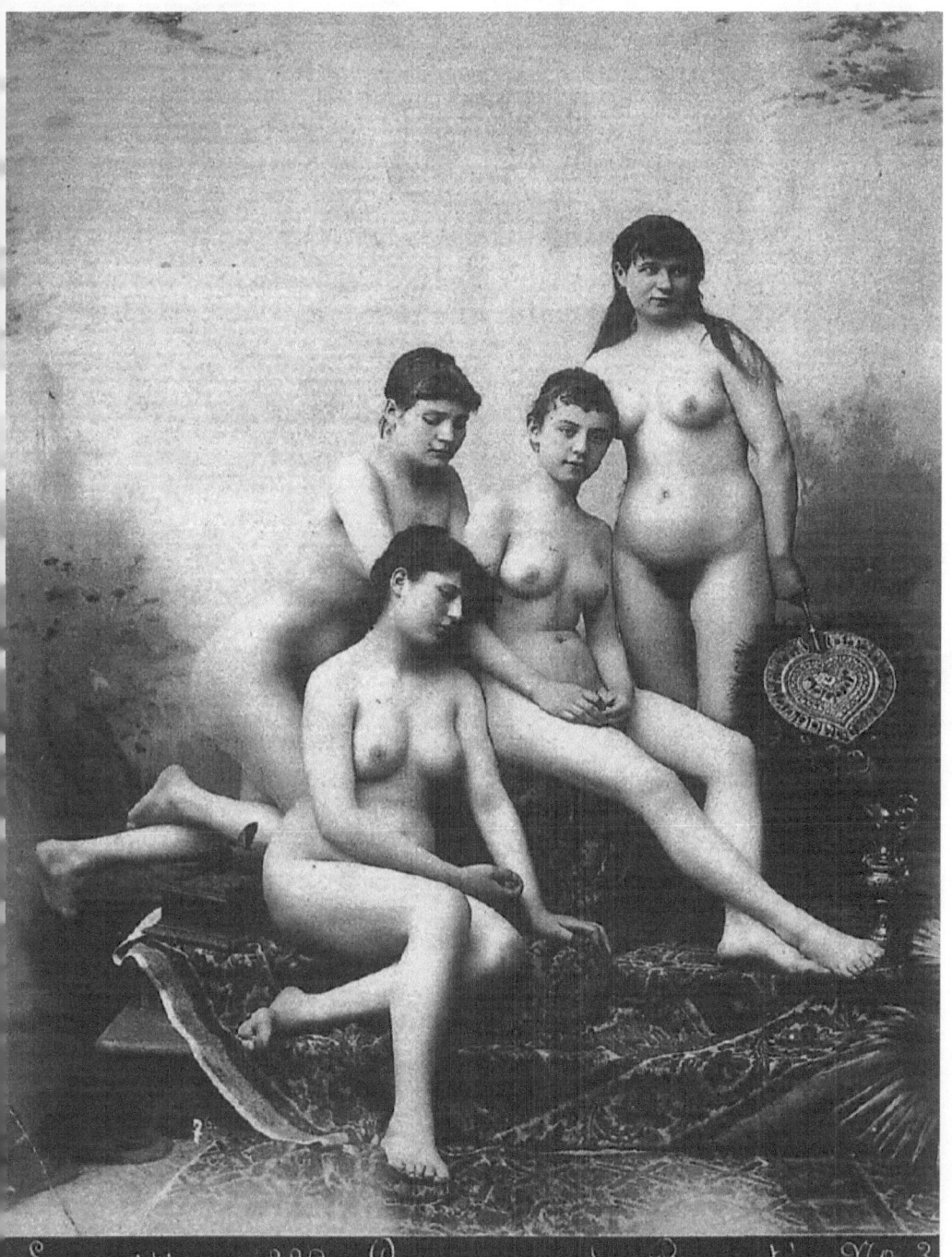

Exposition 1889. Concours de Beauté. N° 3

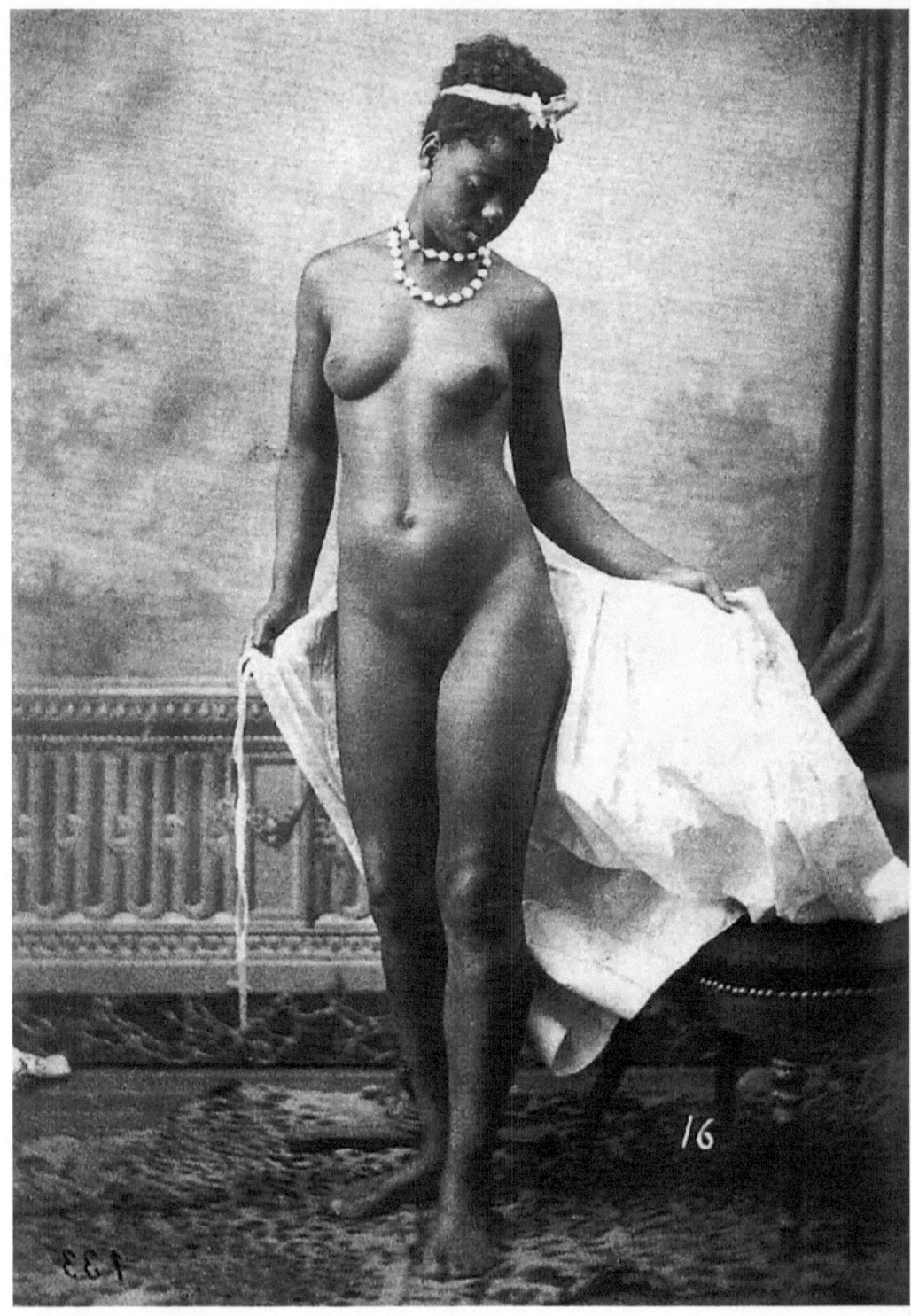

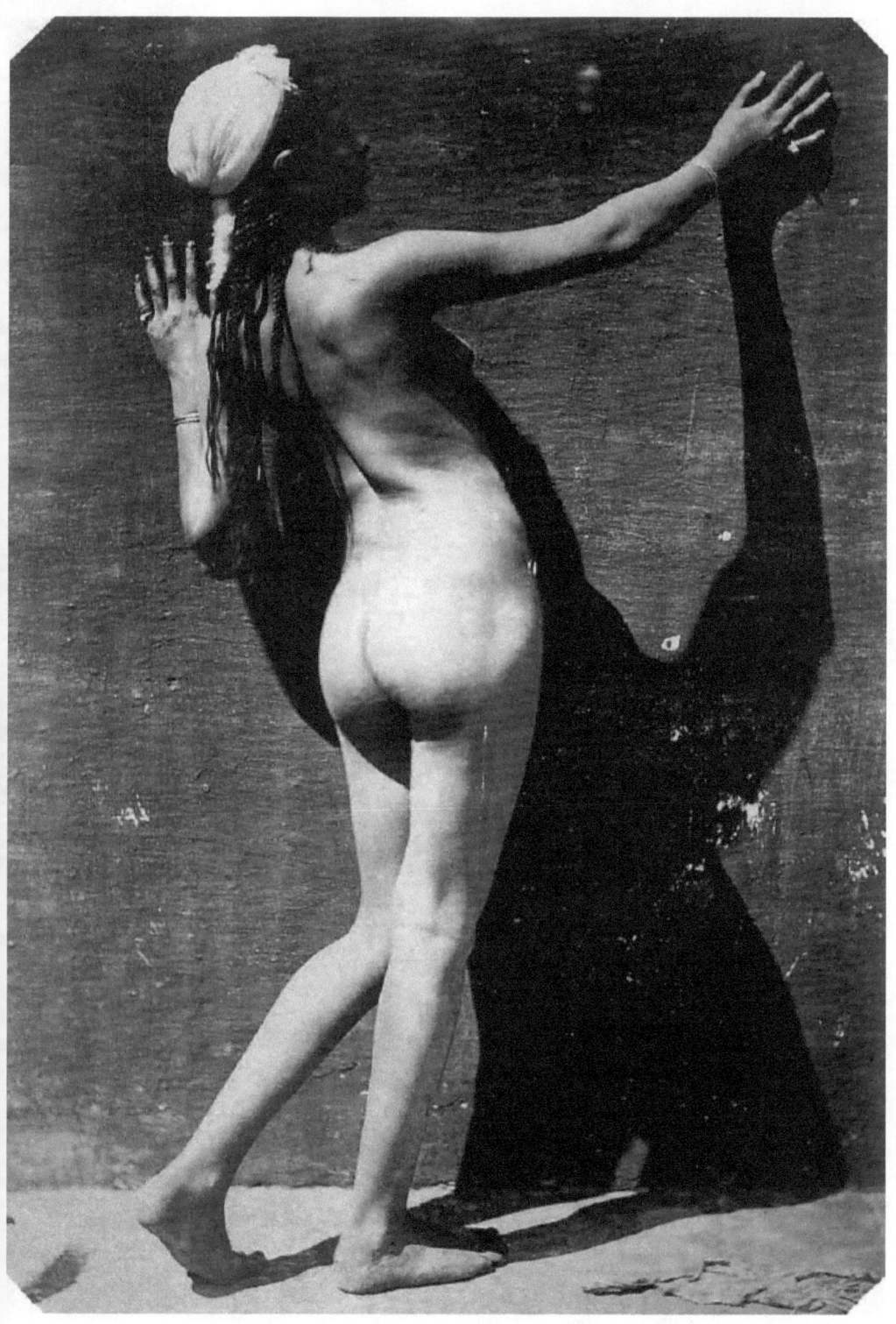

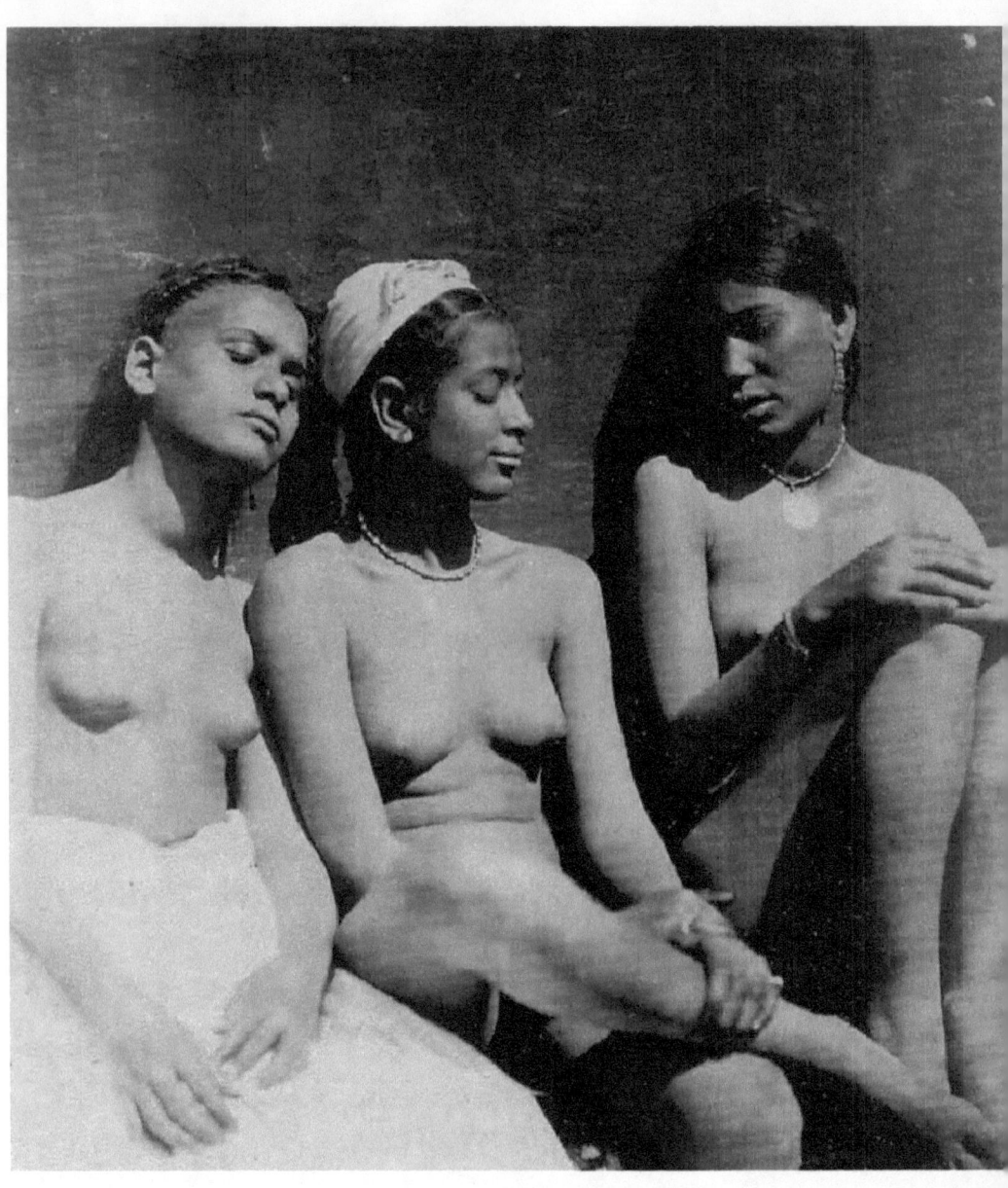

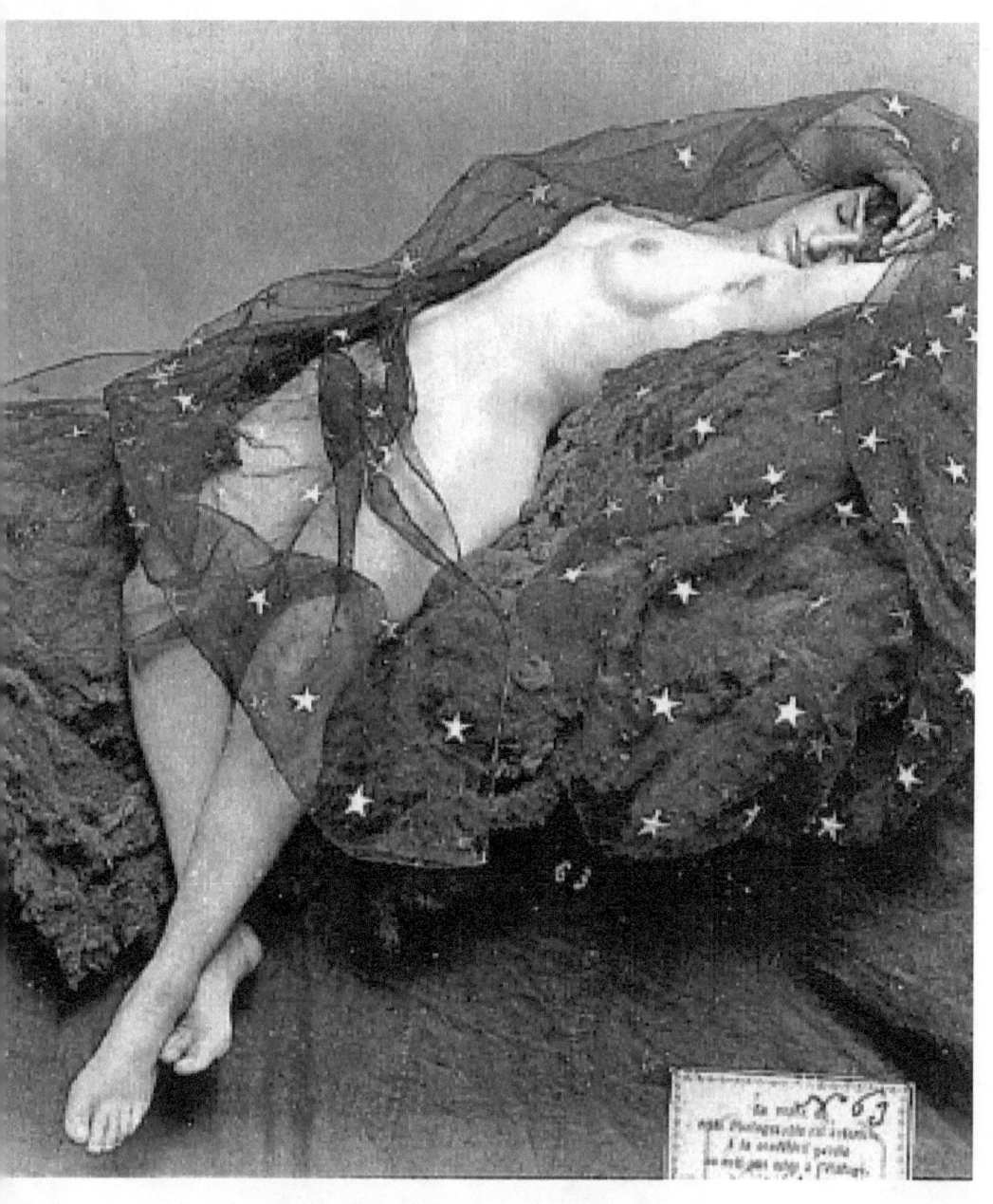

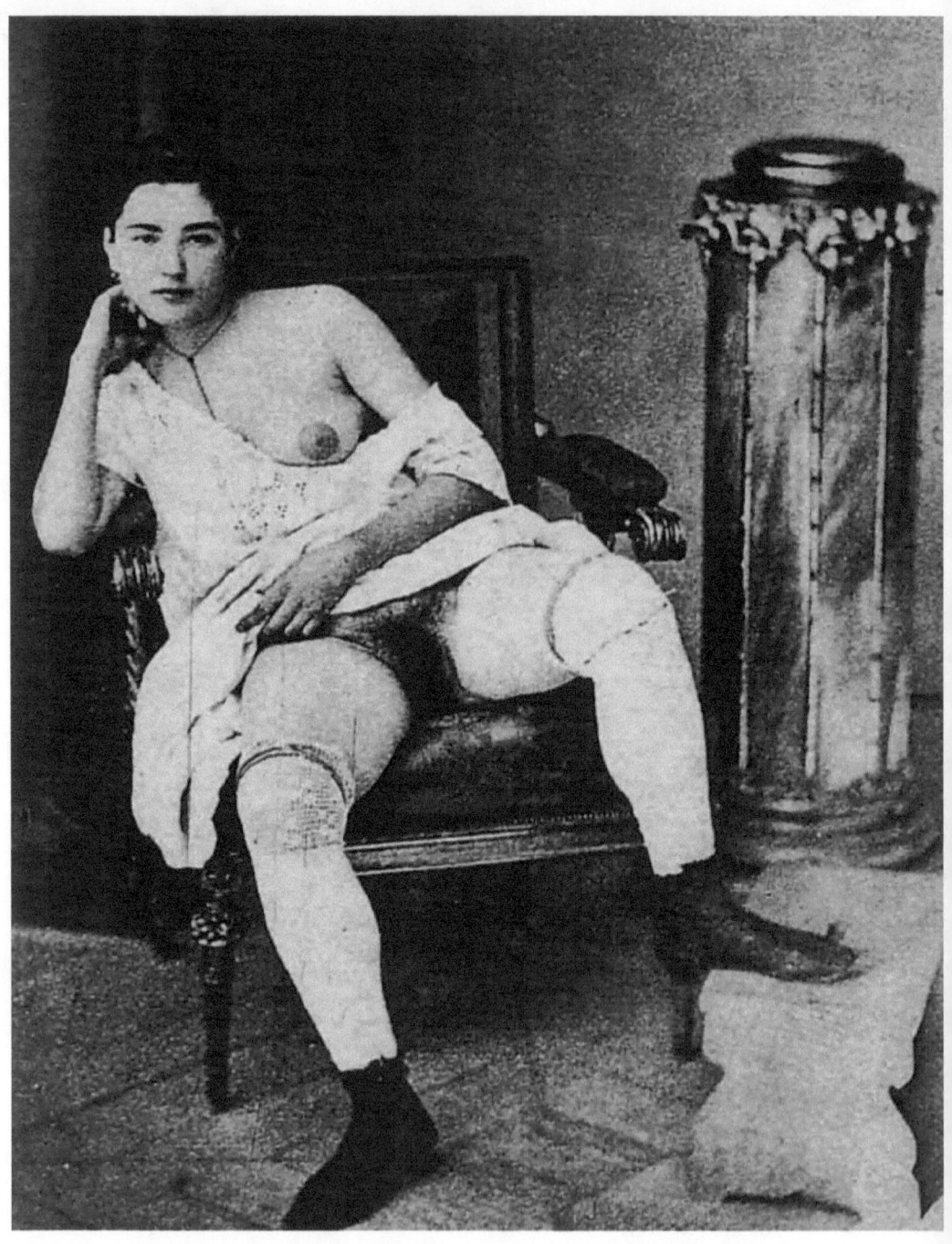

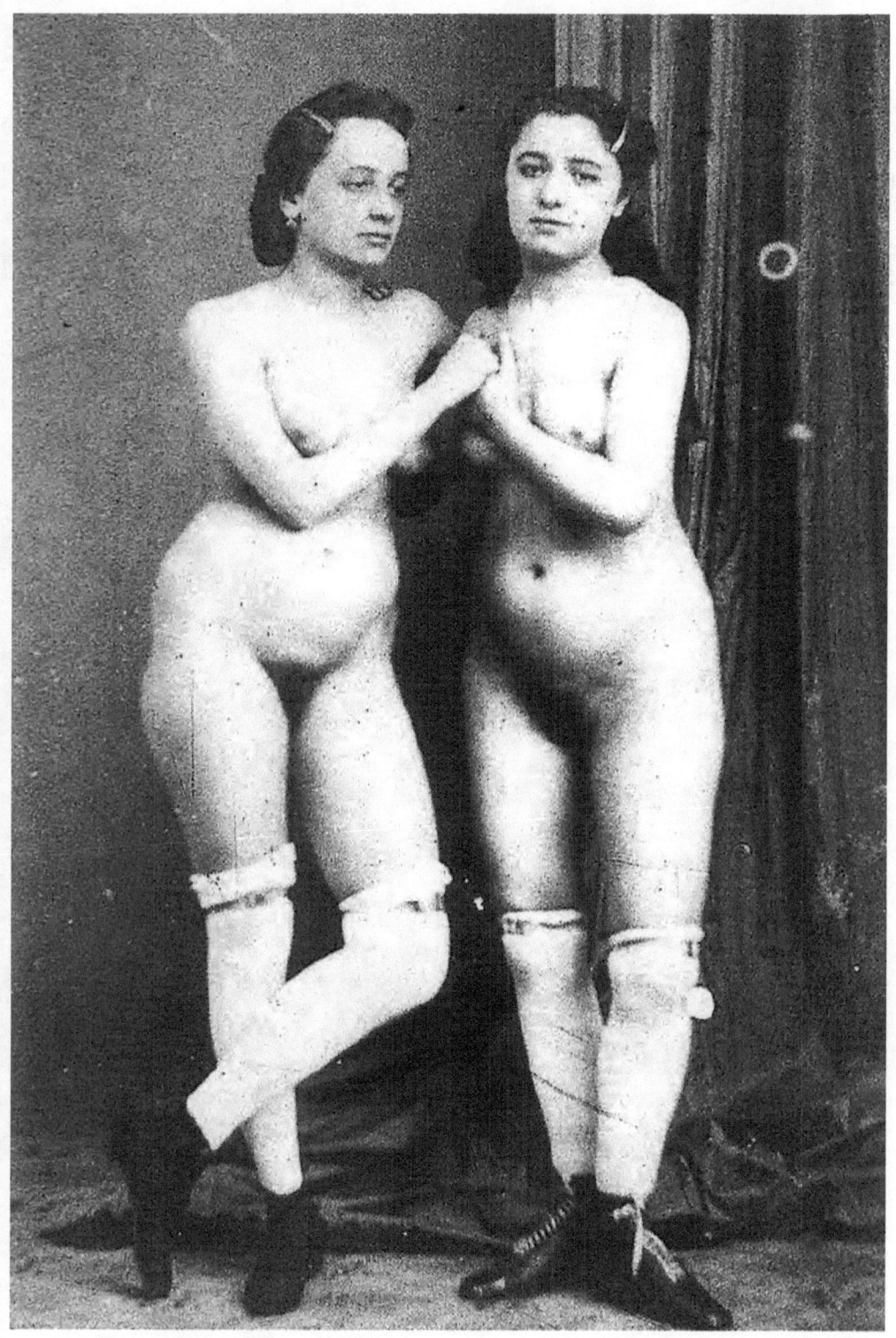

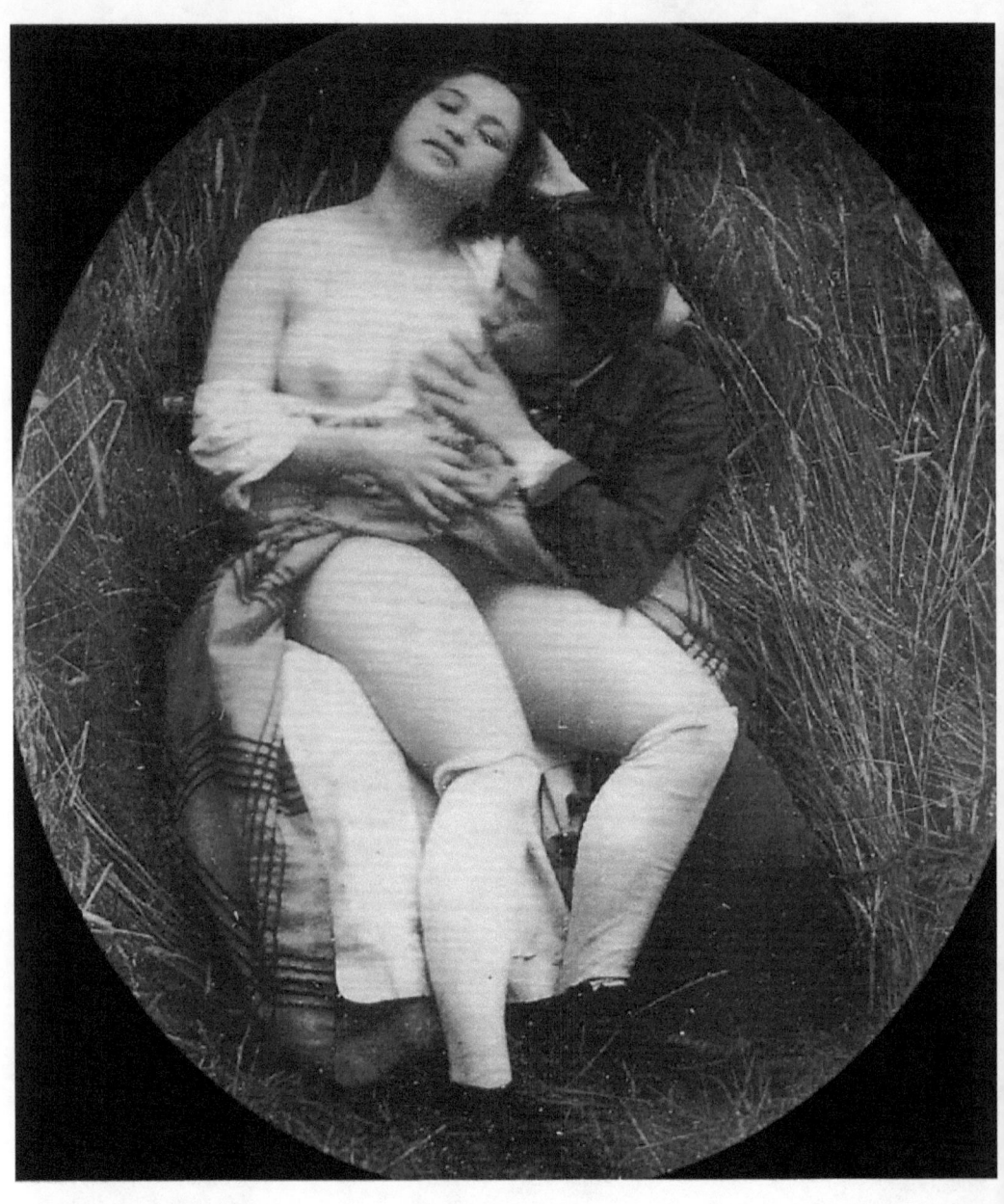

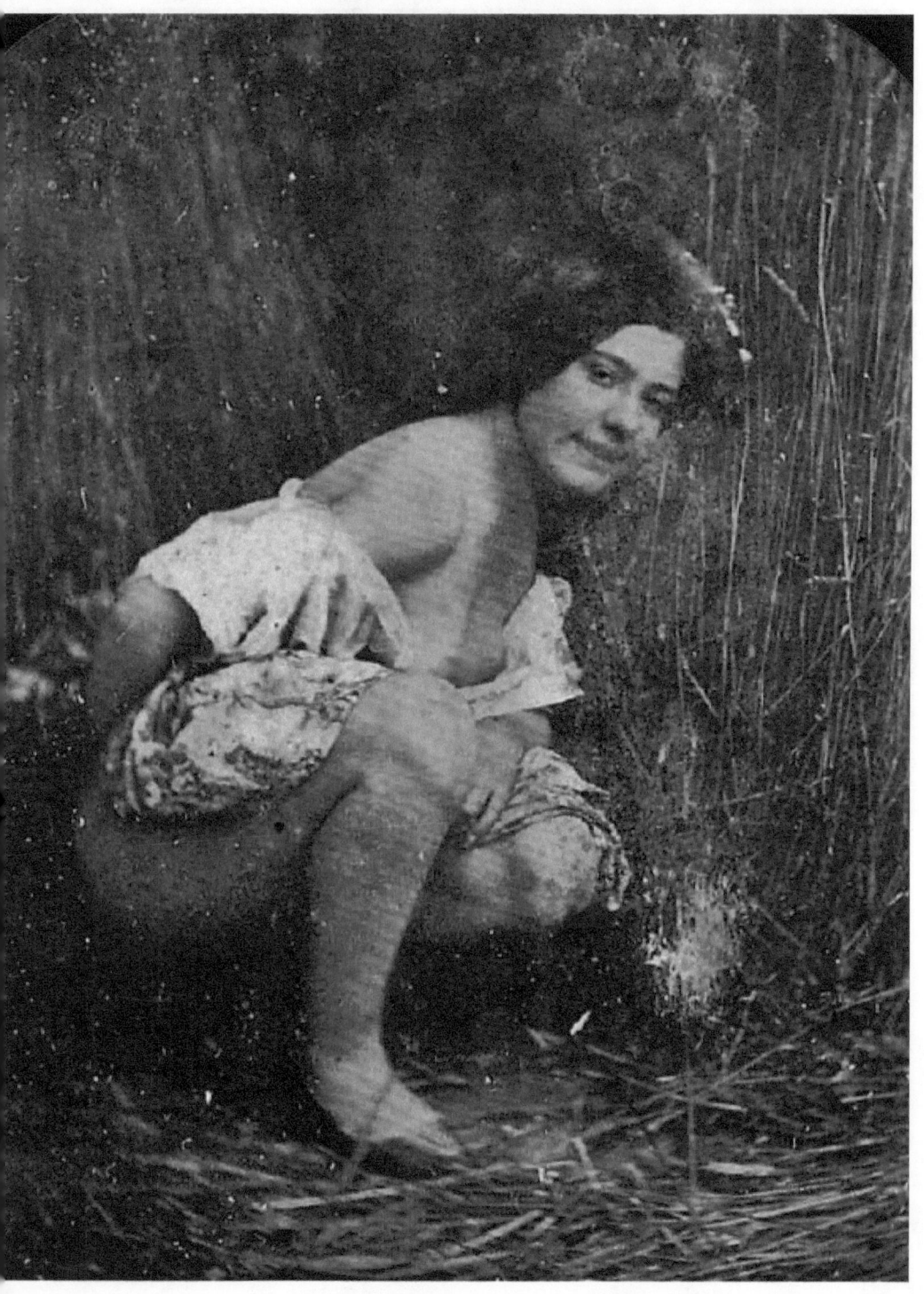

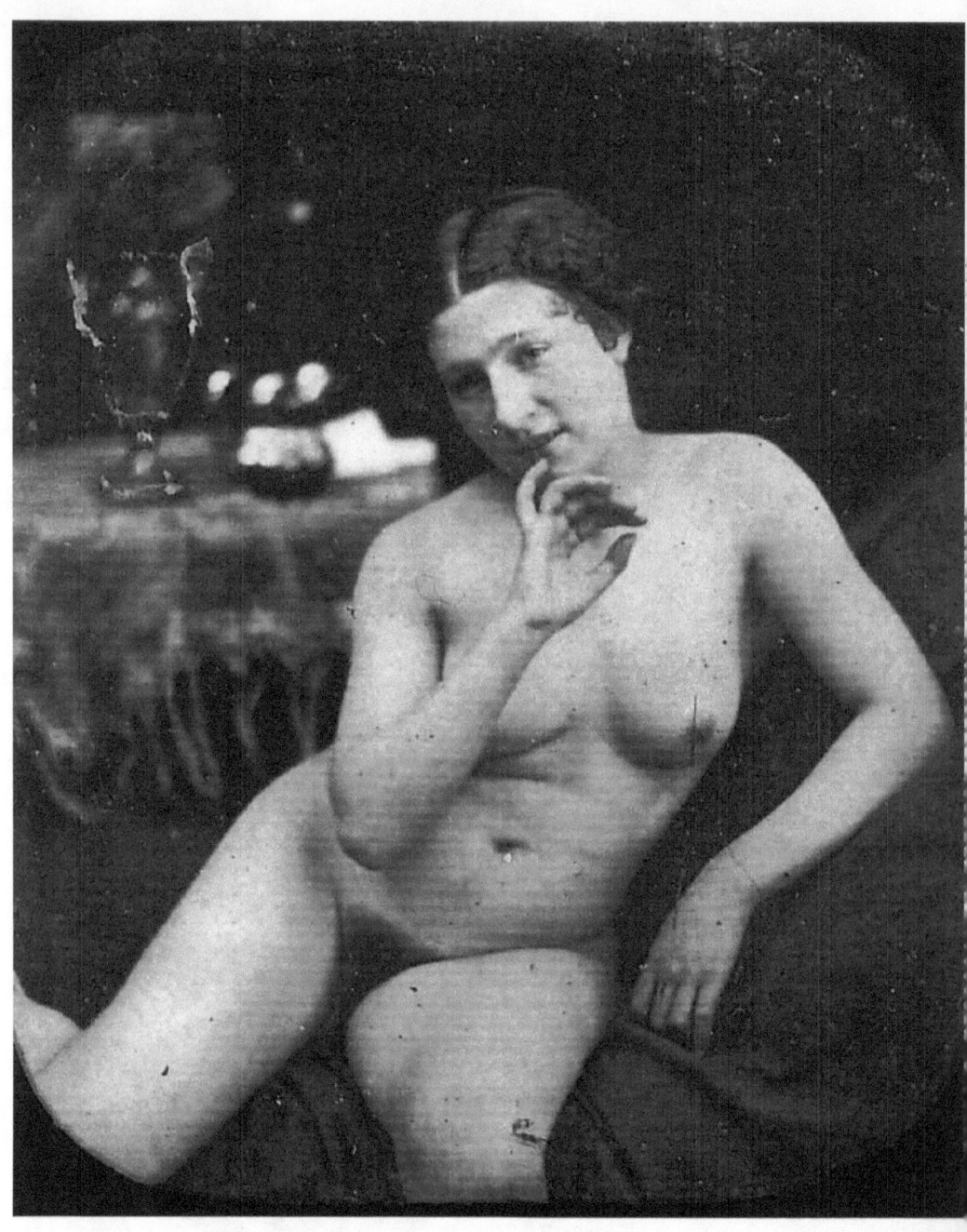

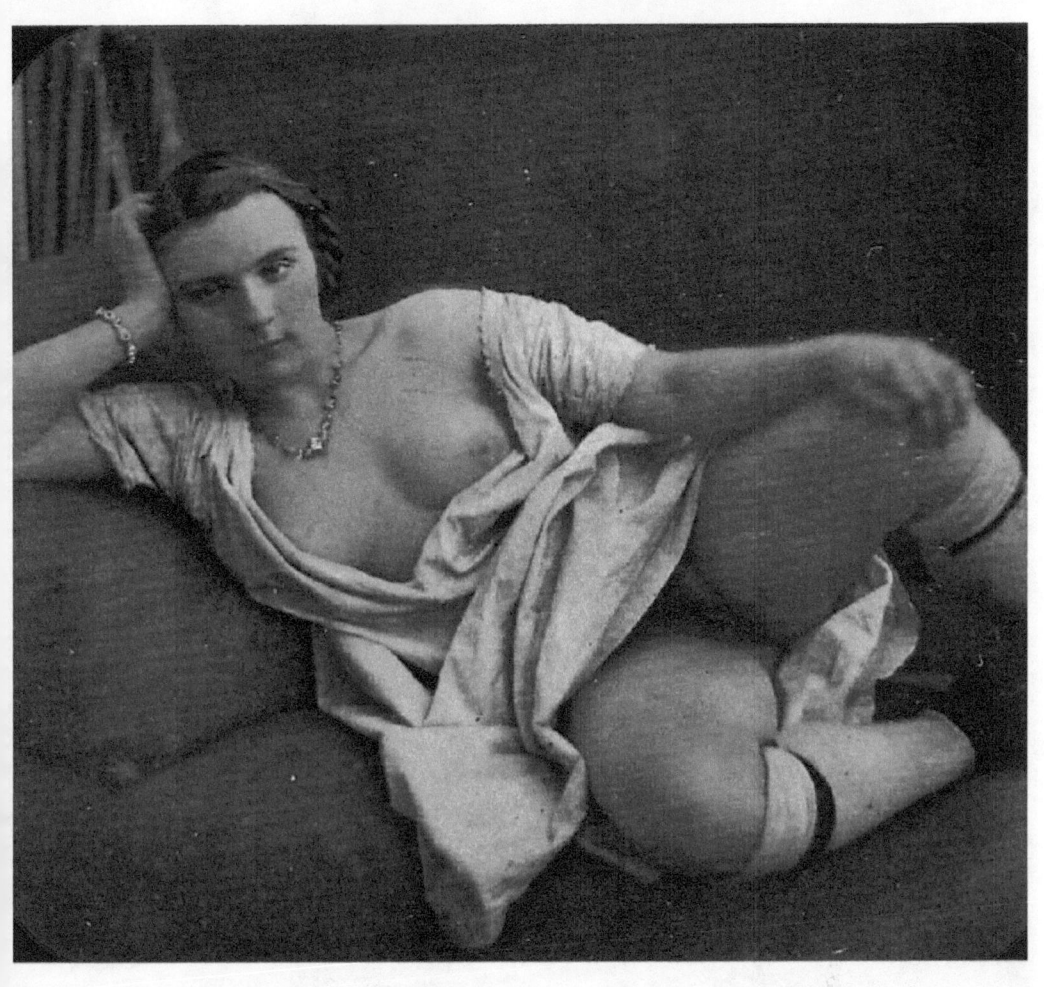

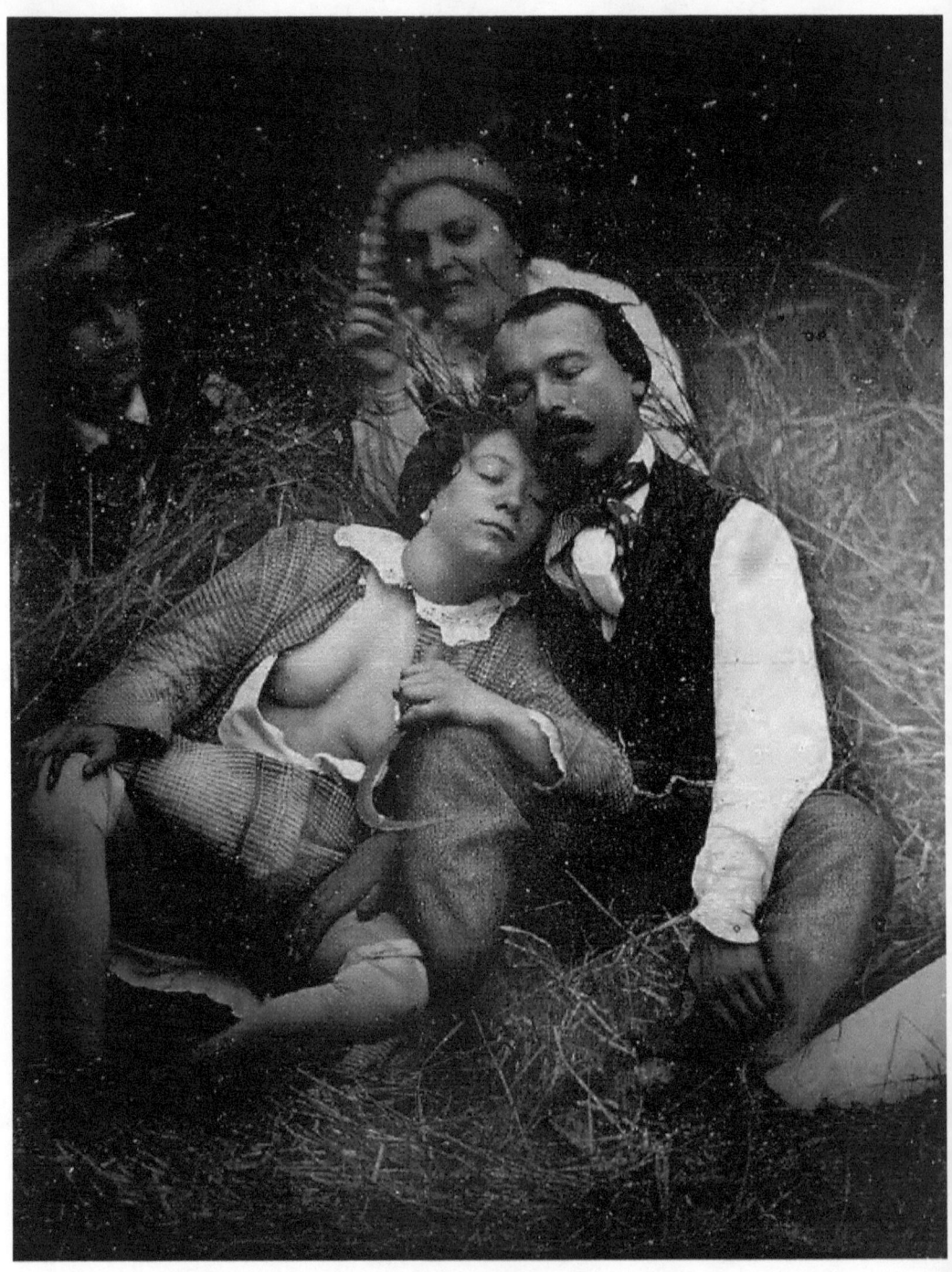

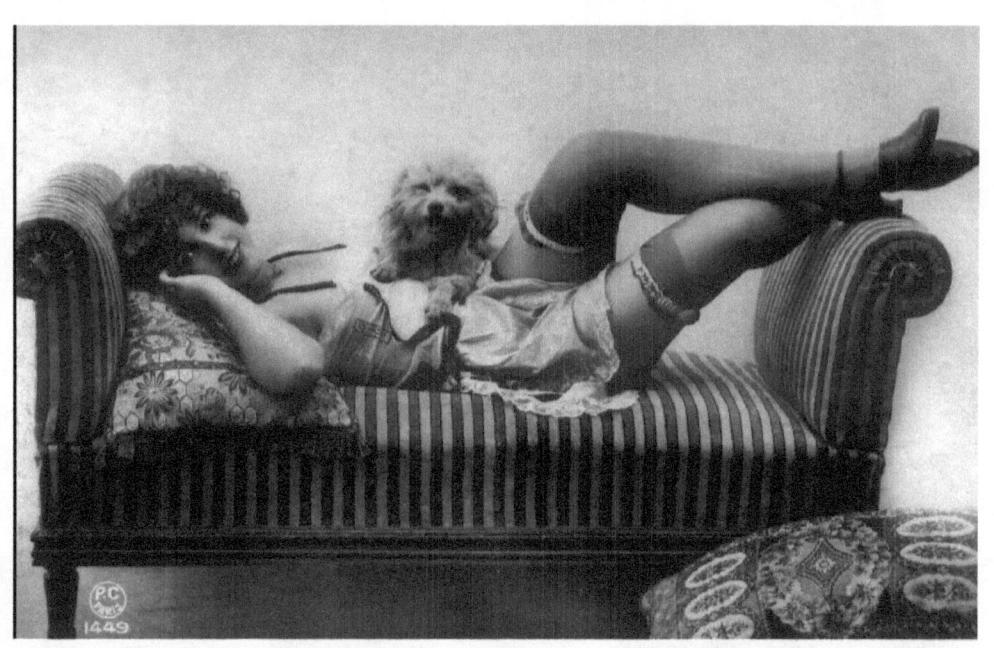

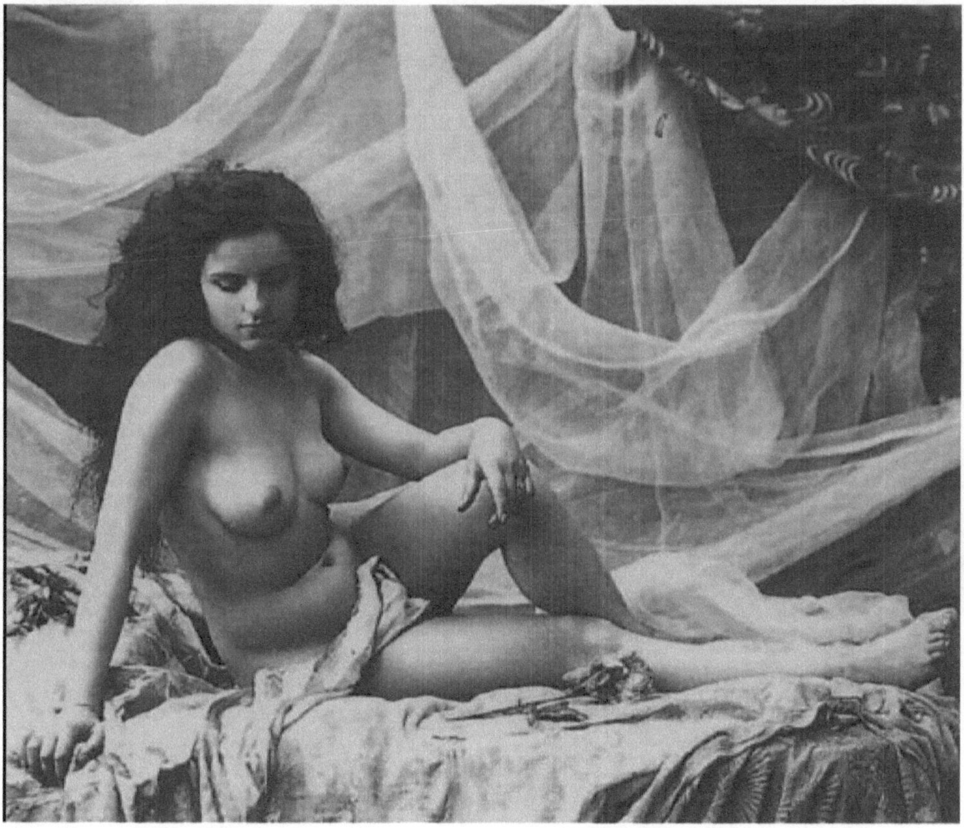

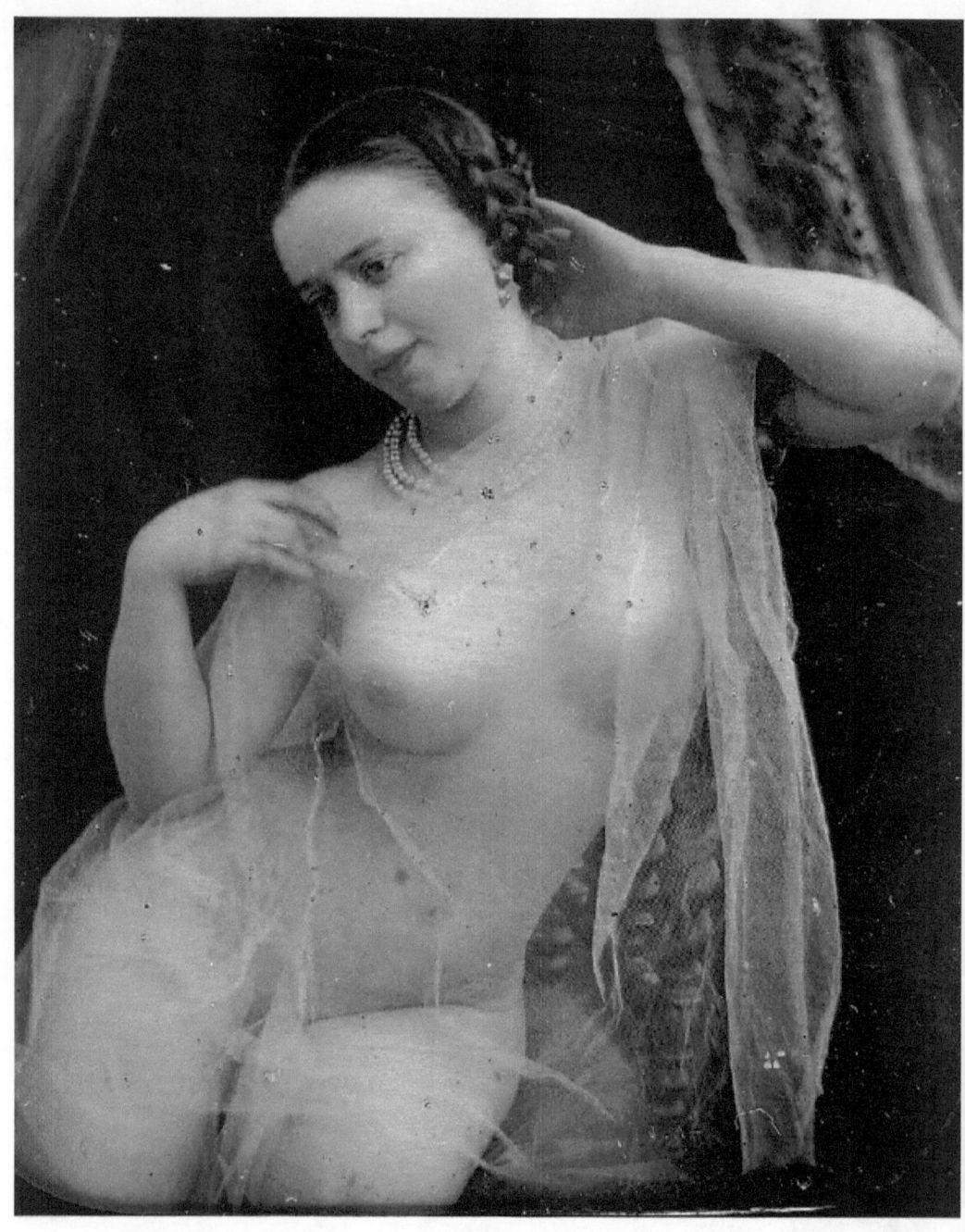

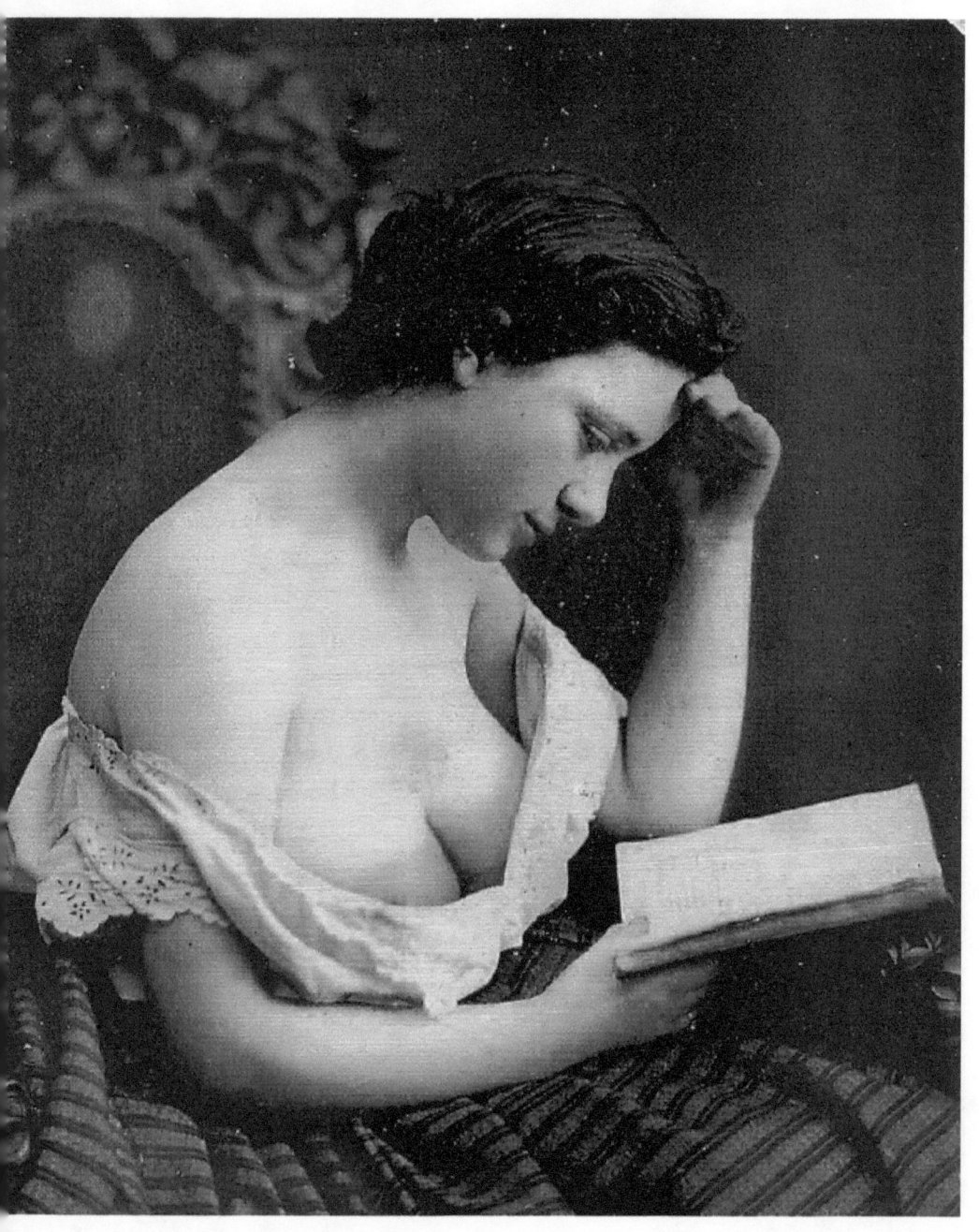

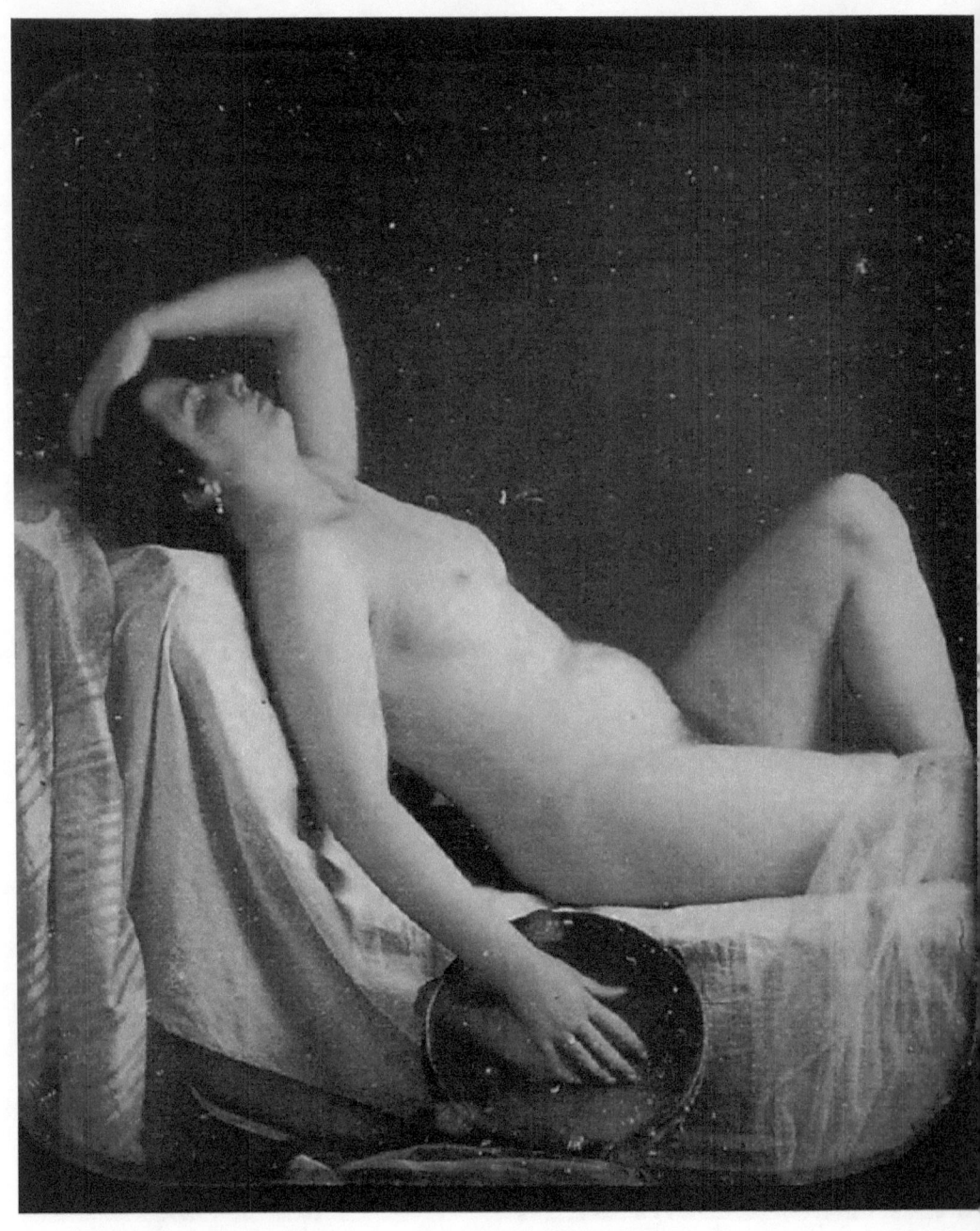

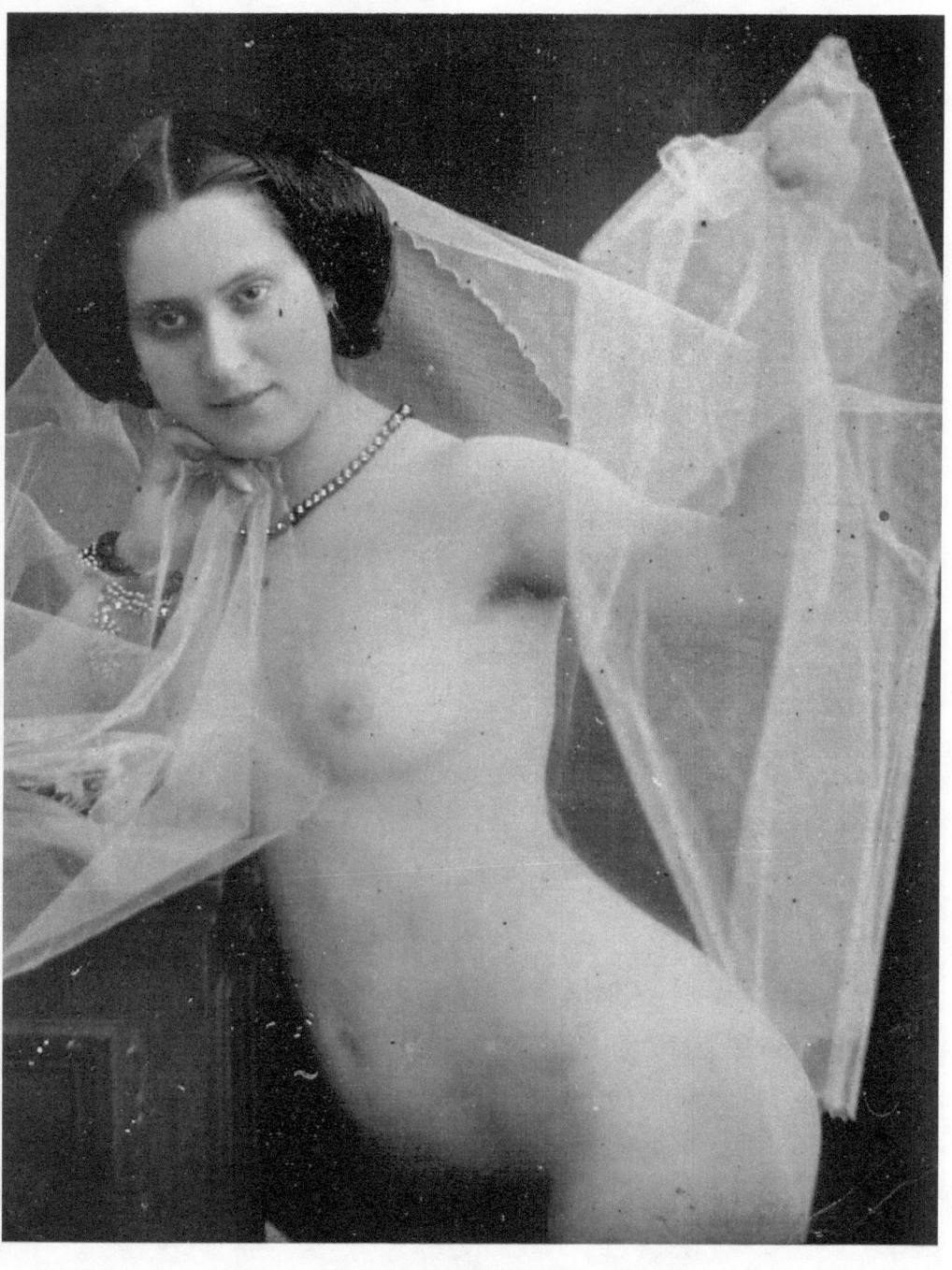

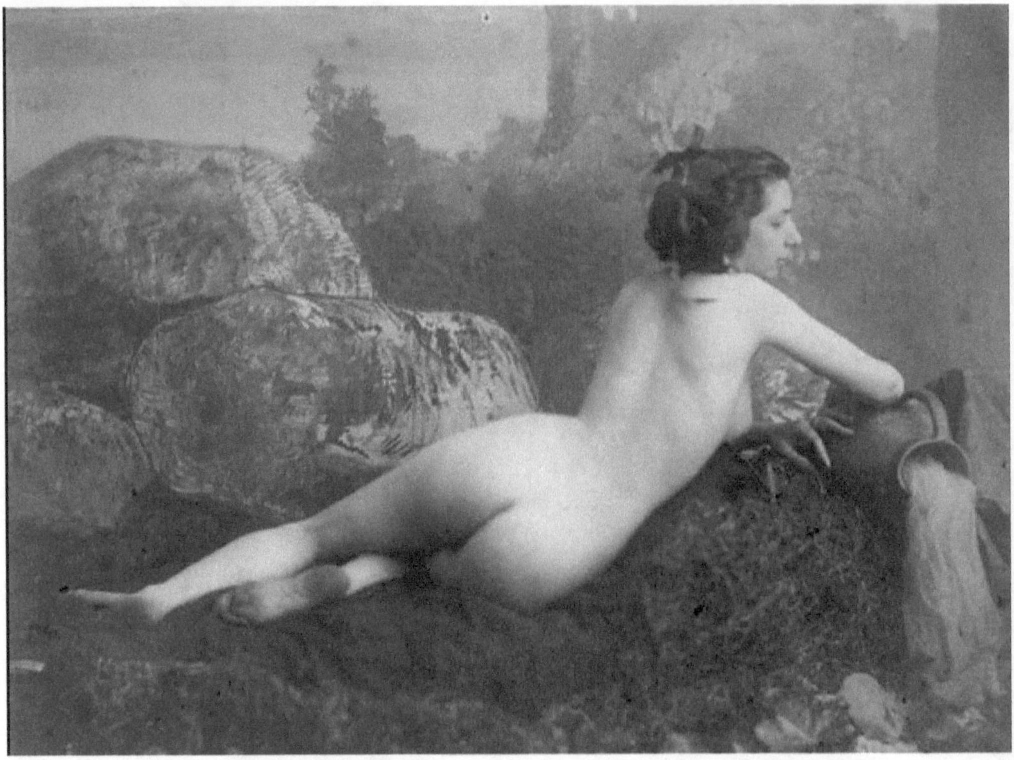

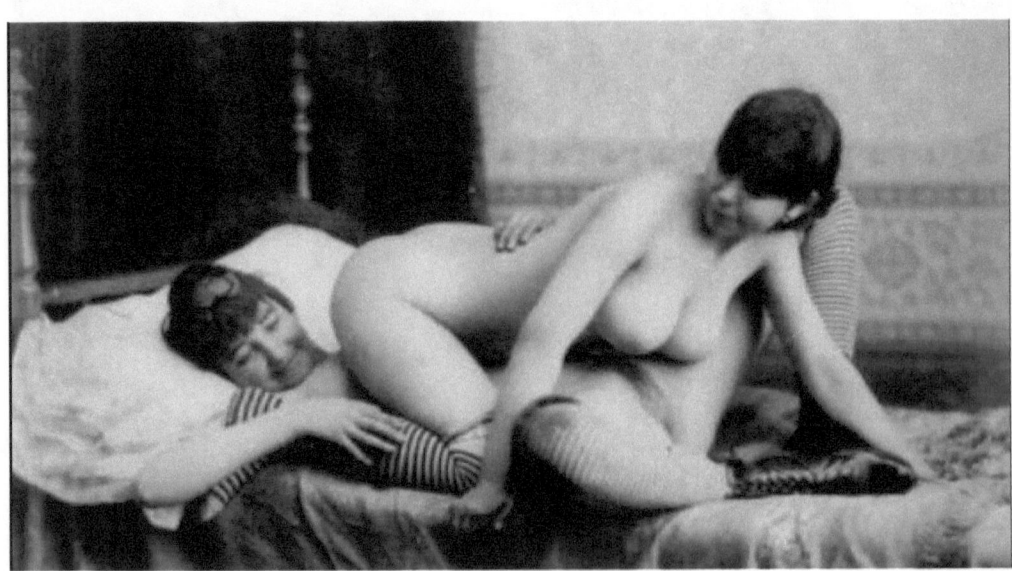

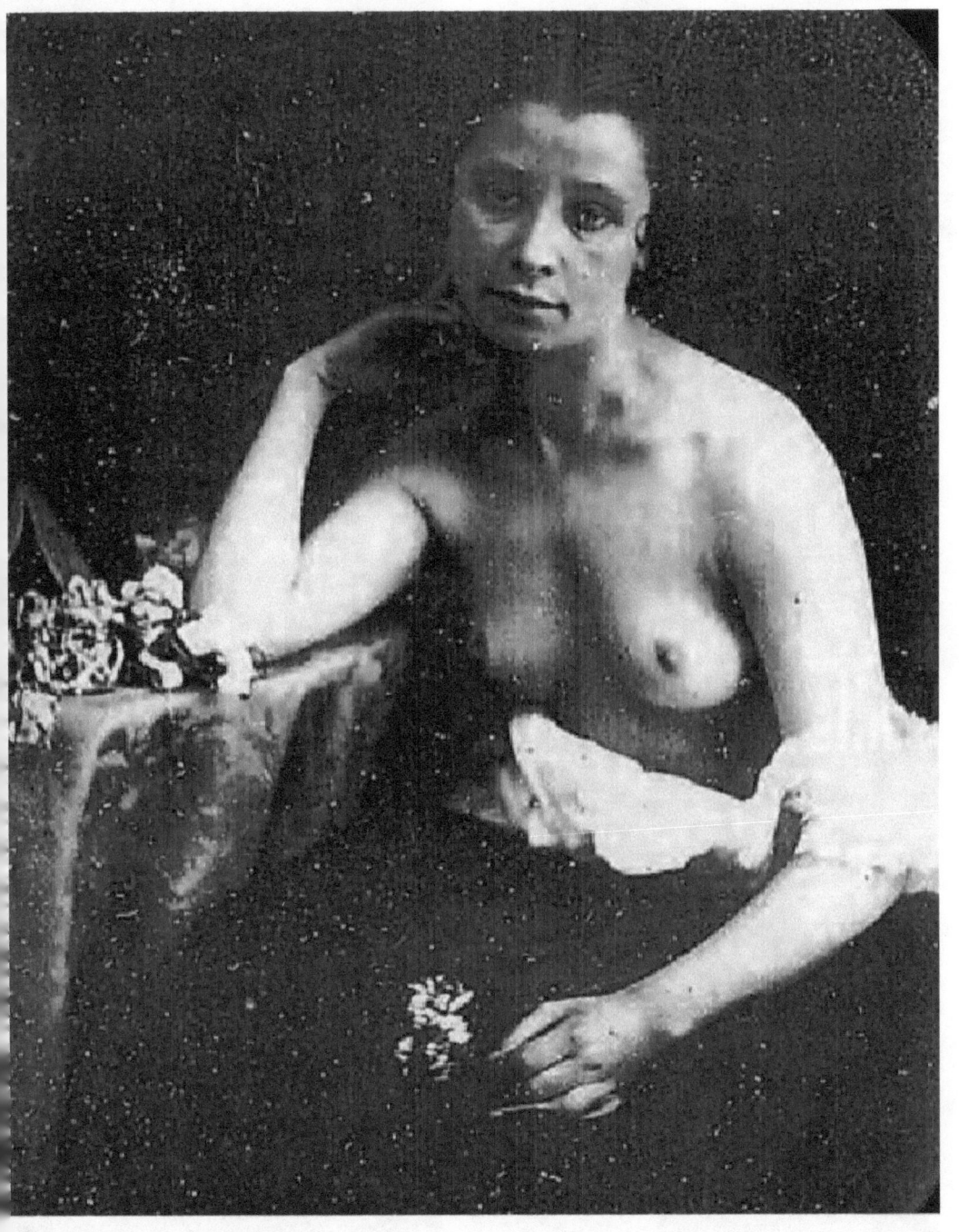

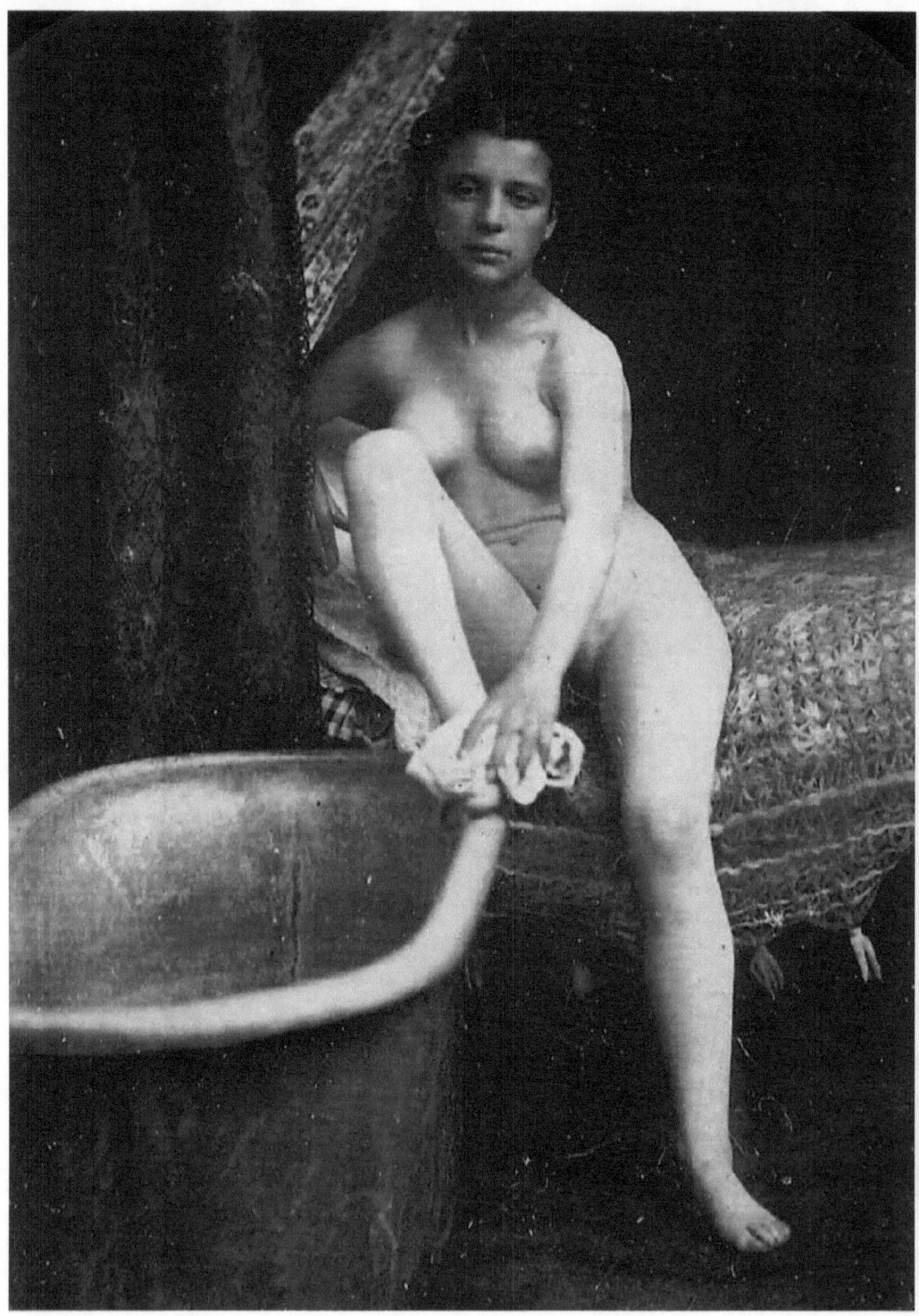

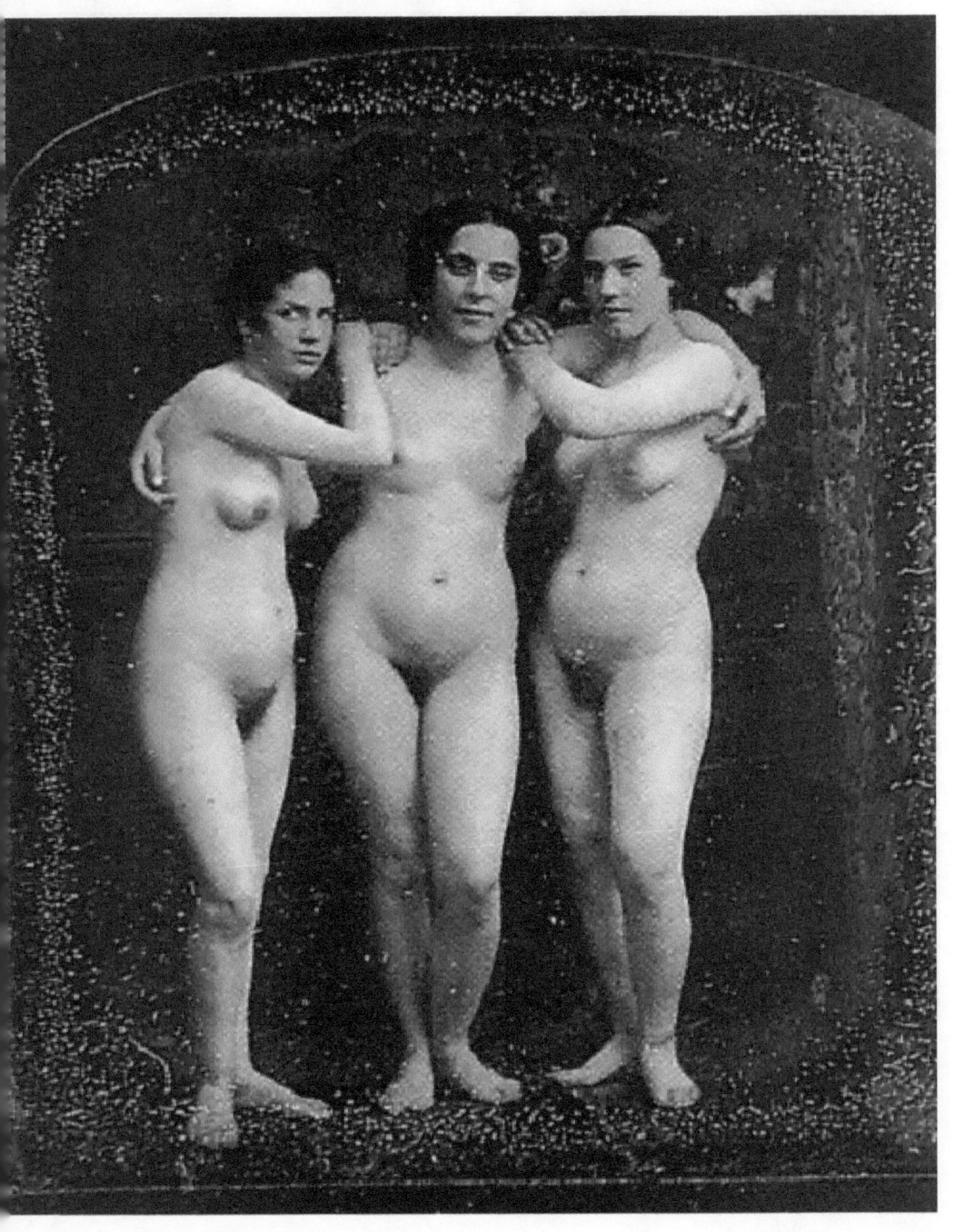

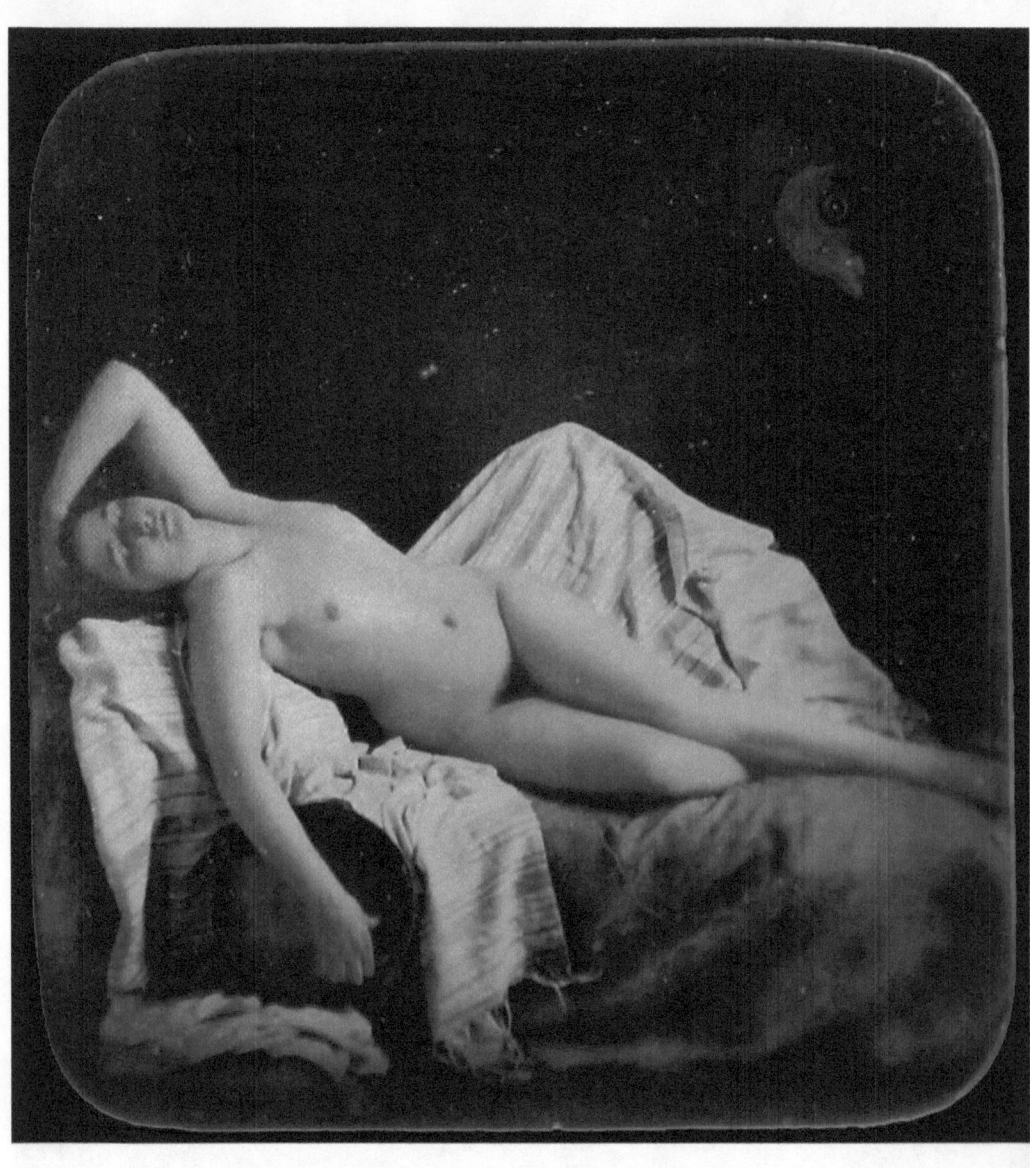

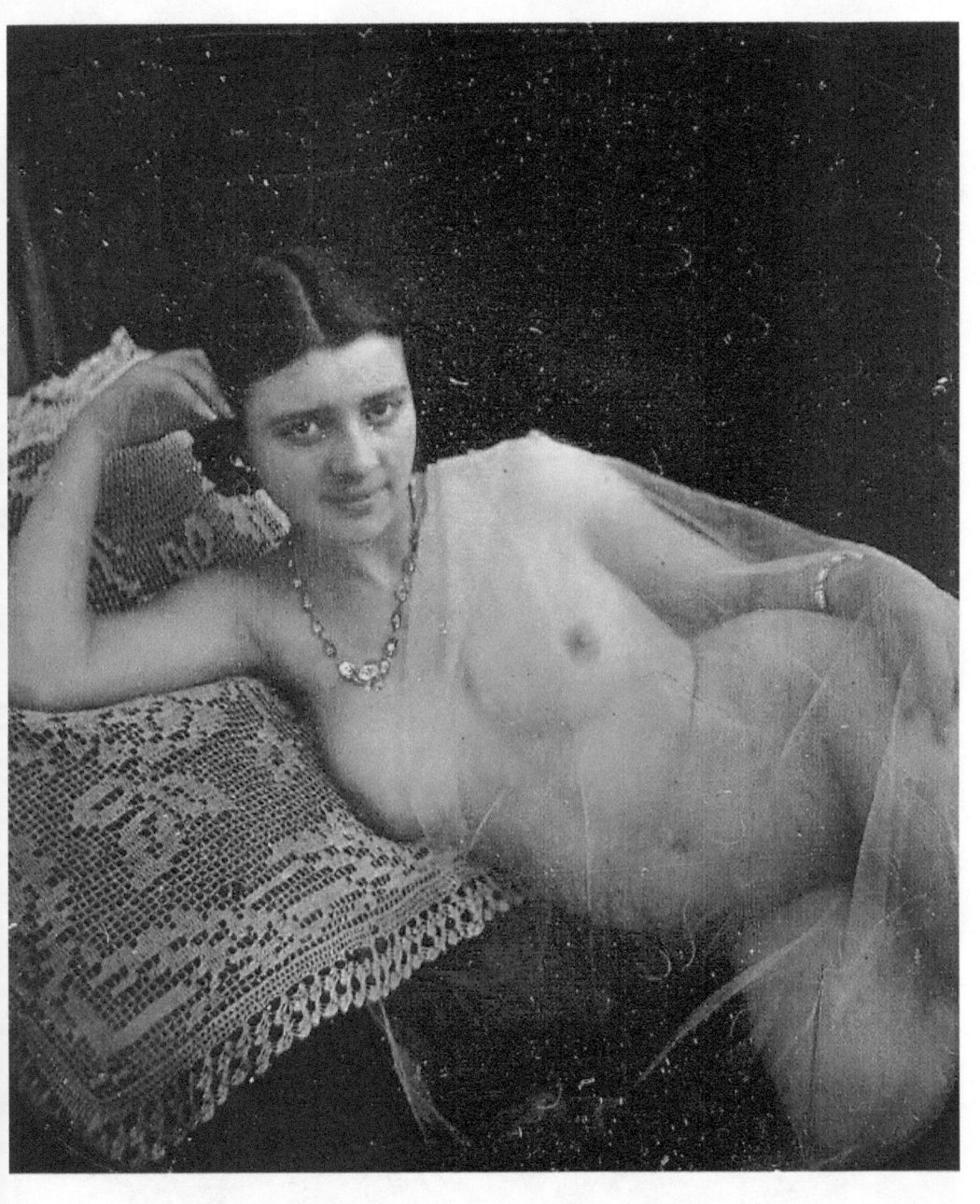

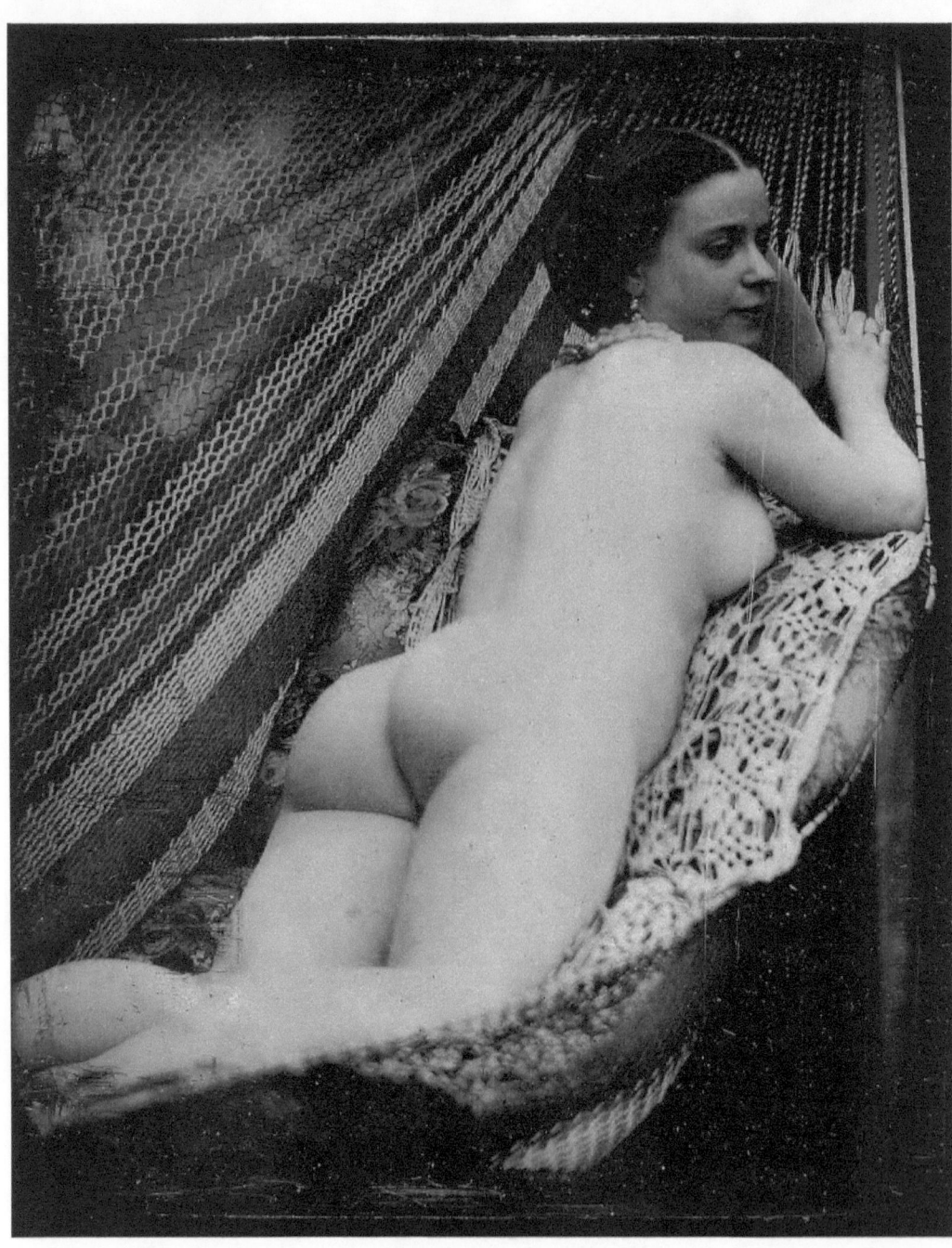

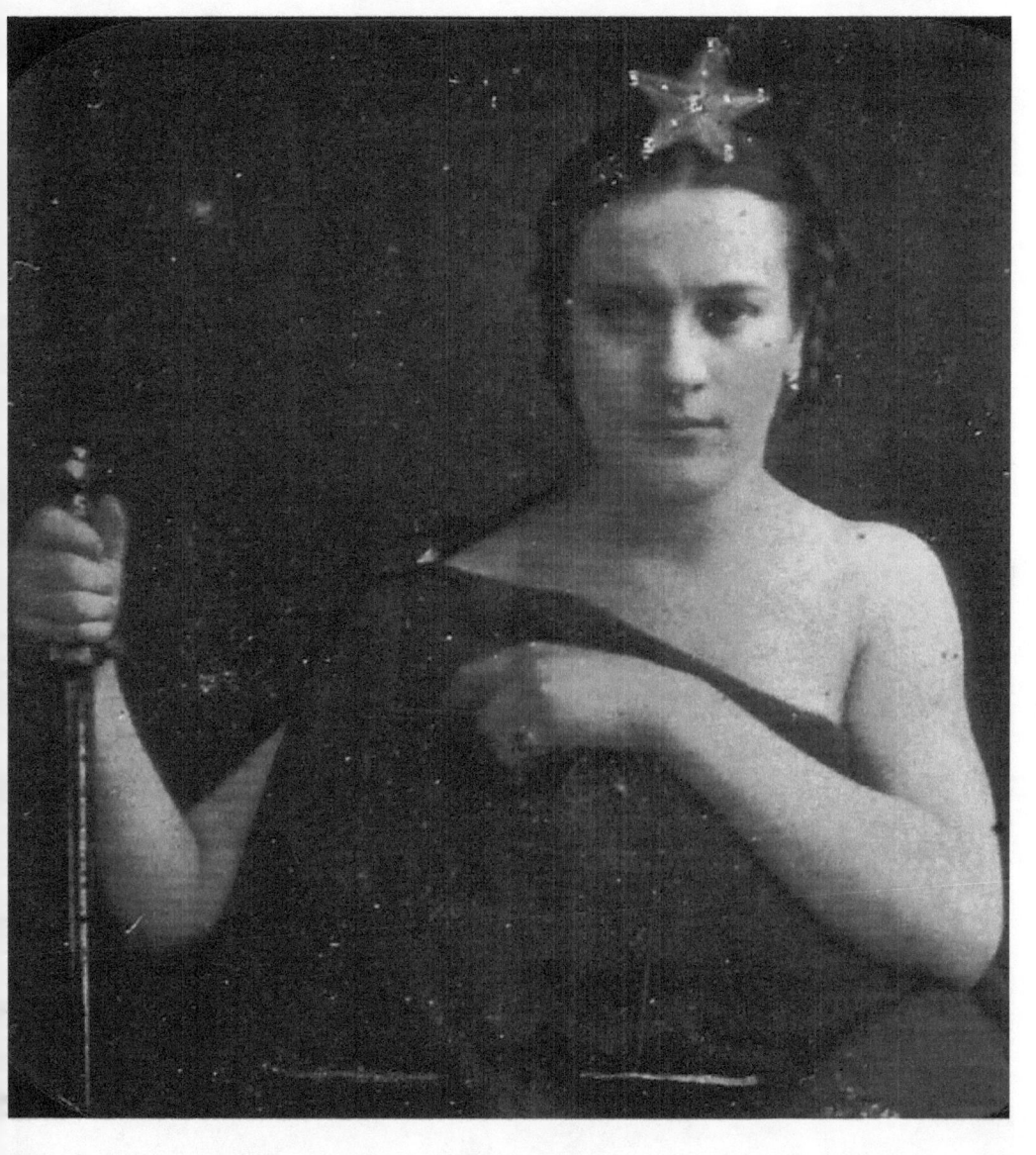

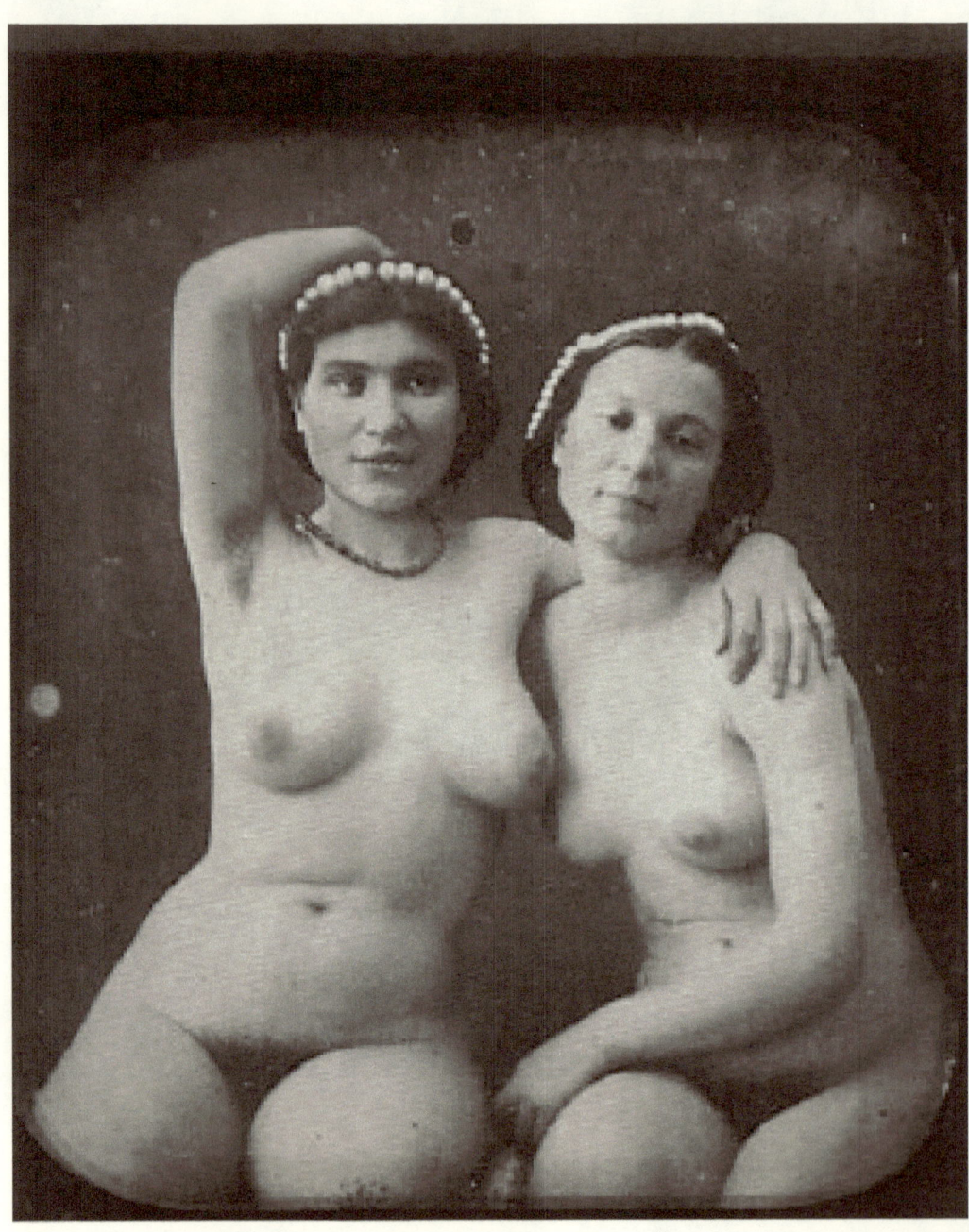

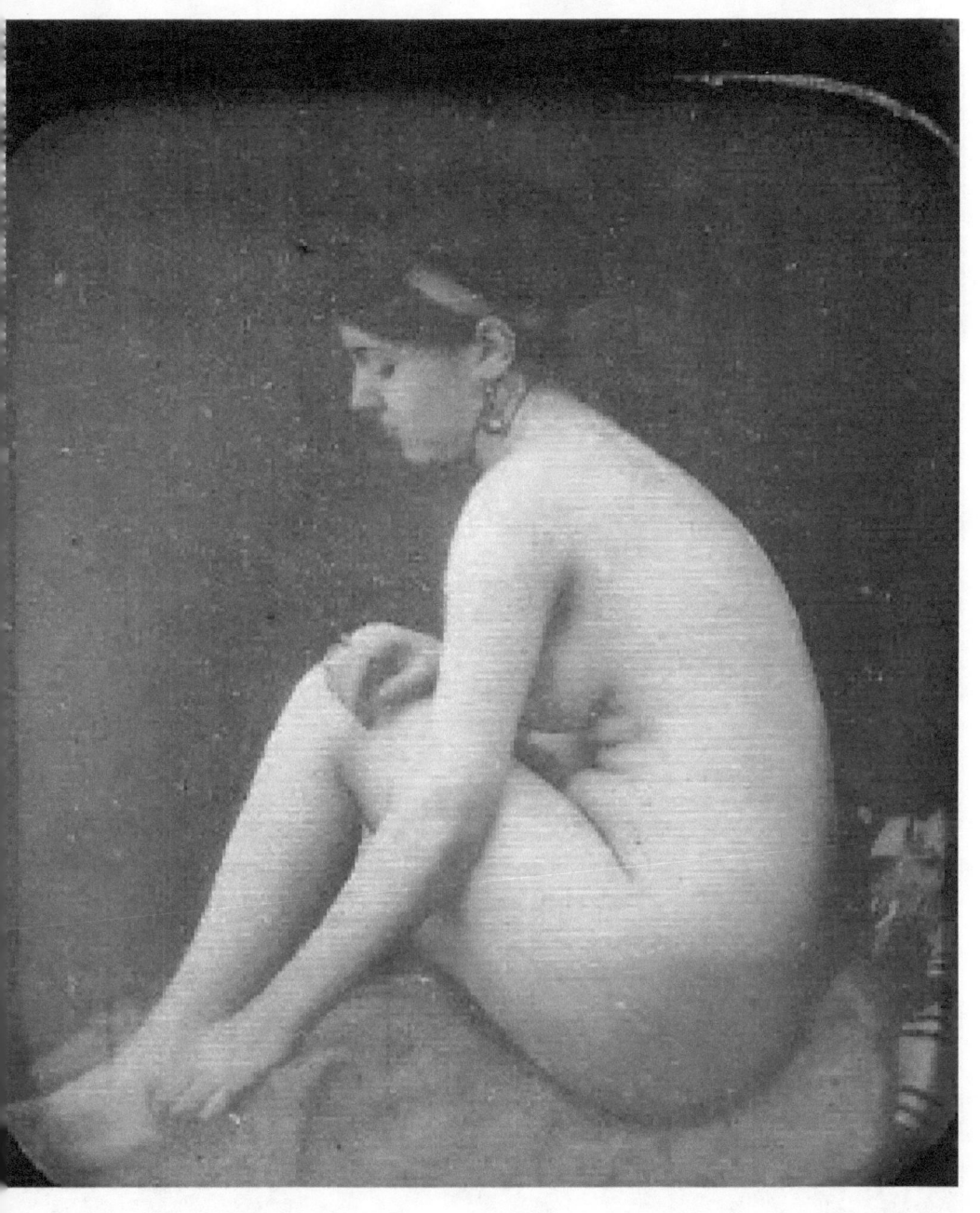

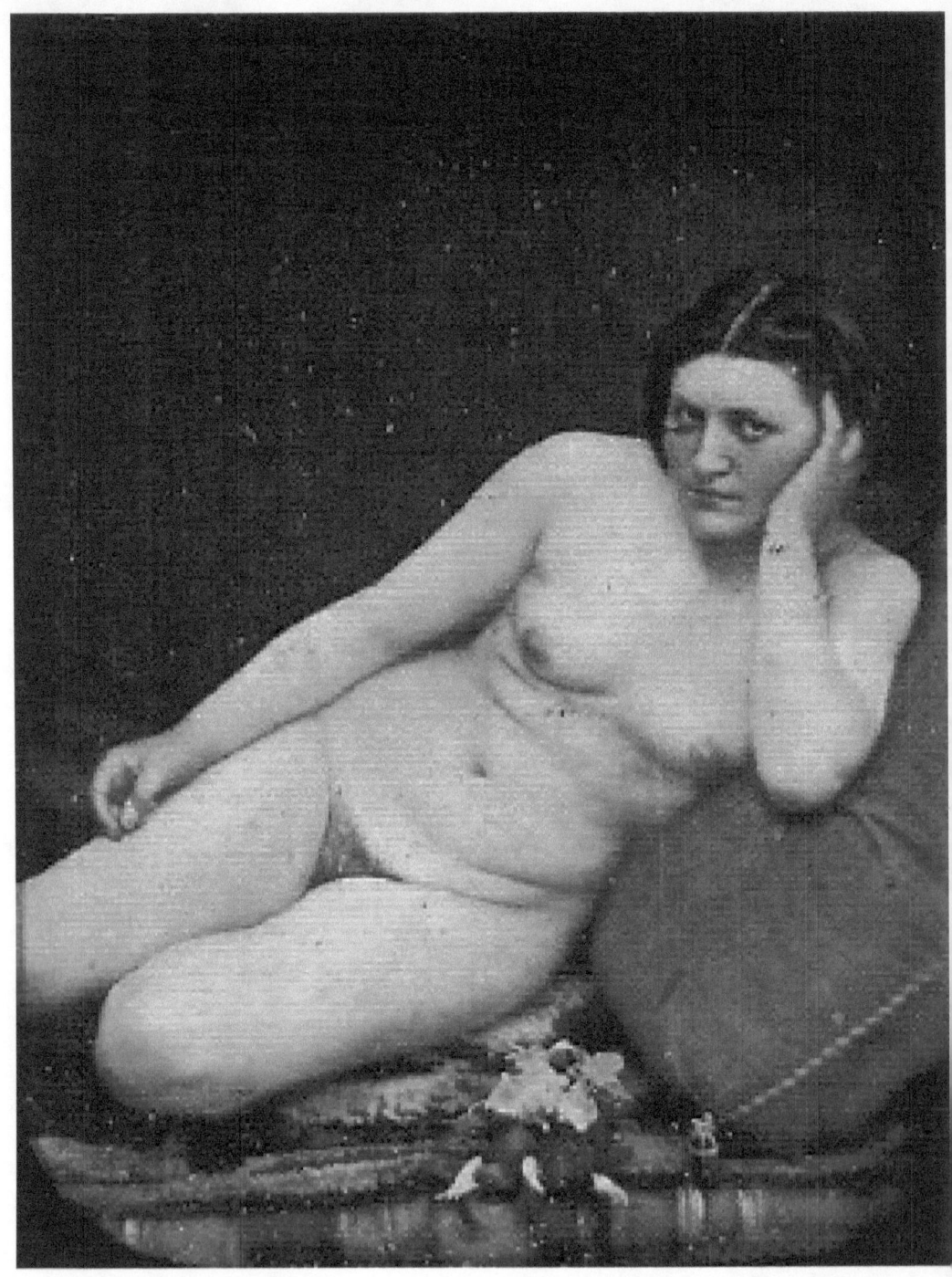

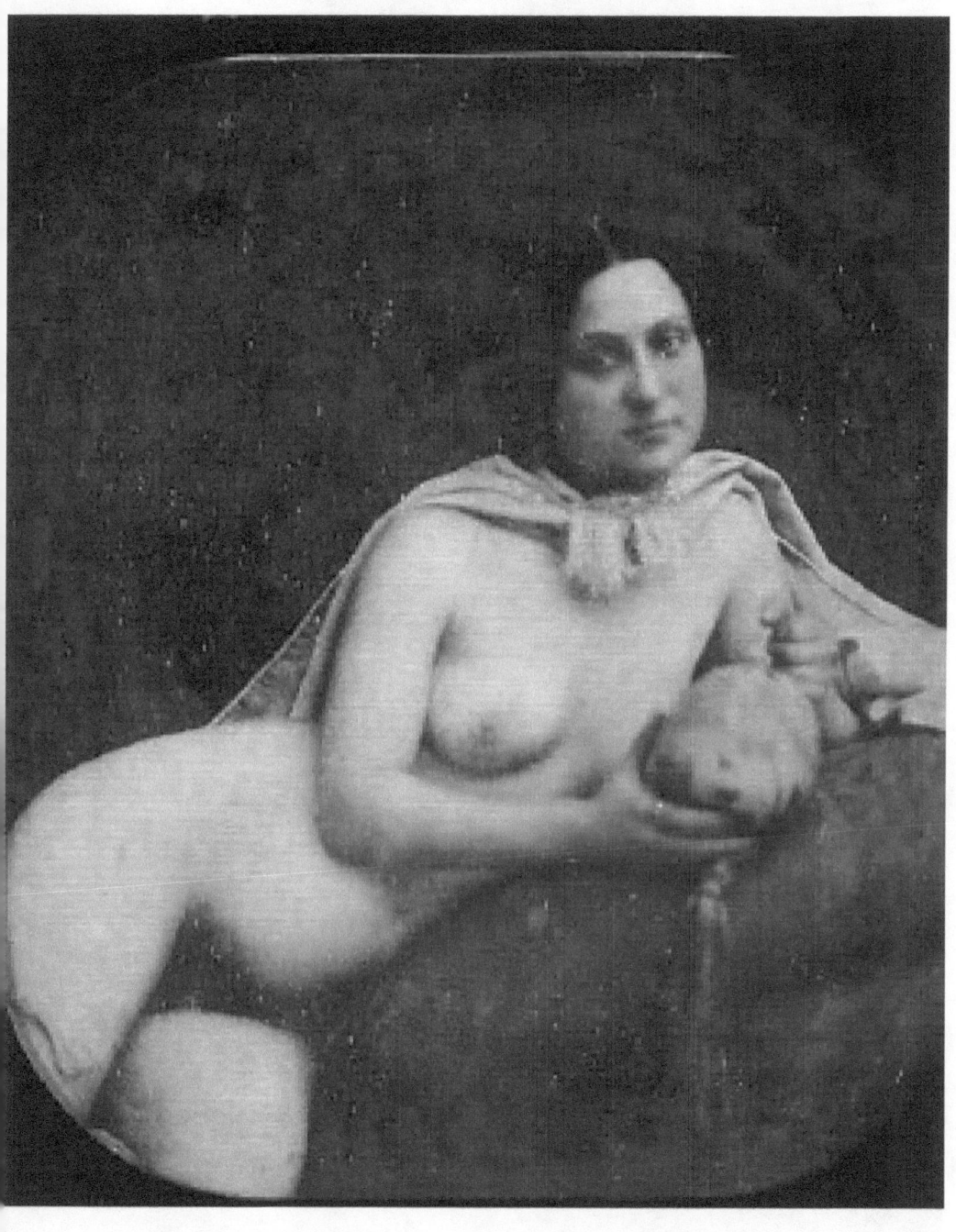

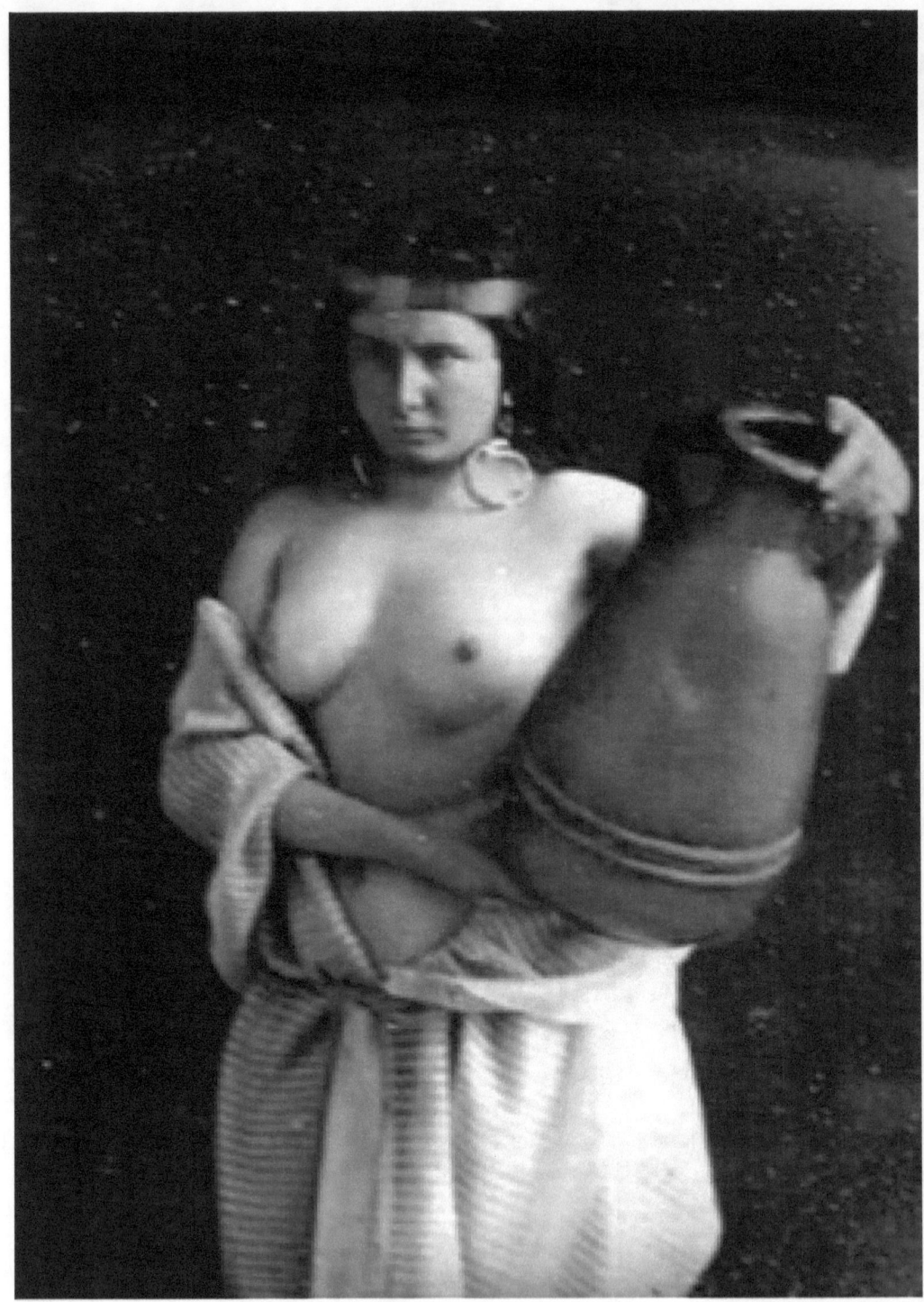

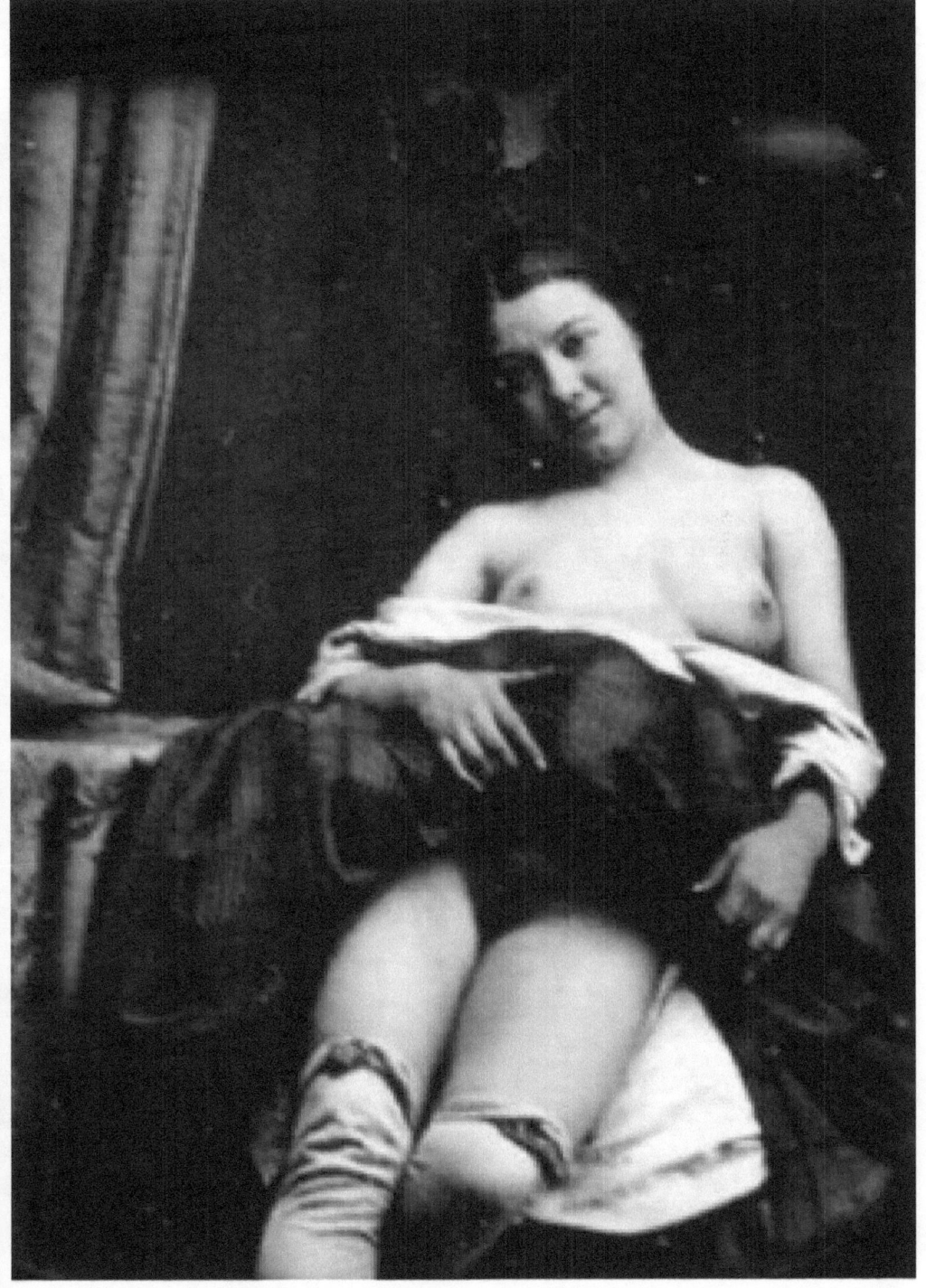

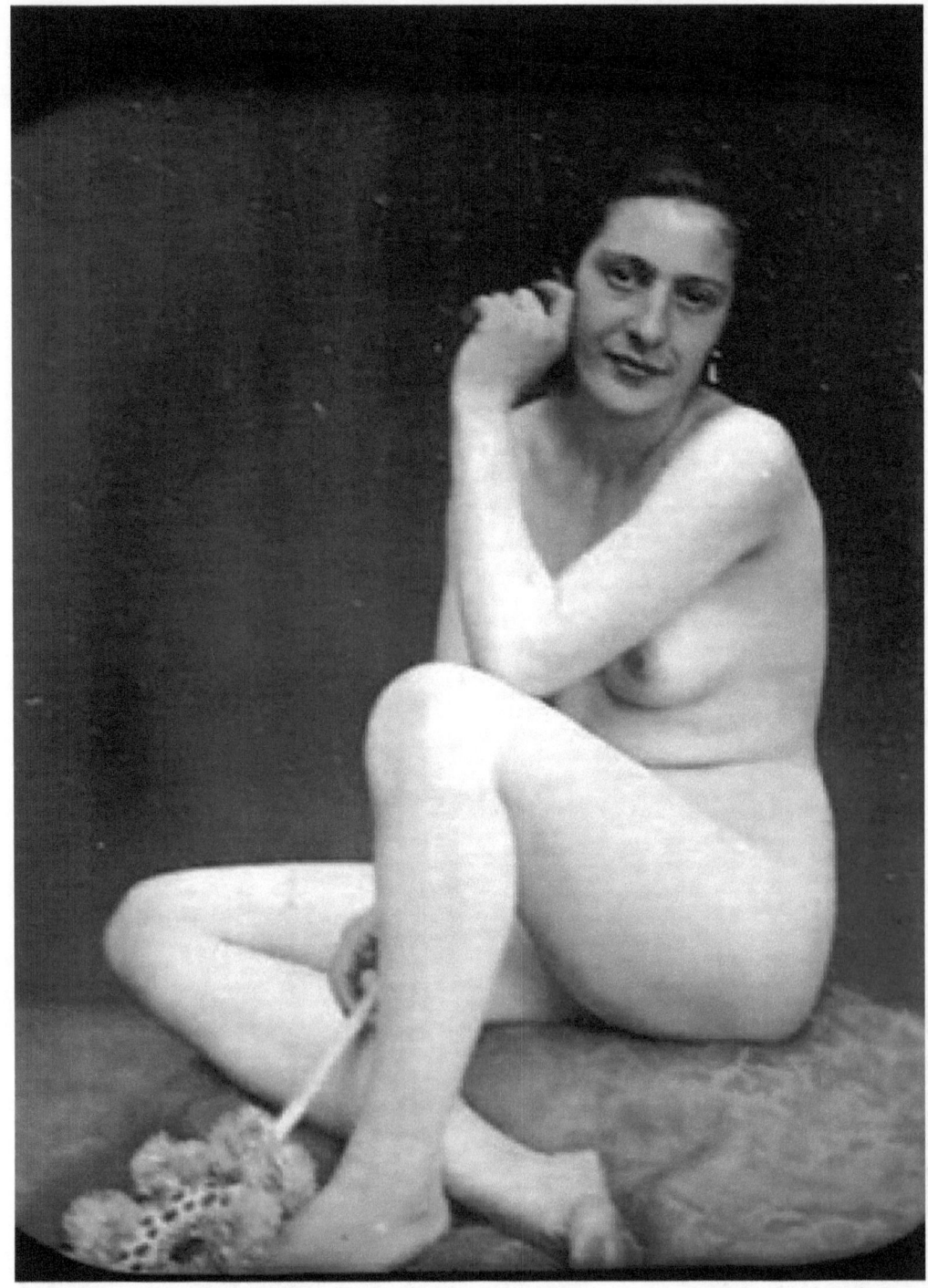

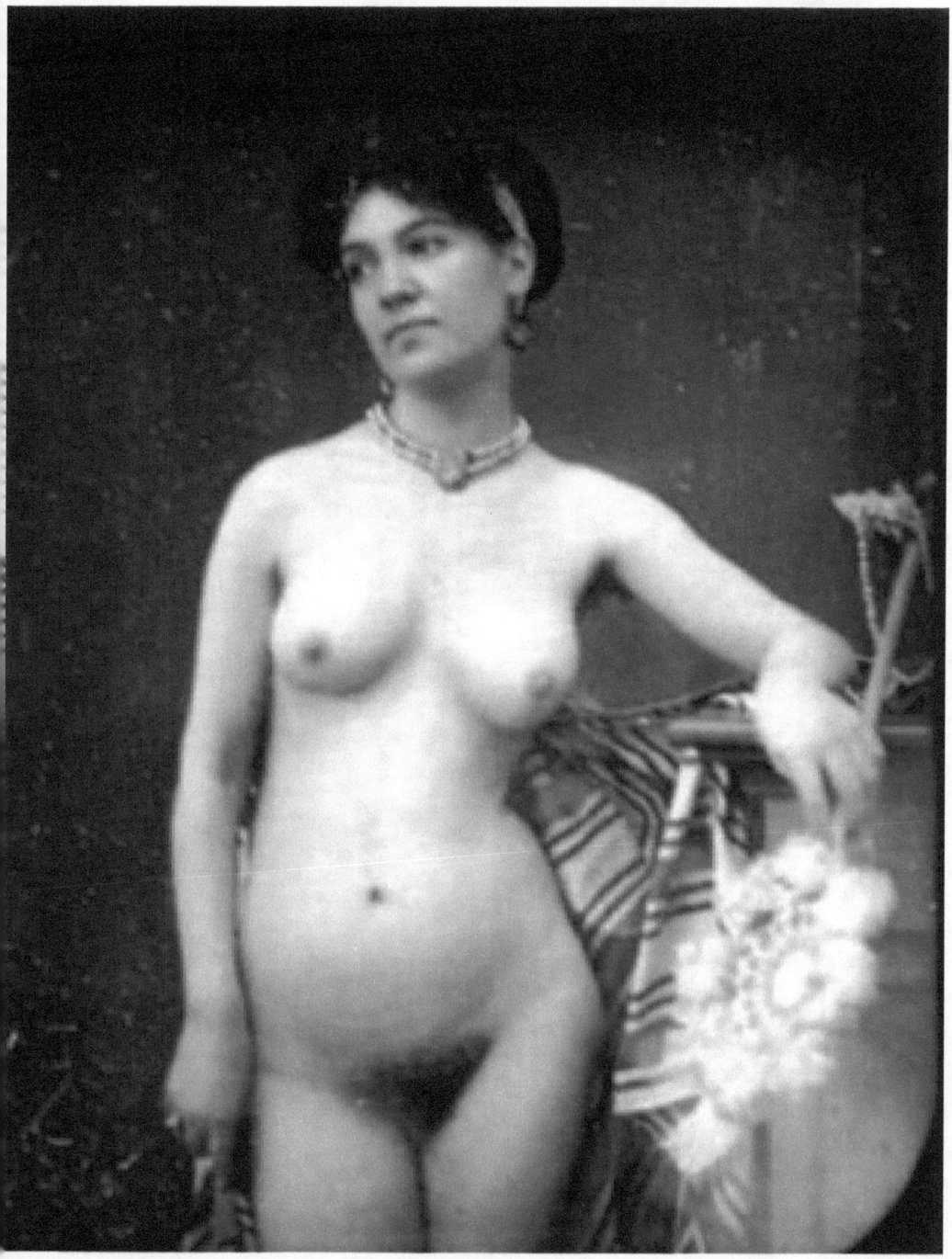

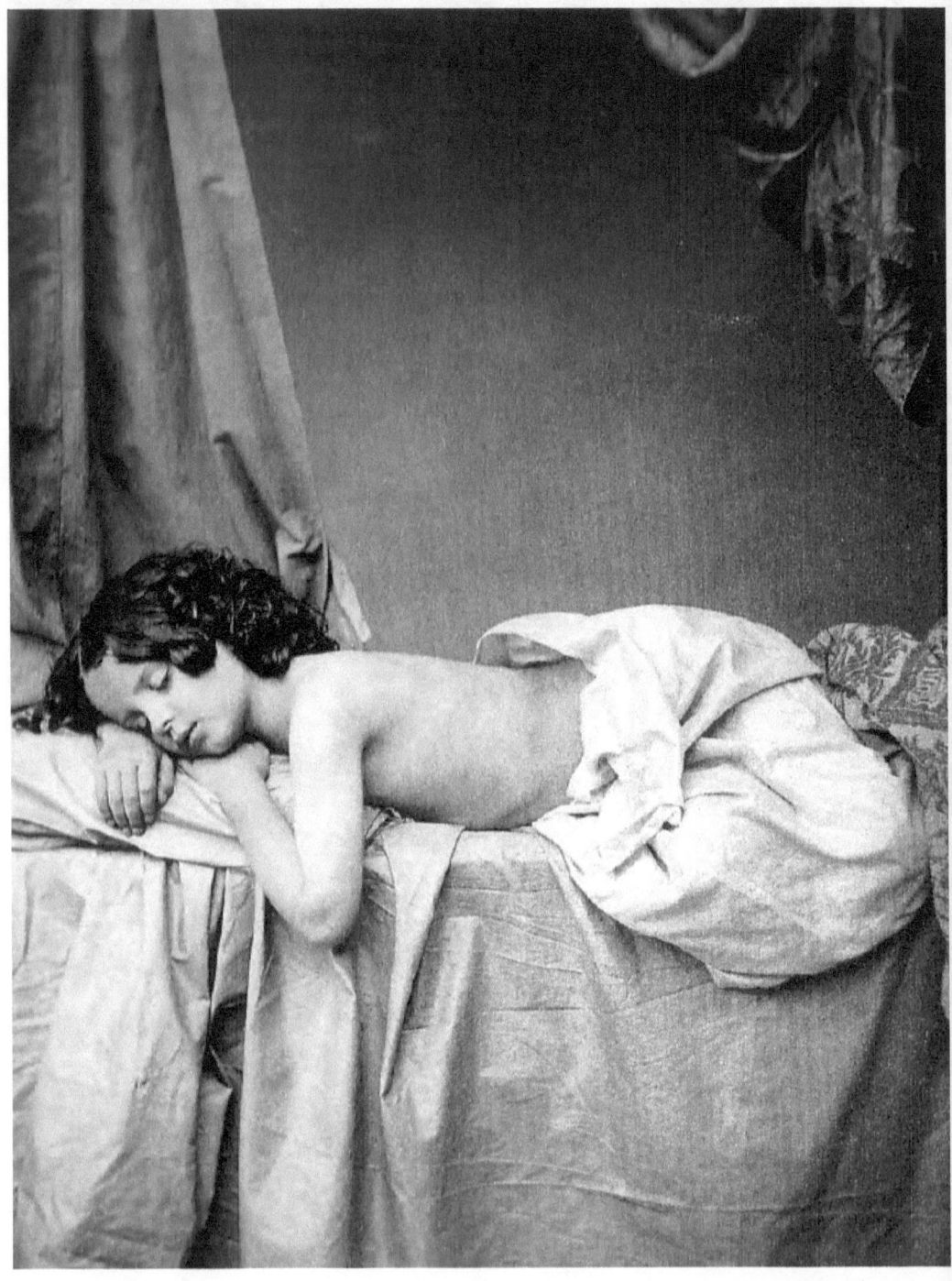

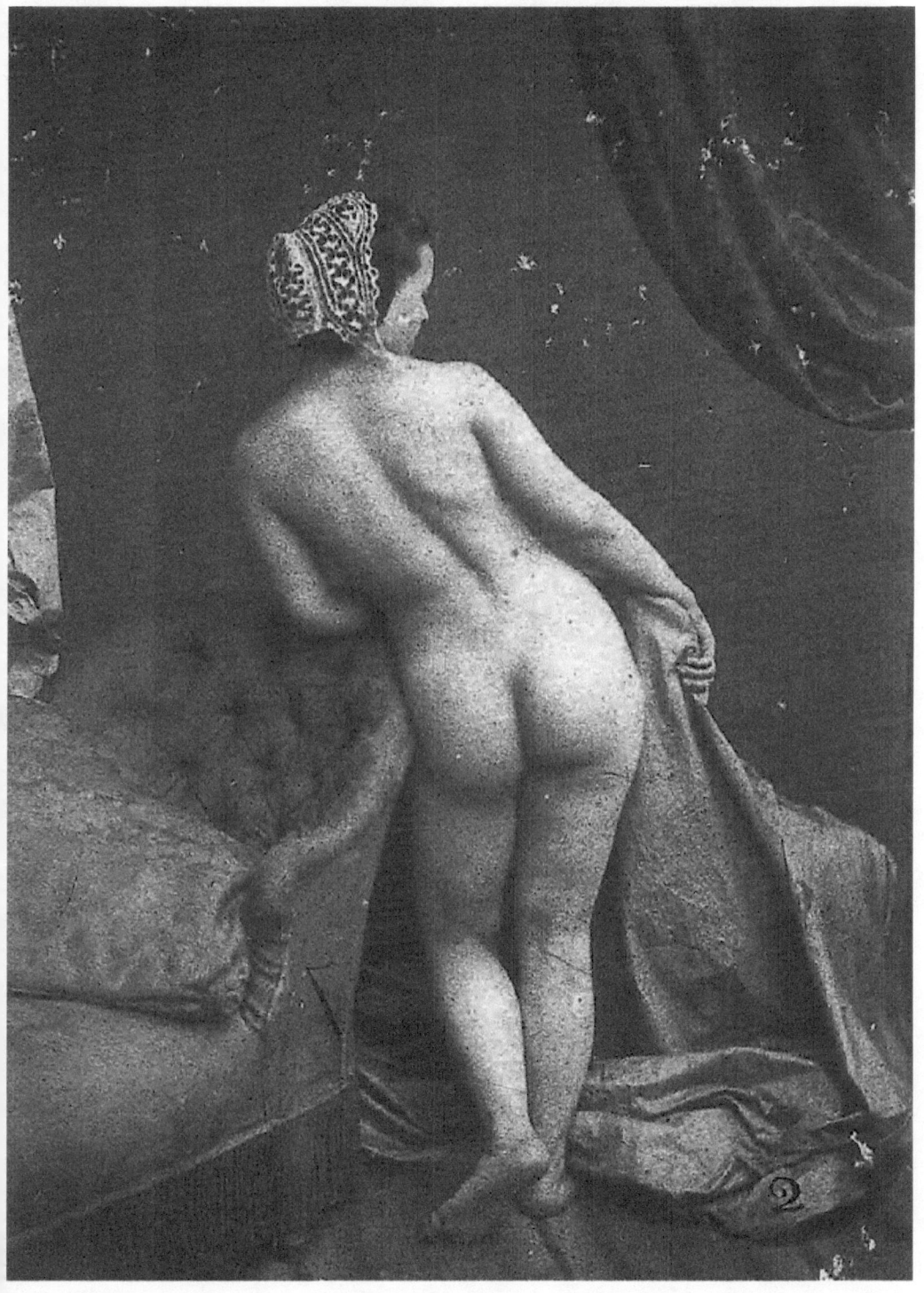

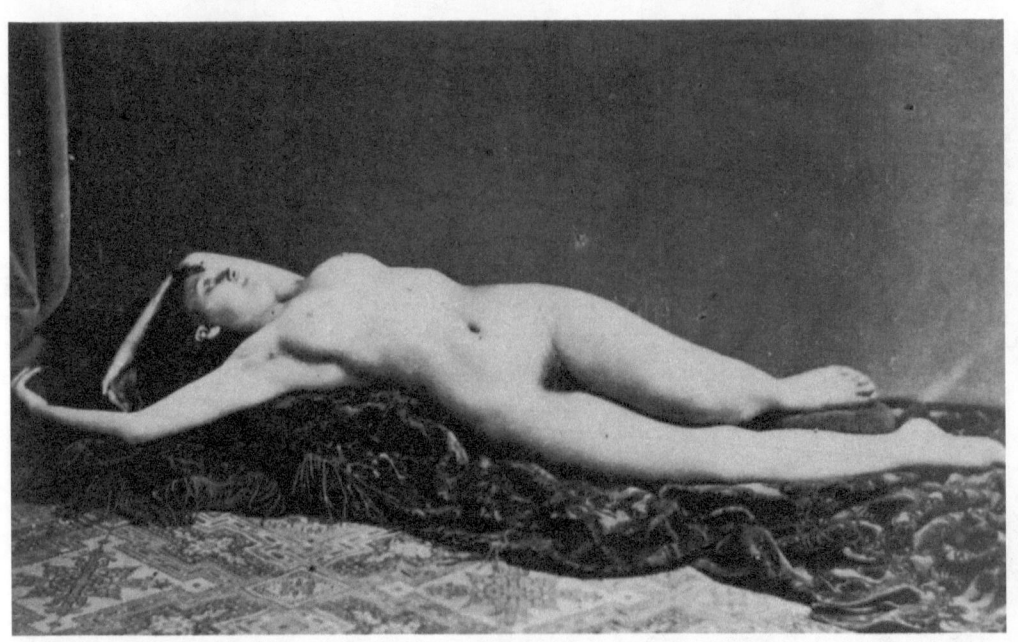

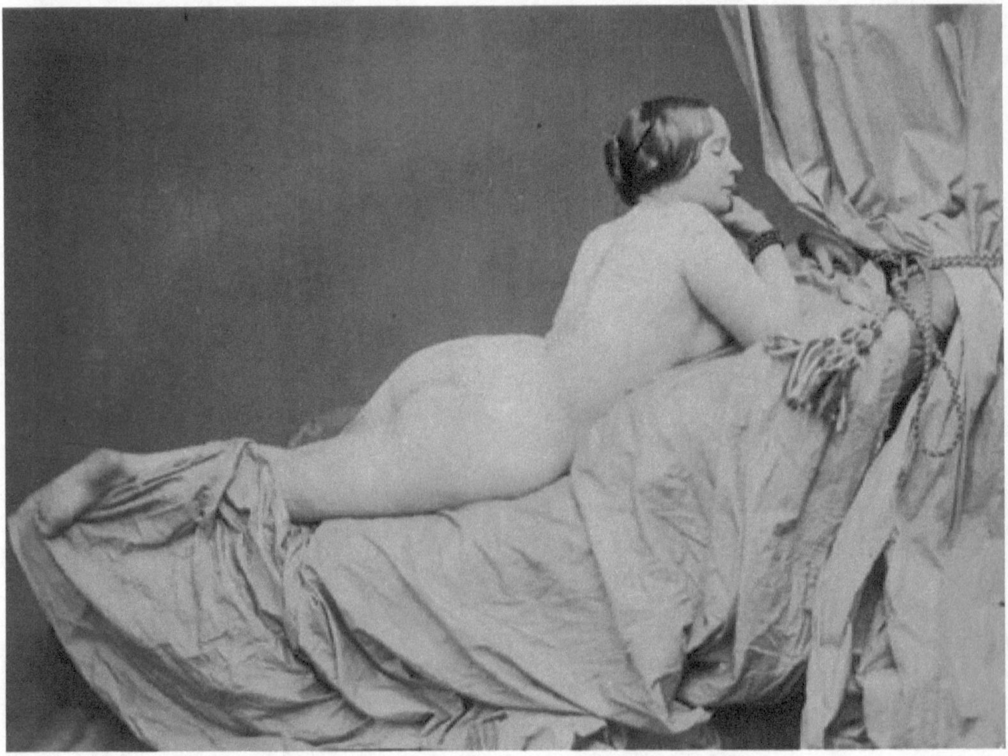

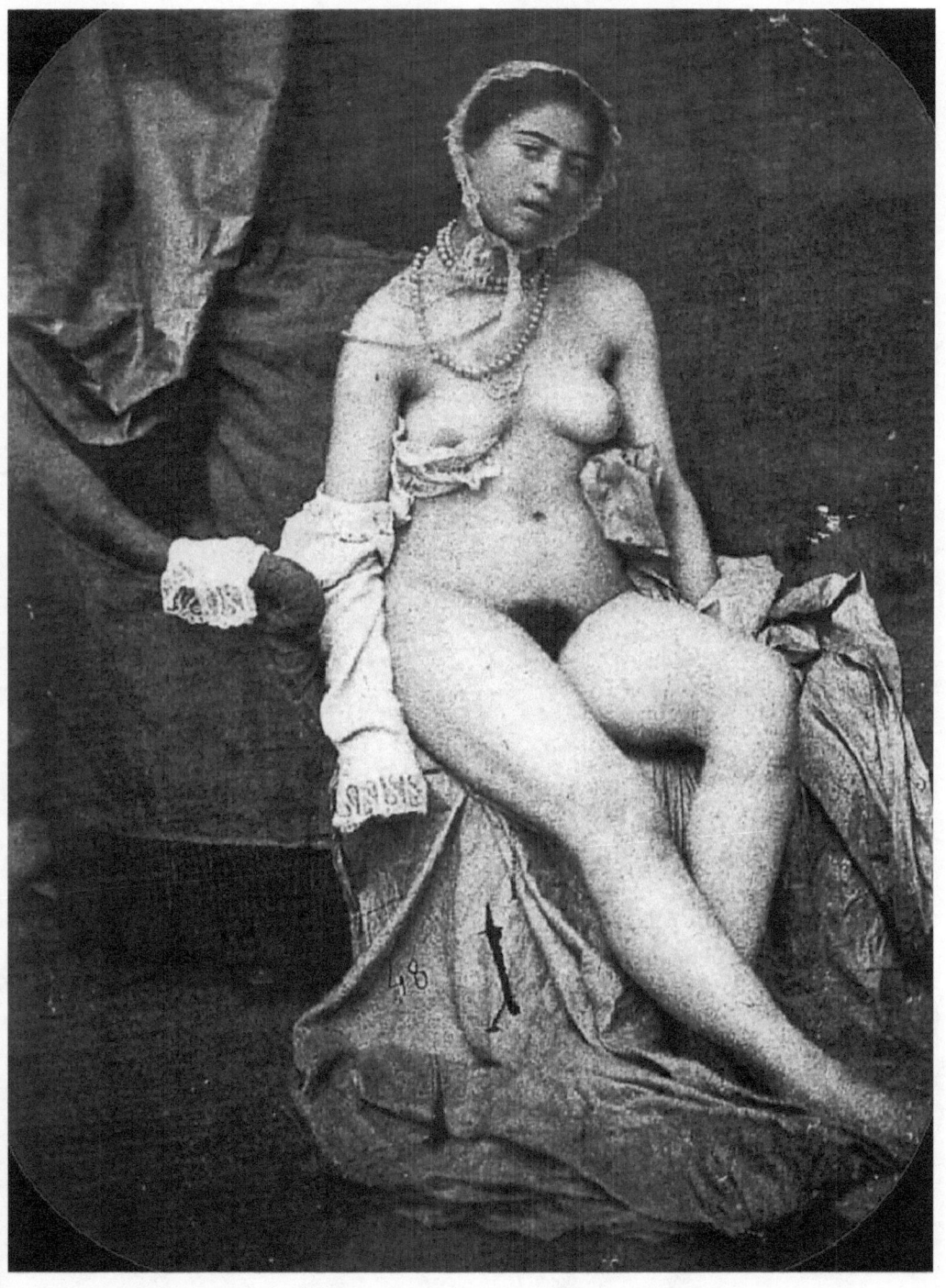

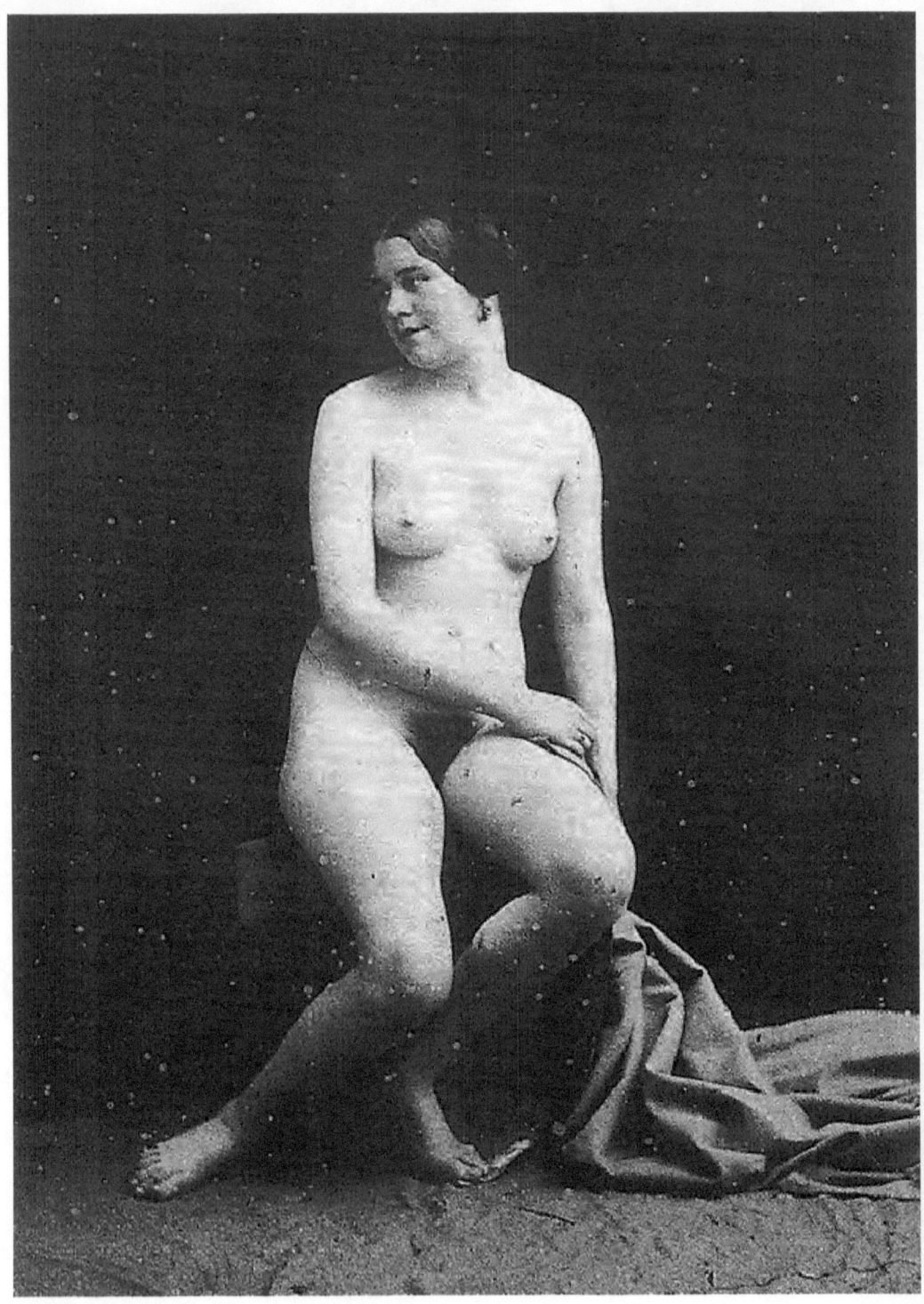

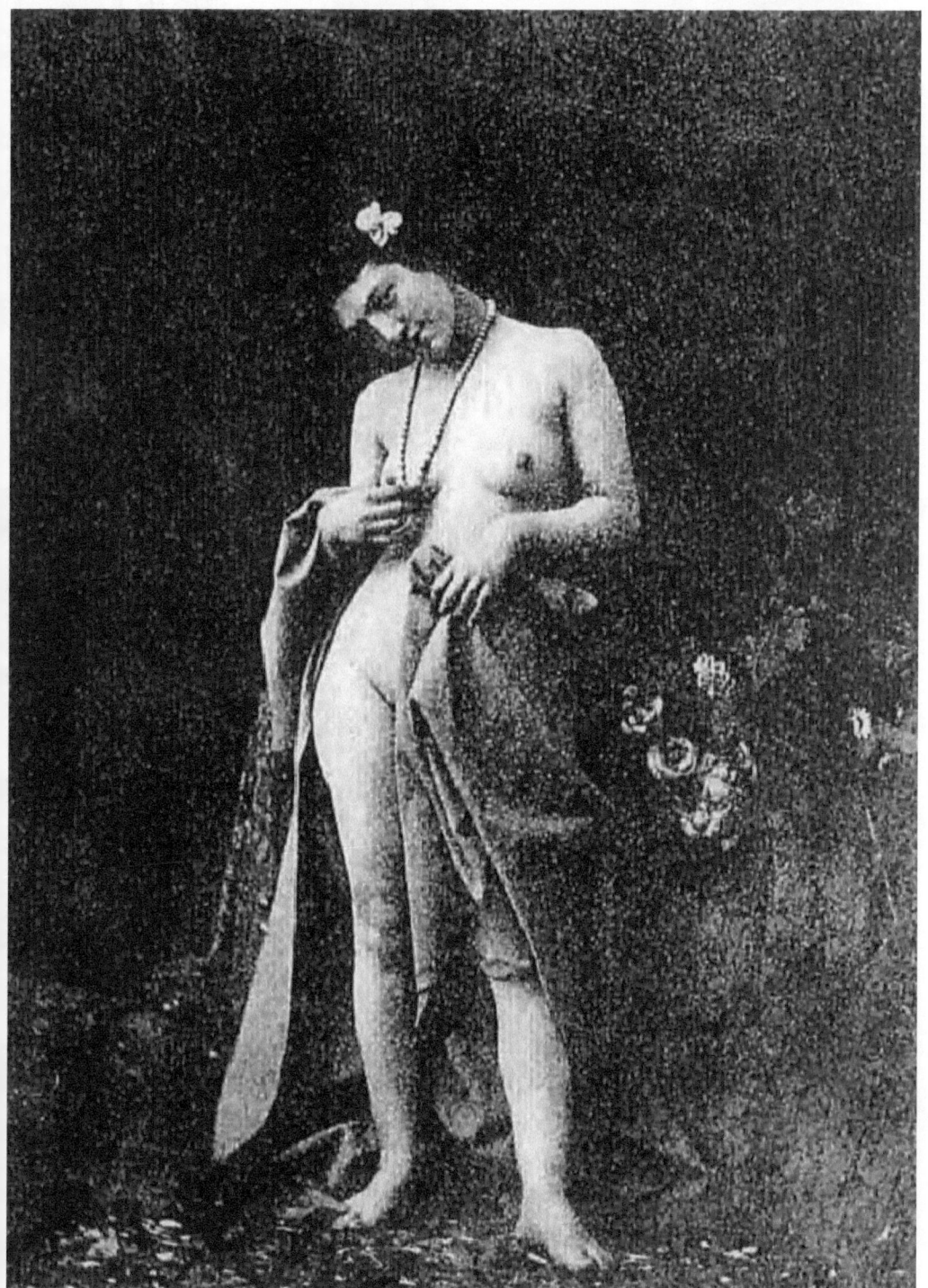

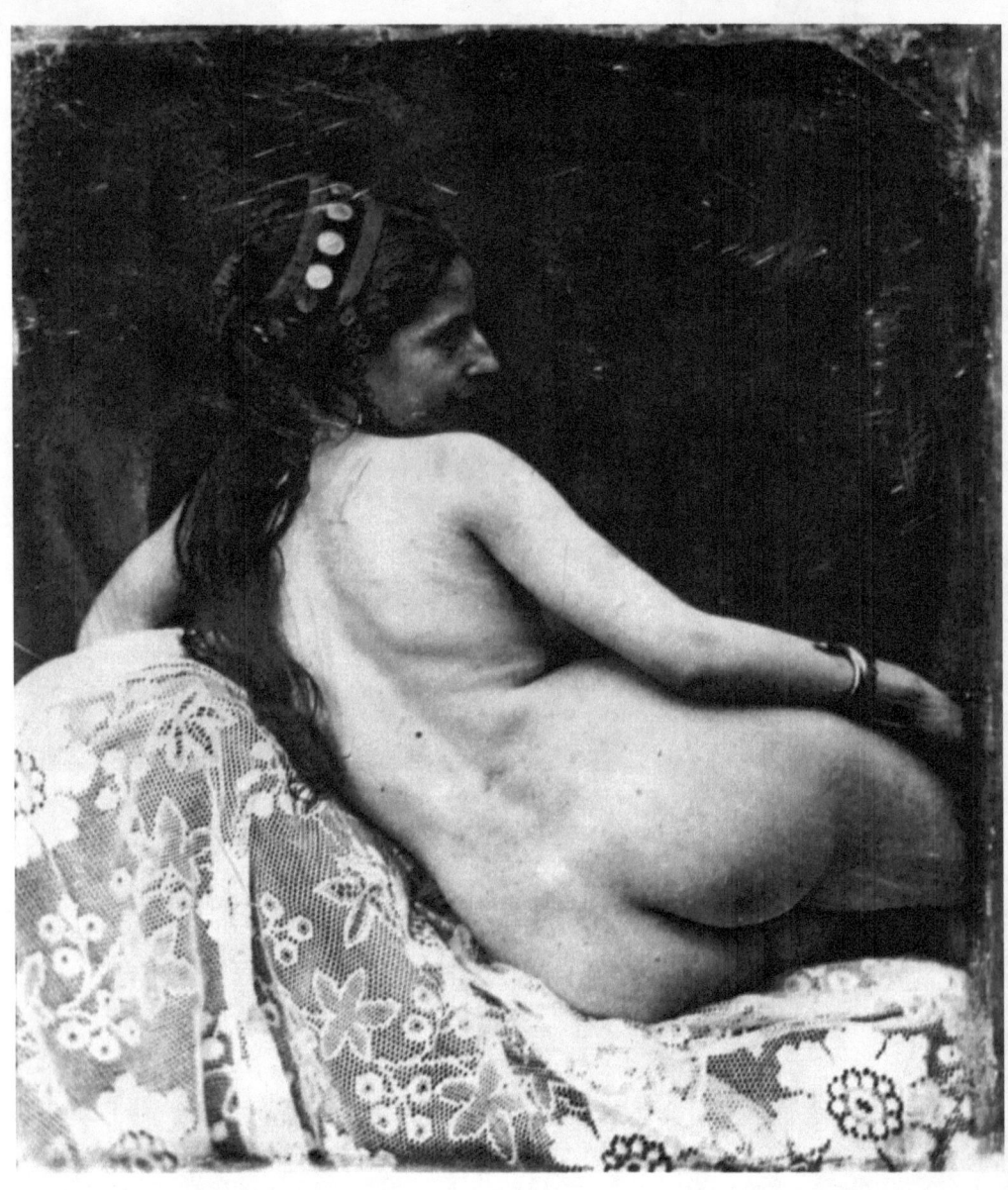

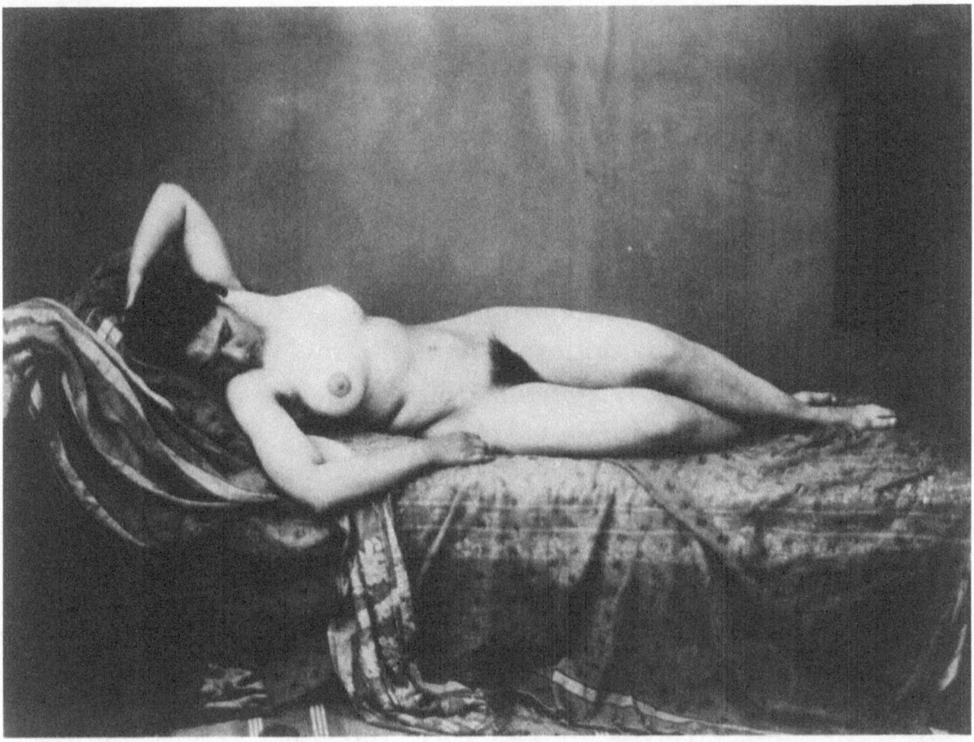

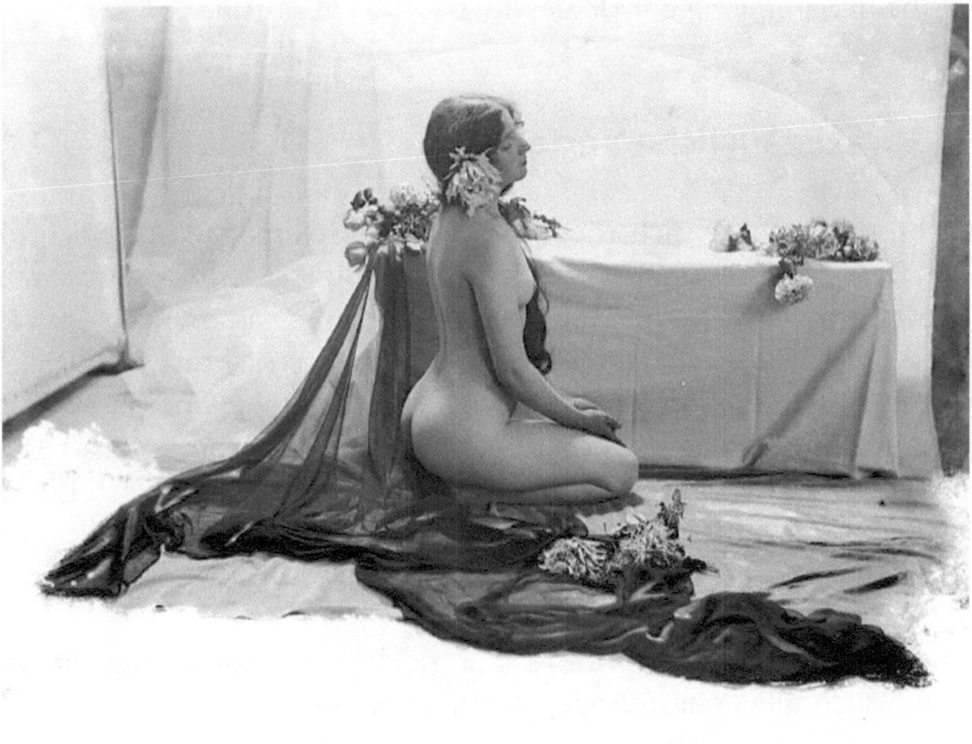

Die erste Fotografie

Ab etwa 1815 begann der reiche Advokat Joseph Nicéphore Niépce sich mit der Lithografie zu beschäftigen. Mit seinem von ihm selbst als Heliographie bezeichneten Verfahren gelang ihm 1822 eine Direktkopie eines Lithographie-Porträts auf einer asphaltbeschichteten Zinnplatte, welche nach Auflösen der unbelichteten Asphalt-Partien mit Lavendelöl graviert wurde und so vervielfältigt werden konnte. Parallel hierzu versuchte er bereits seit 1816 mit der Camera obscura Positivbilder auf verschiedenen Materialien herzustellen.

1829 benutzte er zusammen mit Daguerre eine mit Asphalt, Jod und Silber beschichtete Kupferplatte. Die vermutlich 1826 bis 1827 entstandene, erst 1952 wieder aufgefundene, älteste erhaltene Heliographie (wiederum auf Zinn) erforderte noch eine Belichtungszeit von mehreren Stunden. Sie zeigt den Blick aus dem Arbeitszimmer im Teil des Niépce-Landsitzes in Le Gras. Das Bild gehört heute zur Gernsheim-Sammlung der University of Texas at Austin.

Erste praxistaugliche Verfahren

Im Jahr 1829 schloss sich Niépce, wohl aus Geldmangel, brieflich mit Louis Daguerre zusammen, um die Erfindung weiterzuentwickeln. Niépce starb vier Jahre später, und Daguerre gelang es nach Niépces Tod erst 1837 eine belichtete, mit Silberiodid beschichtete Silberplatte in Quecksilberdämpfen zu entwickeln und anschließend in warmer Kochsalzlösung zu fixieren. Er verbesserte das Verfahren noch bis 1839 und François Arago, Leiter des Pariser Observatoriums, stellte es schließlich am 19. August 1839 der Pariser Akademie der Wissenschaften und damit der Öffentlichkeit als Daguerreotypie vor.

Daguerres Verfahren erforderte nur noch eine Belichtungszeit von einem Bruchteil einer Stunde, schuf aber lediglich ein Unikat. Die immer noch verhältnismäßig lange Belichtungszeit konnte aber bereits Anfang 1840 ganz erheblich von 15 Minuten unter günstigen Lichtverhältnissen auf 45 Sekunden gesenkt werden, als die aufgrund ihrer Operngläser bekannte und seit 1756 bestehende Wiener Firma Voigtländer das erste analytisch berechnete Objektiv, das Petzvalobjektiv, vorstellte.

Seit 1834 arbeitete auch William Henry Fox Talbot an einem fotografischen Verfahren mit lichtempfindlichem Papier; er bezeichnete es als photogenische Zeichnung. 1840 stellte er das erste Negativ-Verfahren vor, das er als Kalotypie (auch Talbotypie genannt) bezeichnete. Auch Talbots Verfahren benötigte noch lange Belichtungszeiten, sein Papiernegativ ließ sich jedoch beliebig oft reproduzieren.

Aus jenem fiktiven Veröffentlichungsjahr der Fotografie 1839 sind diverse weitere konkurrierende fotografische Verfahren bekannt; so hatte beispielsweise Hippolyte Bayard wohl ebenfalls ein Direktpositiv-Verfahren entwickelt.

Verbesserung der Verfahren

Nach 1839 arbeiteten zahllose Forscher an der Verbesserung der fotografischen Verfahren. Weitere lichtempfindliche Silbersalze wurden entdeckt, die Linsen für die Camera obscura wurden verbessert, erste lichtstarke Objektive wurden gebaut (Petzval – Lichtstärke 3,7 für die Voigtländer-Metallkamera). Dadurch konnten die Belichtungszeiten verkürzt werden.

Zu den Verbesserungen der Verfahren zählen die Verwendung von:

- albuminisierten Glasplatten (Abel Niépce de St. Victor, 1847; Albumin-Verfahren),

- albuminisiertem Papier (Louis Désiré Blanquart-Evrard, 1850)
- Wachspapier (Gustave Le Gray, 1850) und der
- Kollodium-Nassplatte (Frederick Scott Archer, 1851; engl. wet plate process).
- Uran-Kollodium (Wothlytypie von Jacob Wothly, 1864)

Die Belichtungszeiten konnten bereits beim Albuminverfahren auf etwa 20 Sekunden reduziert werden, was erstmals die Abbildung von lebenden Objekten ermöglichte (Visitenkartenporträts, insbesondere von André Adolphe-Eugène Disdéri ab 1854). Die Kollodium-Nassplatte verkürzte die Belichtungszeit weiter auf wenige Sekunden.

Diese Verfahren hatten jedoch noch eine Reihe von Nachteilen:

Die Platten mussten vor Ort vorbereitet und sofort entwickelt werden; dies war sehr aufwendig und schränkte die Mobilität der Fotografie ein. Aufgrund des nassen Kollodiumverfahrens musste ein Reisefotograf beispielsweise immer ein Dunkelkammerzelt mit sich führen. Die Fotoschichten waren verschieden empfindlich für die unterschiedlichen Anteile des Lichts (Farben) und überwiegend für Blau sensibilisiert. Das heißt, die Fotografien waren nur begrenzt abbildgetreu und nicht tonwertrichtig. Die Arbeit mit großformatigen Fotoplatten verhinderten Bildfolgen und Reihenaufnahmen.

Ab der zweiten Hälfte des 19. Jahrhunderts wurden auch diese Probleme sukzessive gelöst, so durch Louis-Alphonse Poitevin, der 1855 den Gummidruck und den Pigmentdruck erfand. Man entwickelte verschiedene Trockenplatten (engl. dry plates), die mit Tanninen, Albumin oder Gelatine beschichtet waren (ab 1856), insbesondere die Gelatine-Trockenplatte (Richard Leach Maddox, 1871). Die industrielle Fertigung begann 1879.

Erste Untersuchungen über ein farbfotografisches Verfahren veröffentlichte Louis Ducos du Hauron 1862. Im Jahr 1868 präsentierte er erste farbige Pigmentdrucke und patentierte verschiedene Farbverfahren.

Im Jahr 1869 erfand Edward Muybridge einen der ersten Verschlüsse. Dies ermöglichte einige Jahre später die ersten Reihenaufnahmen von bewegten Motiven. Er setzte dafür bis zu 30 Kameras ein.

Étienne-Jules Marey konstruierte 1883 das fotografische Gewehr, mit dem er eine ganze Serie von Belichtungen auf einer Platte festhalten konnte. Der Chronofotograf mit fester Platte und rotierendem Schlitzverschluss konnte – abhängig von der Belichtungszeit – bis zu hundert Bilder pro Sekunde anfertigen. Ottomar Anschütz konstruierte 1888 eine Kamera mit Schlitzverschluss für extrem kurze Belichtungszeiten.

Um die Wende vom 19. zum 20. Jahrhundert waren die Voraussetzungen für die panchromatische Tonwertwiedergabe und die Farbfotografie geschaffen. Der Begriff der panchromatischen Sensibilisierung bezog sich zu diesem Zeitpunkt jedoch noch ausschließlich auf schwarzweiße Halbtonvorlagen. Panchromatische Platten waren ab 1906 verfügbar; bei ihnen sind die Fotomaterialien für alle Farben des Lichtspektrums sensibilisiert, was die Voraussetzung für eine tonwertrichtige Wiedergabe in Grauwerten und die Farbfotografie ist.

Durch die Trockenverfahren und die Verkleinerung der Amateurkameras am Ende des 19. Jahrhunderts wurde die Fotografie mobil; außerdem wurde eine industrielle Fertigung des fotografischen Aufnahmematerials möglich, da nun die Fotoplatten auch gelagert werden konnten.

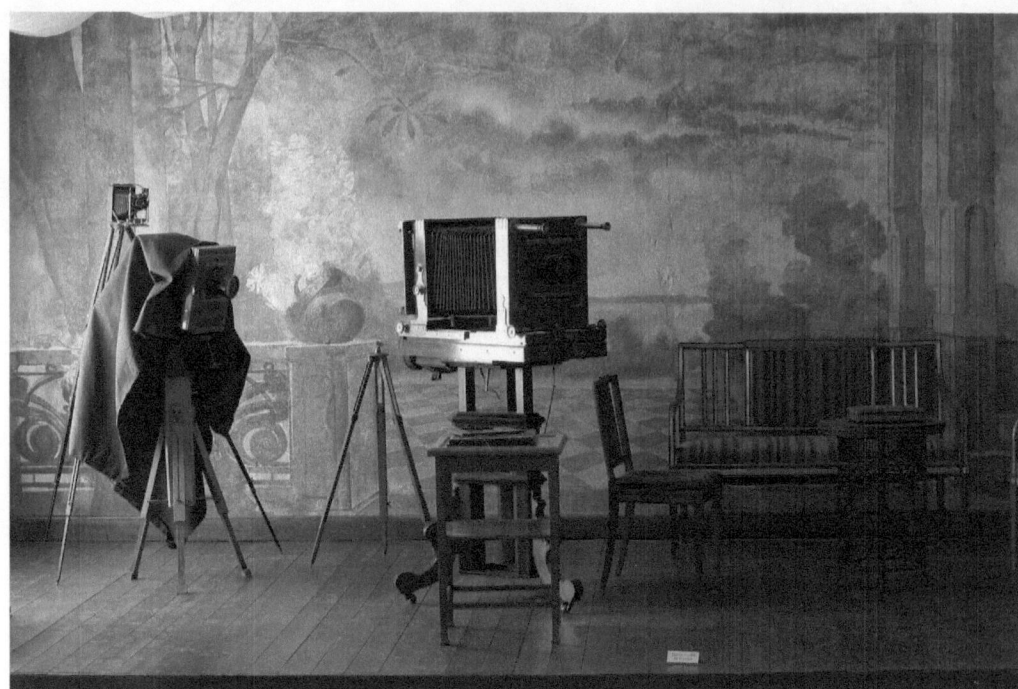

This file is licensed under the Creative Commons Attribution-Share Alike 3.0 Unported license.
Attribution: Ziko van Dijk

Nachbildung eines Fotoateliers um die Jahrhundertwende (1900)

Replica of a photo studio around the turn of the century (1900)

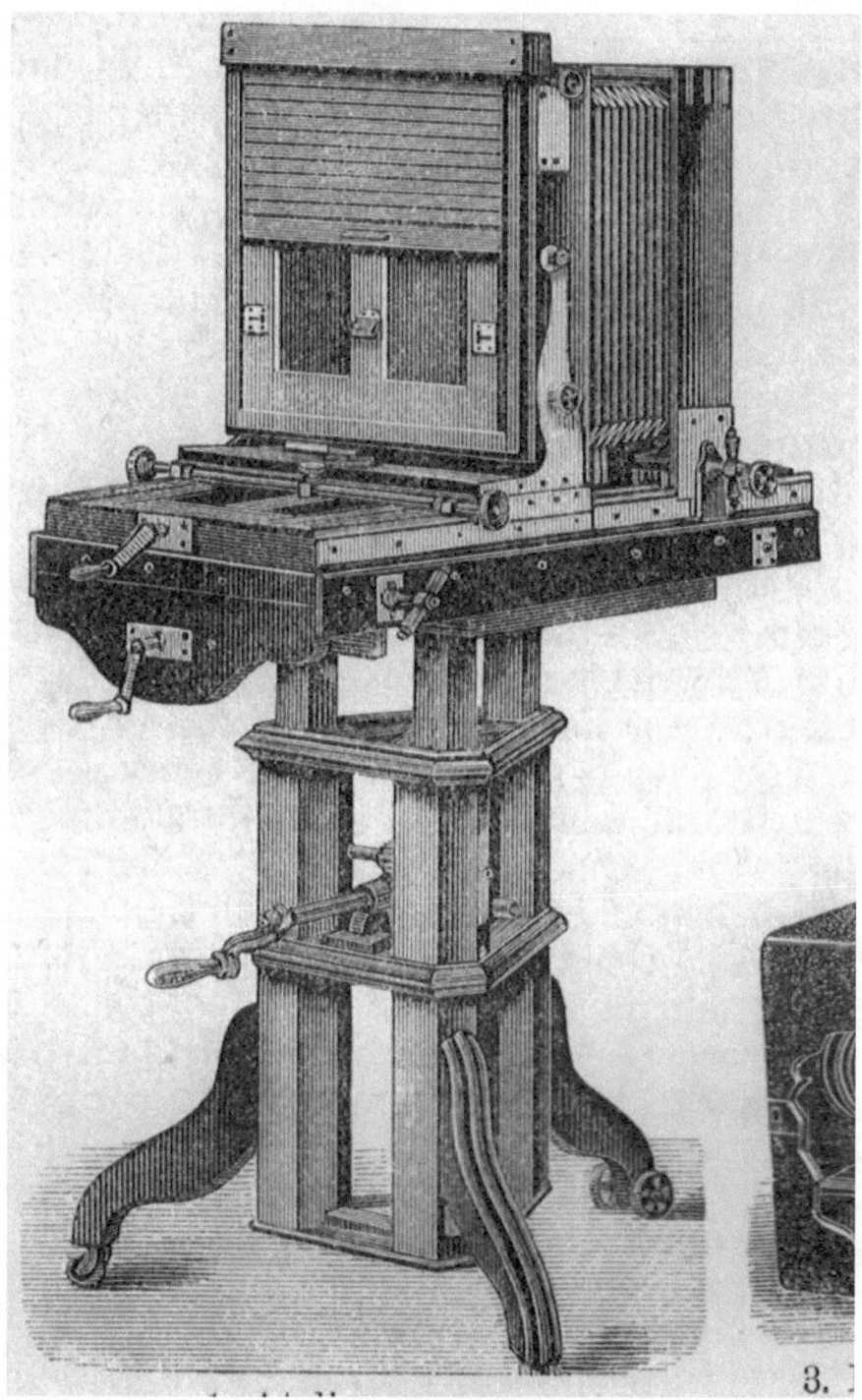

3.

Atelierkamera (Quelle Ausgabe Brockhaus 1893-95)
Studio camera (source lexicon Brockhaus 1893-95)

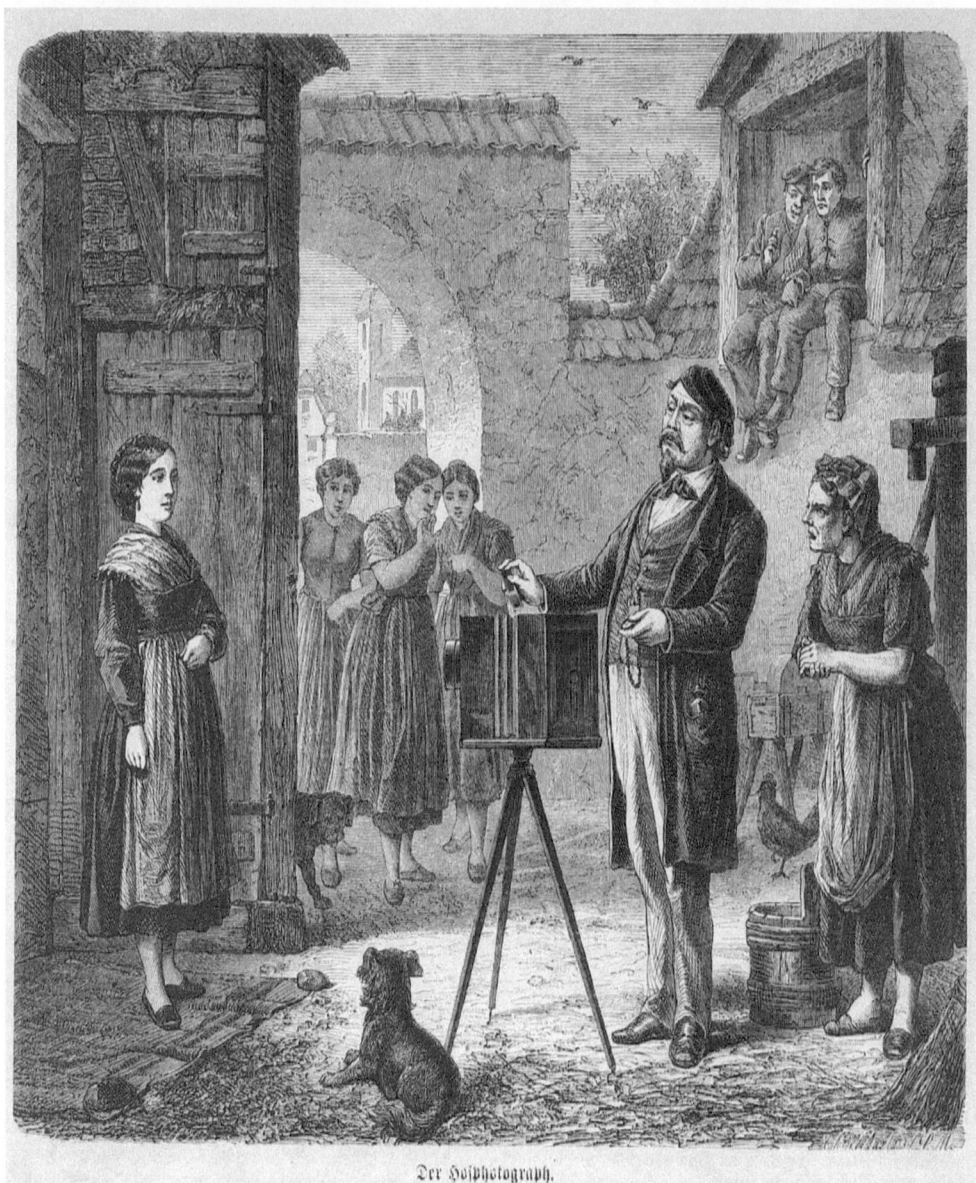

Der Hofphotograph.

Etwa 1875
Date around 1875

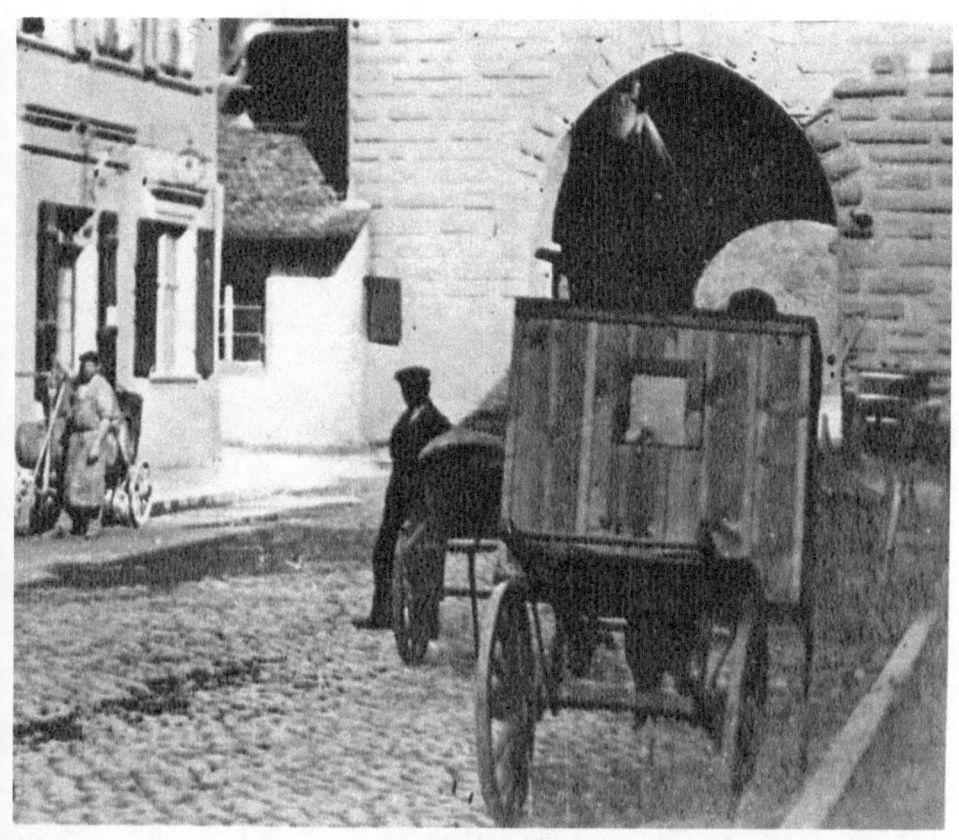

Jakob Höflingers fahrbare Dunkelkammer, wie sie in den Straßen Basels in den Jahren 1860-1875 zu sehen war. Die Platten wurden im Dunkel dieses Kastens erst kurz vor der Aufnahme gesilbert, das heißt lichtempfindlich gemacht, und mussten sofort verwendet werden. Unter dem Wagen sind die Beine des Präparators sichtbar, der gerade an der Arbeit ist. Ein zweiter Wagen führt Chemikalien, Geräte und Waschwasser mit. Der Meister benötigte zu seinen Freilichtaufnahmen drei Gehilfen.

Foto eines unbekannten Fotografen, entstanden zwischen 1860 bis 1875

Jakob Höflingers mobile darkroom, as it was seen in the streets of Basel in the years 1860-1875 . Plates were silvered in the darkness of this box just before the recording to make them sensitive to light and they had to be used immediately. A second carriage carried chemicals, equipment and washing water. The master needed for his outdoor shots three assistants .

Photo by unknown photographer, created between 1860-1875

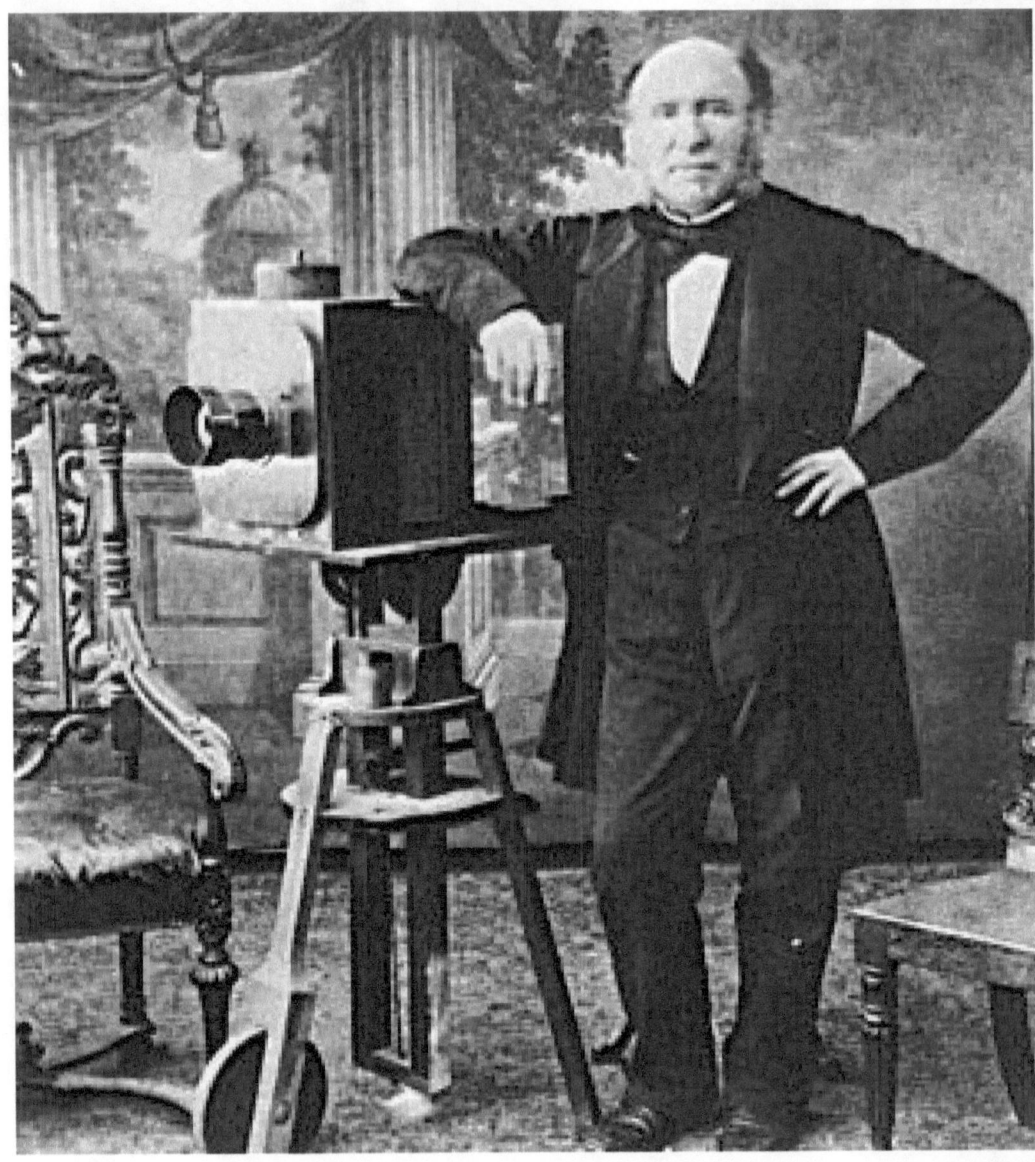

Englischer Portraitfotograf in seinem Studio, um 1850
English portrait photographer in his studio, 1850s

Development of chemical photography

Around the year 1800, Thomas Wedgwood made the first known attempt to capture the image in a camera obscura by means of a light-sensitive substance. He used paper or white leather treated with silver nitrate. Although he succeeded in capturing the shadows of objects placed on the surface in direct sunlight, and even made shadow-copies of paintings on glass, it was reported in 1802 that "the images formed by means of a camera obscura have been found too faint to produce, in any moderate time, an effect upon the nitrate of silver." The shadow images eventually darkened all over because "no attempts that have been made to prevent the uncoloured part of the copy or profile from being acted upon by light have as yet been successful." Wedgwood may have prematurely abandoned his experiments due to frail and failing health; he died aged 34 in 1805.

In 1816 Nicéphore Niépce, using paper coated with silver chloride, succeeded in photographing the images formed in a small camera, but the photographs were negatives, darkest where the camera image was lightest and vice versa, and they were not permanent in the sense of being reasonably light-fast; like earlier experimenters, Niépce could find no way to prevent the coating from darkening all over when it was exposed to light for viewing. Disenchanted with silver salts, he turned his attention to light-sensitive organic substances.

The oldest surviving permanent photograph of the image formed in a camera was created by Niépce in 1826 or 1827. It was made on a polished sheet of pewter and the light-sensitive substance was a thin coating of bitumen, a naturally occurring petroleum tar, which was dissolved in lavender oil, applied to the surface of the pewter and allowed to dry before use. After a very long exposure in the camera (traditionally said to be eight hours, but in fact probably several days), the bitumen was sufficiently hardened in proportion to its exposure to light that the unhardened part could be removed with a solvent, leaving a positive image with the light regions represented by hardened bitumen and the dark regions by bare pewter. To see the image plainly, the plate had to be lit and viewed in such a way that the bare metal appeared dark and the bitumen relatively light.

In partnership, Niépce (in Chalon-sur-Saône) and Louis Daguerre (in Paris) refined the bitumen process, substituting a more sensitive resin and a very different post-exposure treatment that yielded higher-quality and more easily viewed images. Exposure times in the camera, although somewhat reduced, were still measured in hours.

In 1833 Niépce died suddenly, leaving his notes to Daguerre. More interested in silver-based processes than Niépce had been, Daguerre experimented with photographing camera images directly onto a mirror-like silver-surfaced plate that had been fumed with iodine vapor, which reacted with the silver to form a coating of silver iodide. As with the bitumen process, the result appeared as a positive when it was suitably lit and viewed. Exposure times were still impractically long until Daguerre made the pivotal discovery that an invisibly slight or "latent" image produced on such a plate by a much shorter exposure could be "developed" to full visibility by mercury fumes. This brought the required exposure time down to a few minutes under optimum conditions. A strong hot solution of common salt served to stabilize or fix the image by removing the remaining silver iodide. On 7 January 1839, this first complete practical photographic process was announced at a meeting of the French Academy of Sciences, and the news quickly spread. At first, all details of the process were withheld and specimens were shown only at Daguerre's studio, under his close supervision, to Academy members and other distinguished guests. Arrangements were made for the French government to buy the rights in exchange for pensions for Niépce's son and Daguerre and present the invention to the world (with the de facto exception of Great Britain) as a free gift. Complete instructions were published on 19 August 1839.

After reading early reports of Daguerre's invention, William Henry Fox Talbot, who had succeeded in creating stabilized photographic negatives on paper in 1835, worked on perfecting his own process. In early 1839 he acquired a key improvement, an effective fixer, from John Herschel, the astronomer, who had previously shown that hyposulfite of soda (commonly called "hypo" and now known formally as sodium thiosulfate) would dissolve silver salts. News of this solvent also reached Daguerre, who quietly substituted it for his less effective hot salt water treatmen

Talbot's early silver chloride "sensitive paper" experiments required camera exposures of an hour or more. In 1840, Talbot invented the calotype process, which, like Daguerre's process, used the principle of chemical development of a faint or invisible "latent" image to reduce the exposure time to a few minutes. Paper with a coating of silver iodide was exposed in the camera and developed into a translucent negative image. Unlike a daguerreotype, which could only be copied by rephotographing it with a camera, a calotype negative could be used to make a large number of positive prints by simple contact printing. The calotype had yet another distinction compared to other early photographic processes, in that the finished product lacked fine clarity due to its translucent paper negative. This was seen as a positive attribute for portraits because it softened the appearance of the human face. Talbot patented this process, which greatly limited its adoption, and spent many years pressing lawsuits against alleged infringers. He attempted to enforce a very broad interpretation of his patent, earning himself the ill will of photographers who were using the related glass-based processes later introduced by other inventors, but he was eventually defeated. Nonetheless, Talbot's developed-out silver halide negative process is the basic technology used by chemical film cameras today. Hippolyte Bayard had also developed a method of photography but delayed announcing it, and so was not recognized as its inventor.

In 1839, John Herschel made the first glass negative, but his process was difficult to reproduce. Slovene Janez Puhar invented a process for making photographs on glass in 1841; it was recognized on June 17, 1852 in Paris by the Académie Nationale Agricole, Manufacturière et Commerciale. In 1847, Nicephore Niépce's cousin, the chemist Niépce St. Victor, published his invention of a process for making glass plates with an albumen emulsion; the Langenheim brothers of Philadelphia and John Whipple and William Breed Jones of Boston also invented workable negative-on-glass processes in the mid-1840s.

In 1851 Frederick Scott Archer invented the collodion process.

Herbert Bowyer Berkeley experimented with his own version of collodion emulsions after Samman introduced the idea of adding dithionite to the pyrogallol developer. Berkeley discovered that with his own addition of sulfite, to absorb the sulfur dioxide given off by the chemical dithionite in the developer, that dithionite was not required in the developing process. In 1881 he published his discovery. Berkeley's formula contained pyrogallol, sulfite and citric acid. Ammonia was added just before use to make the formula alkaline. The new formula was sold by the Platinotype Company in London as Sulpho-Pyrogallol Developer.

Nineteenth-century experimentation with photographic processes frequently became proprietary. The German-born, New Orleans photographer Theodore Lilienthal successfully sought legal redress in an 1881 infringement case involving his "Lambert Process" in the Eastern District of Louisiana.

Popularization

The daguerreotype proved popular in response to the demand for portraiture that emerged from the middle classes during the Industrial

Revolution. This demand, which could not be met in volume and in cost by oil painting, added to the push for the development of photography.

In 1847, Count Sergei Lvovich Levitsky designed a bellows camera that significantly improved the process of focusing. This adaptation influenced the design of cameras for decades and is still found in use today in some professional cameras. While in Paris, Levitsky would become the first to introduce interchangeable decorative backgrounds in his photos, as well as the retouching of negatives to reduce or eliminate technical deficiencies. Levitsky was also the first photographer to portray a photo of a person in different poses and even in different clothes (for example, the subject plays the piano and listens to himself).

Roger Fenton and Philip Henry Delamotte helped popularize the new way of recording events, the first by his Crimean war pictures, the second by his record of the disassembly and reconstruction of The Crystal Palace in London. Other mid-nineteenth-century photographers established the medium as a more precise means than engraving or lithography of making a record of landscapes and architecture: for example, Robert Macpherson's broad range of photographs of Rome, the interior of the Vatican, and the surrounding countryside became a sophisticated tourist's visual record of his own travels.

By 1849, images captured by Levitsky on a mission to the Caucasus were exhibited by the famous Parisian optician Chevalier at the Paris Exposition of the Second Republic as an advertisement of their lenses. These photos would receive the Exposition's gold medal; the first time a prize of its kind had ever been awarded to a photograph.

That same year in 1849 in his St. Petersburg, Russia studio Levitsky would first propose the idea to artificially light subjects in a studio setting using electric lighting along with daylight. He would say of its use, "as far as I know this application of electric light has never been tried; it is something new, which will be accepted by photographers because of its simplicity and practicality".

In 1851, at an exhibition in Paris, Levitsky would win the first ever gold medal awarded for a portrait photograph.

In America, by 1851 a broadside by daguerreotypist Augustus Washington was advertising prices ranging from 50 cents to $10. However, daguerreotypes were fragile and difficult to copy. Photographers encouraged chemists to refine the process of making many copies cheaply, which eventually led them back to Talbot's process.

Ultimately, the photographic process came about from a series of refinements and improvements in the first 20 years. In 1884 George Eastman, of Rochester, New York, developed dry gel on paper, or film, to replace the photographic plate so that a photographer no longer needed to carry boxes of plates and toxic chemicals around. In July 1888 Eastman's Kodak camera went on the market with the slogan "You press the button, we do the rest". Now anyone could take a photograph and leave the complex parts of the process to others, and photography became available for the mass-market in 1901 with the introduction of the Kodak Brownie.

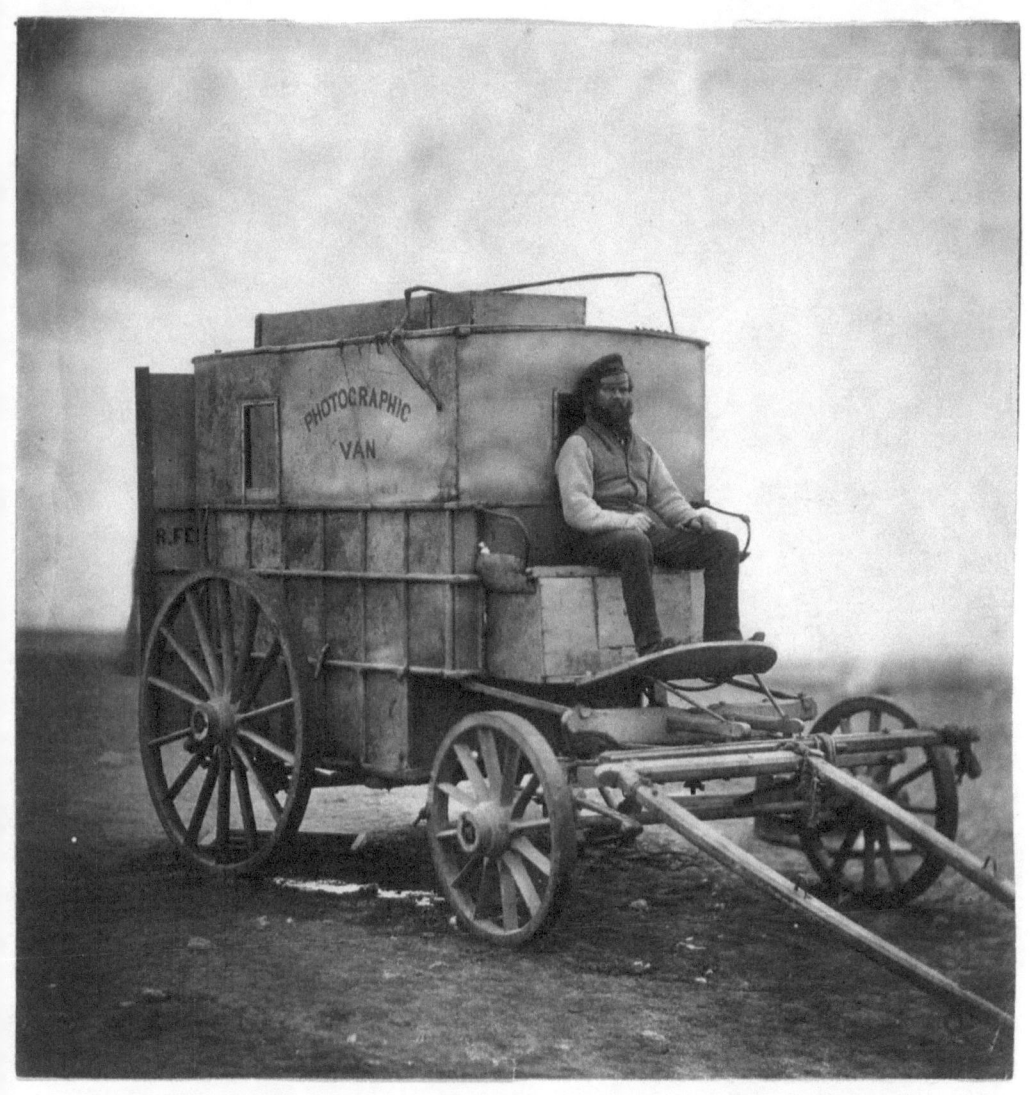

Roger Fentons Photographic Van 1855

Der Fotografenkarren von Roger Fenton 1855

www.ingramcontent.com/pod-product-compliance
Lightning Source LLC
Chambersburg PA
CBHW030854180526
45163CB00004B/1568